MONTANA
HORSE RACING

MONTANA
HORSE RACING
—— *A History* ——

BRENDA WAHLER

THE
History
PRESS

Published by The History Press
Charleston, SC
www.historypress.com

First published 2019

Manufactured in the United States

ISBN 9781467140324

Library of Congress Control Number: 2019936990

In memory of Gordon Schlack (1923–2015)

Thanks, Dad, for passing on your love of horses and photography.

CONTENTS

CONTENTS

ACKNOWLEDGEMENTS

I t is an understatement to say that this book was possible thanks to the help of many people. I cannot list everyone here, but please know that all who contributed have my deepest thanks.

First, my thanks to those whose invaluable help kept this project going and saved me from assorted disasters:

Eric Wahler
Larisa Wahler
Ellen Baumler
Jane Berger
Kim Briggeman
Toni Hinton
Dawn Lynn

Lyndel Meikle
Ken Robison
Don Richard
Victoria Short
Tom Tucker
Bill Whitfield, Ravalli County
 Museum

My further thanks to:

Montana Board of Horse Racing
Great Falls Turf Club
Western Montana Turf Club
Billings Gazette: Darrell Ehrlick,
 Chris Jorgensen, Larry Mayer

Joe Bird Rattler and family
Holly Burrows
Tom Chapman
Marylynn Donnelly
Roda Ferraro, Keeneland Library

Acknowledgements

Holly Gervais
Rita Gibson, Montana State Law
    Library
Darlene Gould and everyone at the
    Marcus Daly Mansion
Jeff Malcolmson, MHS photo
    archives
Kelly Manzer
Bunny Miller, Range Riders
    Museum

Kendra Newhall and everyone at
    the Montana Historical Society
Shawn Real Bird
Melanie Sanchez, Powell County
    Museum
Candice Score
Suzy Wilson

Special thanks:

Patty Briggs, for encouragement.
Everyone at The History Press for their patience and support.
Ray Paulick and Alicia Wincze-Hughes for directing me to valuable national
    research sources.
My friends on Wikipedia who helped with this project.

NOTES TO THE READER

The following may help readers who are unfamiliar with the topics discussed in this book.

ABOUT HORSES

1. Many horse and horse racing terms are defined in the glossary beginning on page 221.
2. Racing statistics are formatted as in this example: (20:11-6-1). The first number is the total races the horse has run, numbers after the colon are the races where the horse finished first, second, or third.
3. Horse parentage is shown as (Sire name x Dam name). Horses are "by" their sire and "out of" their dam.
4. Horse names can be confusing, particularly as it was once popular to name racehorses after actual people. One example was Sam Lucas, Marcus Daly's farm trainer. Daly honored him by naming a horse "Sam Lucas." Further confusion occurs because multiple horses sometimes had the same name (such as Strideaway)—or one horse might be given different names over his or her lifetime (such as Mambrino Diamond, also called Black Diamond).

Native American Culture

America's First People have many distinct cultures, languages and historic experiences. I acknowledge my understanding is incomplete and apologize in advance for my errors. Speaking generally, "Native" (deliberately capitalized) and "American Indian" are used colloquially, and use herein is intended with respect. Academics prefer "Native American," and "Indian" has a specific meaning in U.S. law.

When possible, I describe people by tribal affiliation. Sometimes historic records or unclear sources limit my options, and words used sometimes vary with context. For example, "Crow Indian Reservation" is a legal entity; the people living there ask to be called Apsáalooke. For the Blackfoot Confederacy (Niitsitapi), "Blackfoot" describes the Canadian Kainai ("Bloods") and Siksika; while "Blackfeet" is used in the United States for the Piikani/Amskapi Pikuni (previously "Piegan").

Monetary conversions to current value are from MeasuringWorth.com. The most conservative estimates are given in most cases.

Photos

Some photo credits are abbreviated as follows. My thanks to all who provided images:

Allen: Gene and Bev Allen, Helena
Barrett: Bob and Lisa Barrett, Helena
Daly: Daly Mansion, Hamilton
Elison: Elison family, Missoula
GF: The History Museum, Great Falls
GHM: Gallatin History Museum, Bozeman
Hinton: Toni Hinton and Jim Johnson, Missoula
LOC: Library of Congress
MOR: Museum of the Rockies, Bozeman
Overholser: Overholser Historical Research Center, Fort Benton
PCM: Powell County Museum and Arts Foundation, Deer Lodge

Peters: Photography by Mary Peters
RCM: Ravalli County Museum, Hamilton
RR: Range Riders' Museum, Miles City.
TBHAM: Twin Bridges Historical Association Museum
Tomaskie: John and Beverly Tomaskie, Helena
Wahler: Photography by Brenda Wahler
Wilson: Suzy Wilson, Fort Worth, Texas
WMTC: Western Montana Turf Club, Missoula
YCM: Yellowstone County Museum, Billings

MONTANA'S HORSE RACING HISTORY

To my idea Montana is the greatest country on earth in which to race or hold races because the people there look upon racing as a sport worthy of patronage and they have the money to gratify their notions. Wages are good and the men who toil are amongst the best patrons of both the gate and the pool box. The women bet almost as much as the men.
—Ed Tipton, 1896[1]

The horse is born to run; speed is a survival tool. To hone this skill, the urge to compete comes naturally. Young horses race to play; stallions retired to stud challenge one other by running along adjoining fence lines. Open a corral gate, and the herd gallops to pasture. Brief fights may settle disputes within a herd, but most conflicts end before injuries occur. Horses only battle predators when desperate—flight allows the horse to live another day.

Humans also have a competitive streak and use play to hone survival skills. Games of speed, skill, and chance have existed since prehistory. When horses and humans became a team, someone inevitably boasted, "I bet my horse is the fastest," and others begged to differ. Our two species' instincts dovetailed in horse racing.

Today, racing as a sport provides humans a link to the natural world and our ancient roots. For domesticated horses, it is one of the few remaining outlets for instincts once crucial for survival. In modern Montana, horse racing faces many challenges. But just as in the early West, a "good horse" is often synonymous with a fast horse.

This page: Young horses use play to hone survival skills. *Mike Briggs, 2013.*

Solid scholarship indicates the Shoshone people brought horses to what is today Montana by 1680. Horse racing probably began as soon as horses arrived. As the 1800s brought fur traders, gold miners, ranchers, and other pioneers to Montana, horses ran in match races outside of trading forts and down the streets of mining towns. Before long, local officials outlawed street races as a public hazard and oval tracks were built. Helena led the way to "respectable" racing with Madam Coady's one-mile "circular race course" hosting Montana's first territorial fair in 1868. Fairs and horse races ran hand in hand for over a century. Racing often survived even when fairs did not.

Marcus Daly. *Courtesy Daly.*

In 1889, the Kentucky Derby win of Noah Armstrong's Spokane challenged statehood itself as Montana's top news story of the year and marked the start of Montana's first golden age of racing. In the 1890s, Marcus Daly, founder of the Anaconda Copper Company, became king of the Montana turf. His 22,000-acre Bitter Root Stock Farm near Hamilton was home to 1,200 horses. With wealth flowing from mining and related industries, his tracks at Butte and Anaconda drew hundreds of racehorses.

Progressive Era reforms limited races and wagering, and gambling on horse races was banned altogether in 1915. Drought and economic downturns hit Montana after World War I, and for racing, the 1920s were the "slough of despond." When parimutuel betting was authorized by the 1929 legislature, Montana racing revived over the next decade—in spite of that year's stock market crash. Great Falls, planning carefully, built a new fairgrounds and resurrected racing at the 1931 North Montana Fair. Horses still run there today.

In the 1950s, as Native Dancer became TV's first Thoroughbred star, Gallatin County entrepreneur Lloyd Shelhamer brought "Kentucky Derby–style racing" to his showplace Beaumont Club near Belgrade. He also founded United Tote in 1957, starting with a mobile tote board he hauled to county fair meets across the state, and retiring as a multimillionaire.

In the 1960s, the need to protect horses and improve the integrity of racing led to greater oversight and regulation throughout the United States. The second golden age of Montana racing began when the legislature created the Montana Horse Racing Commission in 1965. State authority opened up conflicts between factions of strong-minded horsemen. Larry Elison, racehorse trainer and University of Montana law professor, joined the fledgling commission in 1969. He and his fellow commissioners established the state's authority to enforce professional standards at the tracks.

Montana's new 1972 Constitution allowed gambling "by acts of the legislature or by the people through initiative or referendum."[2] Racing days exploded, peaking in the mid-1980s when fourteen Montana tracks held over 140 days of racing—pushing the climate edges of Montana's short summers—pulling in an annual handle of almost $12 million. Unfortunately, the gambling provisions that initially helped racing became a threat: In the late 1980s, legalized video gaming machines drew bettors' money from tracks to taverns. Political missteps cost the racing industry revenue from gaming taxes that could have offset losses. Rising costs put unprecedented financial pressure on the Montana turf.

By 2000, except for Shelby's boisterous Marias Fair, most small-town county fairs had given up on racing. Montana's five largest tracks hung on by a thread. Depression-era infrastructure was aging, and undeveloped acres inside racetrack ovals drew the eye of county governments looking for profitable land uses. Helena succumbed first when its grandstands were demolished in 2000. Montana's nadir hit in 2012, when only one parimutuel track ran in the state: Miles City, which had long and successfully melded racing with its annual Bucking Horse Sale.

Horses have competitive spirits. Riderless horse finishes third. Missoula, 1972. *Vertical file clipping, Missoula Public Library.*

Indian Relay, Crow Fair 2015. *Larry Mayer.*

In 2013, Montana racing proved ever-resilient when Miles City was rejoined by Great Falls. With cooperation between horsemen, public officials, volunteers, and the local community, the Electric City developed a model for twenty-first-century Montana racing.

Native American communities have produced successful owners, trainers, jockeys, and horses. Examples include the Bird Rattler and Real Bird families, who for generations have won major stakes races in Montana and other states. Today, Montana's sovereign Blackfeet and Crow Reservations hold horse race meets. The growing popularity of Indian Relay has also revived several tracks off Montana's reservations.

Today, the Big Sky is still horse country. Montana races draw large and enthusiastic crowds that belie the claim that racing is a dying sport. On the national scene, from 1889's Spokane to twenty-first-century Medaglia d'Oro, champions of the turf developed strong lungs and solid bodies under the Big Sky.

TIMELINE OF MONTANA HORSE RACING

c. 10,000 BCE	Horses become extinct in America.
1519	Horses return to American mainland via the Spanish.
c. 1680	Horses arrive in Montana via the Shoshone.
c. 1725	Intertribal races, including "Racetrack," Deer Lodge Valley.
1806	Lewis and Clark's Nez Perce guides hold horse races at Traveler's Rest.
1843	Alexander Culbertson and Natawista Iksina stage horse races at Fort Union.
1855	Match races at Fort Benton and Fort Owen. (Hellgate Treaty signed.)
1860	*Key West* arrives in Fort Benton, horse races staged. Mullan Road active.
1863	Virginia City blocks off Jackson and Wallace Streets every Sunday for horse races.
1864	Virginia Slade's famous ride on Billy Bay (Montana Territory created).
1868	Montana's first organized races, "Fashion Course," Helena.
1869	Horse racing at "Olin's Course," Deer Lodge.
1870	Montana State Fairgrounds Racetrack built at present-day Lewis and Clark County Fairgrounds, Helena. (Last races 1999. Homestretch paved over 2007.)
1876	Missoula hosts first race meet. (Last races, 2010. Track torn out 2018.)
1877	Horse racing in Coulson, near Billings.

1878	First race meet in Butte. (Last races, 1936.)
1880	Horse racing at Fort Keogh, near Miles City.
1886	Marcus Daly buys Bitter Root Stock Farm, Hamilton.
1888	Anaconda Driving Park opens. Racing ends c. 1915.
1889	Spokane wins the Kentucky Derby. (Montana statehood.)
1890	Racing at Custer County Fair, Miles City.
1890	North Montana Racing Association holds organized races in Great Falls.
1892	Horse race meets organized in Billings. Racing suspended after 2011.
1897	Scottish Chieftain wins Belmont Stakes.
1900	Marcus Daly dies, horses sold.
1902	Horse racing at Northwest Montana Fair, Kalispell. Racing suspended after 2011.
1904	First Crow Fair (c. 1904–5). Racing continues today.
1909	Statutes restrict betting to "inclosed" tracks and limit length of meets. *Rose* and *Sylvester* convictions upheld.
1912	Montana Supreme Court decision *State v. Gemmell*, 45 Mont. 210 (1912) upholds meet limits.
1915	Legislature bans gambling on horse races.
1917–21	Multiple, unsuccessful attempts to legalize parimutuel betting. "Slough of despond" for racing.
1926	Montana Supreme Court decision *Toomey v. Penwell*, 76 Mont. 166 (1926) allows "co-ownership" pools.

1929	Legislature legalizes parimutuel betting; thirty-seven county fairs, most with races. (Stock market crash, October 1929.)
1931	Great Falls revives race meet. Racing continues today.
1935–43	WPA builds and rebuilds county fairgrounds across the state.
1951	North American Indian Days begins. Racing continues today.
1954	Beaumont Downs opens, Belgrade. Races run 1954–66.
1963	Horse racing held with Miles City Bucking Horse Sale. Racing continues today.
1965	Legislature authorizes Montana Horse Racing Commission to regulate racing and wagering.
1972	1972 Constitution allows gambling "by acts of the legislature or by the people through initiative or referendum." Parimutuels approved. Commission becomes Montana Board of Horse Racing (MBOHR).
1982	Fourteen tracks run races in Montana.
1984	143 race days; wagering handle $11.8 million. Zenith of modern racing era.
1985	Video poker legalized, expanded in 1987.
1989	Simulcast wagering legalized.
1991	Legislation to transfer tax revenue from video gaming to support live horse racing fails.
1997–2006	Insurance costs increase. Racetracks struggle.
2004	Shelby ends racing at Marias Fair, last small-town county fair meet.

2012   Nadir of Montana racing, only Miles City runs.

2013   Racing resurrects in Great Falls.

2018   U.S. Supreme Court allows states to legalize sports betting.

IN THE BEGINNING

And the Grass Remembered[3]

H orses evolved in North America and in the northern Rockies. Fossils of the horse's earliest ancestor, the fifty-million-year-old dog-sized *Eohippus*, were found in Wyoming's Wind River basin. Fossils of *Epihippus* and *Mesohippus* were unearthed in Montana's Beaverhead, Madison, and Broadwater Counties.

Earl Douglass, who discovered the fossil beds of Dinosaur National Monument in Utah, once taught at a one-room schoolhouse in Madison County. He hunted fossils in his spare time. In 1902, returning to Winston, Montana, as a full-fledged paleontologist, he found fragments of three-toed *Merychippus*, a horse ancestor that lived ten to fifteen million years ago.

As primordial forests gave way to open grassland, single-toed hooves gave early *equidae* the speed to escape predators. The 3.5-million-year-old *Equus simplicidens*, the "Hagerman Horse," was the first member of genus *Equus*—the horse and donkey family. It is now Idaho's state fossil.

During the most recent ice age, the horse evolved into its modern form. As dropping oceans exposed Beringia, the Bering land bridge, horses migrated into Eurasia. Before long, the horse was distributed across the globe. About ten thousand years ago, after humans reached North America, rising seas closed Beringia. Horse migration between the continents ended. After that, whether because of changing climate, disease, or overhunting by newly arrived humans—a continuing debate among scientists—the horse became extinct in the Americas.

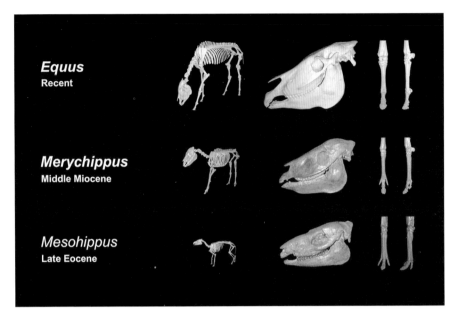

Horses evolved in North America. *Wikimedia Commons.*

RACING'S ANCIENT ROOTS

Horses survived in the Eastern Hemisphere and were first tamed about 5,500 to 5,700 years ago. The speed of the horse served ancient humans well—warfare and horsemanship became inextricably intertwined. Racing honed critical skills.

The earliest treatise on conditioning horses was written about 1345 BCE by Kikkuli. He developed speed and endurance in Hittite chariot horses with techniques now called "interval training." In the eighth century BCE, Homer described chariot races in *The Iliad*. Horse races in the Olympics of Ancient Greece started in 680 BCE. Two thousand years ago, rules for horse racing were carved on a monument to a jockey at a Roman hippodrome in Turkey.

Wagering has equally ancient roots. We cannot know the first time someone said, "Wanna bet?" We do know bookmakers collected wagers on races in ancient Rome.

From antiquity forward, the horse played a critical role in history—and speed was prized. Horse racing for sport permeated European cultures by the time they began to explore the Americas.

Return to America

In 1519, after an absence of ten thousand years, horses returned to the American mainland. Hernán Cortés landed on the Mexican coast with a Spanish force that included sixteen horses. The Spanish imported more horses as they conquered the Aztec Empire and moved northward.

Horses thrived. Domesticated herds grew rapidly, and some escaped to the wild. These feral Spanish horses, called *mesteño*, became the Mustangs of the American West. A few researchers even argue that horses reoccupied the ecological niche of their extinct ancestors: the Smithsonian's 1991–92 exhibition *Seeds of Change* introduced the return of the horse with the phrase "And the Grass Remembered."[4]

"Meeting of Cortez and Montezuma." *Wikimedia Commons.*

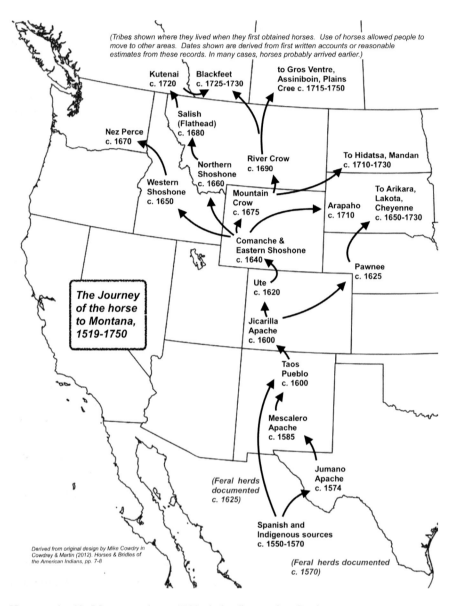

(Tribes shown where they lived when they first obtained horses. Use of horses allowed people to move to other areas. Dates shown are derived from first written accounts or reasonable estimates from these records. In many cases, horses probably arrived earlier.)

Kutenai c. 1720

Blackfeet c. 1725-1730

to Gros Ventre, Assiniboin, Plains Cree c. 1715-1750

Salish (Flathead) c. 1680

Nez Perce c. 1670

River Crow c. 1690

To Hidatsa, Mandan c. 1710-1730

Northern Shoshone c. 1660

Western Shoshone c. 1650

Mountain Crow c. 1675

Arapaho c. 1710

To Arikara, Lakota, Cheyenne c. 1650-1730

Comanche & Eastern Shoshone c. 1640

Pawnee c. 1625

The Journey of the horse to Montana, 1519-1750

Ute c. 1620

Jicarilla Apache c. 1600

Taos Pueblo c. 1600

Mescalero Apache c. 1585

Jumano Apache c. 1574

(Feral herds documented c. 1625)

Spanish and Indigenous sources c. 1550-1570

(Feral herds documented c. 1570)

Derived from original design by Mike Cowdry in Cowdrey & Martin (2012). Horses & Bridles of the American Indians, pp. 7-8

Horses arrived in Montana prior to 1700. *Author diagram, from Cowdrey.*

Horses officially reached what is today New Mexico with conquistador Juan de Oñate in 1598. The Spanish tried to keep indigenous people from possessing horses but also trained men and boys, especially among the Pueblo, to help manage their herds. Local people quickly recognized the value of a speedy and agile companion for hunting and war. Between illegal sales, theft, and estrays, horses spread to Native cultures. By 1607, Spanish officials complained that the Apache were "carrying off the horse herds." In 1659, the Navajo used horses to raid the Spanish.[5]

Two events sped up the transfer of horses. The first was Oñate's expedition to the Arkansas River in 1601, when he claimed he "lost" several hundred horses. The second was the Pueblo Revolt of 1680, when the fleeing Spanish left behind 1,500 horses. As tribes of the southern Plains exchanged horses, distribution moved steadily north.

Horses changed Native cultures dramatically. Mobility and wealth increased. Nomadic life became easier; horse-mounted people covered more ground and transported more goods. Hunting on horseback with a fleet-footed "buffalo horse" was superior to driving herds on foot over a buffalo jump. Some cultures even abandoned agriculture in favor of a nomadic lifestyle focused on bison.[6]

The Road to Montana

Early studies of horse distribution used mostly French and English accounts, conservatively placing the first horses in Montana "no later than" 1700. Later work, using Spanish documents and accounts from Native people, moved the timeline decades earlier.

Researchers initially assumed that horses spread north via theft, capture, and war, as they did in the Southwest. Historian and horseman Francis Haines believed otherwise. He argued that, given the challenges of horse-handling, most northern tribes probably obtained their first horses via trade—theft and capture required expertise, and the chaos of war was no place to learn equitation.[7]

The Apache of the Southwest provided horses to the Ute and the Pawnee. By 1640, the Ute had passed their knowledge and horses to the Comanche and Eastern Shoshone. The Shoshone brought horses north to the Snake River region in Idaho. The Nez Perce were mounted by 1670.[*8]

Horses crossed the Bitterroot Range by 1680. The Salish (Séliš, Sqelixʷ), considered the first people in what is today Montana to possess horses, got

---

* Today, the Nez Perce are known for developing the Appaloosa horse. However, they did not begin to specialize in spotted patterns until sometime after Lewis and Clark, who noted horses of all colors.

Left: Salish pad saddle. Treeless saddles followed Shoshone designs. "[T]he young men scarcely ever use anything more than a small pad of dressed leather stuffed with hair." Meriwether Lewis, August 24, 1805. *Eneas Finley, 1890. X1986.01.90, MHS.*

Below: The Shoshone, called the "Snakes" by early explorers. *Snake Indians Horse Racing*. Early C.M. Russell sketch. *Printing proof,* C.M. Russell's Boyhood Sketchbook, *(1970). R.D. Warren, ed., 2016.35.01, MHS.*

them from the Shoshone. Anthropologist Harry Turney-High documented one origin story: A group of Salish warriors, avenging kin killed in a Shoshone raid, spent three days watching a small herd of trained horses, "content where they were, in association with people." Then they stole them. According to the tale, through trial and error, the men learned to ride.[9]

The Apsáalooke (Crow) people probably obtained their first horses from the Shoshone, though some accounts name the Nez Perce as intermediaries. The Mountain Crow may have had horses in northern Wyoming as early as 1675. They brought horses to their River Crow relatives in Montana by 1690.

In one traditional story, some Apsáalooke people traveled to the Green River and bought or captured a stallion. When they brought him to camp, the horse kicked a man, whose clan carries the name "Kicked in the Bellies" to this day. In another story, a band of Mountain Crow traveled to the Great Salt Lake area and returned with Shoshone horses. The Mountain Crow distributed horses north to people living in what today is northern Montana and southern Saskatchewan, including the Cree and Gros Ventre.[10]

Horses reached Montana's Rocky Mountain Front no later than 1720. Some bands of the Blackfoot Confederacy (Niitsitapi) had horses by 1725, possibly from the Kootenai (Ktunaxa). The Siksika word for horse, *ponokáómitaa*, translates as "elk dog," reflecting the animal's size and usefulness.[11]

The north-central plains saw horses travel north along two routes, though devastating fatalities from an 1837 smallpox epidemic resulted in the loss of significant oral history about how horses arrived. One Shoshone route crossed the Continental Divide in Wyoming, roughly along the route that later became the Oregon Trail. Another source was the Pawnee, who may have brought horses to the Lakota as early as 1675. The Cheyenne (Tsis tsis'tas) had horses by 1730, probably from multiple sources. The last of Montana's tribal nations to be mounted were the Chippewa (Ojibwa), who obtained horses via the Mandan or the Assiniboine (Nakoda).

Once people had horses, some migrated hundreds of miles to new territory. In 1742–43, the Vérendrye brothers, among the first white explorers in the area, mentioned horses and commented on Native riders' skill. Soon after, horses from English and French sources began trickling in from the east.[12]

Horses and racing arrived together. One common route across the Continental Divide went through the Deer Lodge Valley, which became a site for intertribal meetups and competition. As discussed in chapter 4, the community of Racetrack was named on account of stories that Native people held horse races there along a flat straightaway.

The Salish were among the first Montanans to have horses. C.M. Russell, *Lewis and Clark Meeting Indians at Ross' Hole*. Oil on canvas, 1912. *MHS X1912.06.01.*

In 1805–6, Lewis and Clark mentioned the quality of horses they observed. Following the well-documented meeting between their Shoshone guide Sacagawea and her brother Cameahwait, Meriwether Lewis described the fleet-footed horses of Cameahwait's band favorably: "Indeed many of them would make a figure on the South side of James River [in Virginia] or the land of fine horses." Upon encountering the Salish at Ross' Hole in the Bitterroot Valley on September 4, 1805, William Clark was equally impressed, describing the horses there as "ellegant [*sic*]."[13]

Lewis was even more effusive about the quality of Nez Perce horses: "Their horses appear to be of an excellent race; they are lofty, eligantly [*sic*] formed, active and durable…much like our best blooded horses in [V] irginia, which they resemble as well in fleetness and bottom as in form and colours." On July 2, 1806, at Traveler's Rest, near present-day Lolo, Lewis and Clark both journaled about horse races held that day as the party prepared to split up and bid goodbye to their Nez Perce guides.[14]

Frontiersman W.T. "Uncle Billy" Hamilton witnessed intertribal races between the Shoshone and the Crow (Apsáalooke) near the Shoshone River in northern Wyoming about 1845 or 1846. Running multiple heats over a one-mile prairie course, the Shoshone initially ran their second-string animals to lull their opponents into wagering high stakes, then brought out their best horses to win the final race.

Hamilton himself owned a fast buffalo horse of unknown breeding named Runner. Runner was a gift to Hamilton from Swift Runner, son of the Cheyenne leader White Antelope. Hamilton was very fond of the horse and raced him successfully against horses owned by the Ute.[15]

"Blooded Horses" Come West

The Oregon Trail, running through Wyoming and southern Idaho, crossed Shoshone horse-trading territory. Montana tribes acquired horses "north of the Great Salt Lake" long before white settlers came west. Their mounts, the "Spanish horse" that inhabited the West, were compact animals, fast over short distances, noted for hardiness and endurance. Then, as American pioneers arrived from the East, some brought "blooded horses"—running Thoroughbreds and fast trotting horses, later called Standardbreds.

Billy Hamilton described an Oregon-bound migrant train he guided from Plattsburg, Missouri, to Fort Hall (in present-day Idaho) about 1848. The group included people who closely guarded their "blooded Kentucky horses." Hamilton spoke with scorn of other, more naïve travelers, whose lack of wariness resulted in their stock being run off—by both white and Indian raiders.[16]

The Horse Nation

The "horse nation"—horses themselves—integrated completely into Native culture. Joe Medicine Crow provided examples in *From the Heart of the Crow Country: The Crow Indians' Own Stories*.

The Apsáalooke name for the horse was *Ichilay*, a word meaning "to search with." This referred to horses' value for scouting and hunting. Some spiritual leaders had abilities called "horse medicine." In matters of the heart, an exchange of horses might solidify a marriage agreement. When people sought justice, the "Keeper of the Peacepipe" might intercede to negotiate an exchange of horses from the offenders to the victims—preventing retaliatory bloodshed. Wealth and economic status were measured by how many horses someone owned; even in the reservation era of the early 1900s, one traditional giveaway saw four hundred horses exchanged.[17]

Although white settlement and centuries of warfare changed Native culture irrevocably, the horse culture remains alive. As discussed throughout this book, and particularly in chapter 16, Montana's Native people have been part of Montana's racing circuit since formal meets were organized, and tribal members run horses today in both modern flat track races and the growing sport of Indian Relay.

2

FORT UNION TO FORT BENTON

Fast horses were a tradition on the frontier of Whoop-Up country.
—Joel Overholser[18]

F ort Union, on the Missouri River between present-day Sidney,
Montana, and Williston, North Dakota, was founded by John Jacob
Astor's American Fur Company. In 1840, Alexander Culbertson
took charge of the outpost, which had become part of Pierre Chouteau Jr.'s
trading empire.

When John James Audubon visited Fort Union in 1843, Culbertson and
his wife, Natawista Iksina,* staged a horse race, further described in chapter
13. Fort Union is on the present-day Montana–North Dakota border, and the
course was over a mile long, so both states can probably claim this contest.[19]

Native people of the upper Missouri sought trade, and Culbertson opened
posts upstream of Fort Union. In 1846, Culbertson built the uppermost, Fort
Lewis. In 1847, he moved that fort across the river and downstream for
easier access. In 1850, Fort Lewis was renamed Fort Benton, in honor of
Chouteau's political ally, Thomas Hart Benton, senator from Missouri.

The Culbertsons developed Fort Benton into a prosperous trading post.
Served by keelboats and other small craft, Fort Benton was critical to the
Upper Missouri fur trade. It was the innermost river port in America; the
cataracts of the Great Falls stopped most water transport. It became the

---

* According to Wischmann, her name is also spelled Natoyist-Siksina' and Natúyi-
tsíxina. Traditionally translated as "Medicine Snake Woman," "Holy Snake" may be
more accurate.

starting point for the Mullan Road, which connected to Fort Walla Walla on the Columbia River, and for the Whoop-Up Trail, which went to Canada.

Natawista Iksina made much of this possible. She was of the Kainai ("Blood") people of the Blackfoot Confederacy (Niitsitapi). She served as a diplomat and interpreter in 1853–54 when Culbertson guided Isaac Stevens's party while they surveyed potential transcontinental railroad routes.[20] With the arrival of white traders, intertribal horse races became interracial, demonstrated by an oral history of a great race in Fort Benton, estimated to have occurred about 1855:

> *A white man named Weber had an undefeated racehorse and issued a challenge to all comers. The Kainai heard of Weber's challenge. Their leader, Many Spotted Horses, owned a fast blue roan and brought the horse to Fort Benton. Many Spotted Horses had a dream where his spirit helper told him how to win the race: he was to insist the race be held on the sandy river bottomland west of Fort Benton, running clockwise, for a distance of two miles. His terms were accepted, and when the day of the race came, the blue roan won.*[21]

In 1860, both John Mullan's road-building expedition and the shallow-draft steamboats *Key West* and *Chippewa* arrived at Fort Benton, launching its boom years. A member of Major A.H. Blake's Dragoons, who arrived on the steamboats, noted several thousand people, mostly Blackfeet, who camped in the area and set up a four-mile racecourse "on a high bluff" above the fort. The soldiers and the Blackfeet exchanged wagers on races. The following year, 1861, trader Johnny Grant said that he ran "a big racehorse" in Fort Benton.[22]

The discovery of gold at Grasshopper Creek in 1862 increased Fort Benton's steamboat traffic. A town, known for its saloons, brothels, and violence, formed around the fort. Front Street between Fifteenth and Sixteenth Streets was dubbed "the bloodiest block in the west." Newfound wealth flowed freely. In 1869, owners put up $200 each for a match race between Sam Debow's sorrel horse Bob and John Arner's bay mare Kate. News reports said spectators wagered over $3,000. Kate won.

Steamboats carried ten thousand tons of freight to Fort Benton in 1879, but railroads ended the steamboat era. The Utah and Northern Railroad reached Montana in 1880; then the Northern Pacific arrived in Helena in 1883. Fort Benton declined in economic importance. Cattle ranching came to dominate the local economy, and the wild town became a quaint and charming county seat.

But horse racing remained.

Dan Blevins

The prairie lands of Chouteau County provided excellent grazing. The area's best-known horse breeder and trainer was Dan Blevins, who ranched on Highwood Creek. His wife was the part-Blackfoot daughter of fur trader George Weippert. The Blevins family raised running horses and some trotters.

Dan Blevins ran horses at the Fort Benton spring meet in 1877. The following year, he took his horses to Canada and defeated "the Britishers" at "Cypress"—Cypress Hills on the Alberta-Saskatchewan border. In 1886, his horses, Daniel B and Ida Glenn, ran in Butte, Helena, Belleview (Idaho), and Salt Lake City. In twenty-one races, they pulled in fifteen firsts and five seconds. Daniel B set a Helena track record of 1:43 in a mile race in 1887.

Blevins also trained outside horses. In 1884, he conditioned horses at Robert Vaughn's track on the Sun River. He trained for the Bielenbergs of Deer Lodge in the 1880s and purchased some of their young horses, including a brilliant filly named Nevada and a colt named Malcolm.

Success was marred by tragedy. His son, Fisher Blevins, "highly respected as an honest, upright lad," was a jockey. At Helena in 1888, eighteen-year-old

Dan Blevins (*second from right*) and horses (*left to right*): Daniel B, "Zoa" (Ida?) Glenn, Nevada, Nisbet and an unnamed colt. 1888. *Dan Dutro photo, Overholser.*

Fisher picked up a ride for another stable. Fisher was reluctant to take the mount, Green Preuitt, as the horse had a "vicious" reputation, but the trainer convinced the boy to ride by offering an unheard-of jockey mount fee of $25. Rank at the break, Green Preuitt, vision narrowed by blinkers, ran into a fence, flipped and rolled over his rider, breaking the boy's neck. People rushed in as the horse scrambled up, unhurt, but the lad died on the track before his distraught father could reach his side. A grief-stricken Blevins promptly declared he would sell all his racing stock. But he kept his champions—Daniel B, Ida Glenn and Nevada—and ran them in 1889.[23] In 1892, Blevins's horse Fannie B challenged the horses of Marcus Daly and Hugh Kirkendall.

Dan Blevins ultimately became a respected elder statesman of the track. He ran horses at Great Falls in 1907. With a wry sense of humor, he joked in 1908 that he (around age seventy), and his twenty-four-year-old horse, Old Rattler, would both compete in the spring races.

County Fairs

Chouteau County was one of the original nine counties in Montana territory. Counties were added as population grew, and today there are fifty-six. The earliest Chouteau county fairs were held in towns later placed in new counties, including Havre (now in Hill County) and Chinook (now in Blaine County). The Chouteau County Fairgrounds at Fort Benton opened in 1913. Races ran annually until 1918. Fairs and races had hard times after that. The economy sank after World War I ended, and the Montana legislature banned gambling in 1915.* Race reports from Fort Benton are spotty until parimutuel gambling became legal in 1929. Another gap in racing appeared from 1947 through 1958.

In the late 1950s, the North Central Racing Association organized. Its successor, the Chouteau County Turf Club, formed in 1972. Horses ran each summer from 1959 or 1960 until 1976. Some years, there were races every weekend in June, over the Fourth of July, and then the Chouteau County Fair ran additional days in August. Racing was popular: in 1974, parimutuel handle (in a town of two thousand people) was $30,000 for one day and $71,500 over three days.[24]

The meet was organized for many years by the Bramlett family. Horsemen appreciated the good footing on the sandy track overlooking

---

* See chapter 7.

Above: Chouteau County Fairgrounds, 1926. *Overholser.*

Below: Trojeana at Fort Benton, 1976. Bev Tomaskie, trainer, R.D. Smith, jockey. *Courtesy Tomaskie.*

the Missouri River. The main problem was that the meet's purses averaged $100 per race. The winning owner got $50, then paid the trainer if he or she had one, plus the jockey, the pony rider, and the photographer. Even a champion's "paycheck" didn't cover hay, oats, farrier, or gas for the truck.[25]

Parimutuel racing ended in Fort Benton after the 1976 meet, and the Chouteau County Turf Club dissolved in 1981. The fairground's grandstands and rodeo arena are still in use today. The track footprint has faded, but it remains mostly undeveloped, leaving open a possibility—however remote—that racing could return.

3
VIRGINIA CITY

Fast Horses and Vigilantes

With all the energy that love and despair could lend…she urged her fleet charger over the twelve miles of rough and rocky ground that intervened between her and the object of her passionate devotion.
—*Thomas Dimsdale*[26]

Rumors of gold drew miners to Montana from California. John White "found color" in 1862 on Grasshopper Creek, and the town of Bannack formed. On May 26, 1863, Fairweather and Edgar struck it rich in Alder Gulch, and the rush was on. In five years, the area produced $30 to 40 million in gold. A series of small camps sprouted up, dubbed "Fourteen Mile City" for the length of Alder Gulch, and the best known was Virginia City.

Gold rush towns were centers for informal match races, and Virginia City was no exception. People blocked off Wallace and Jackson Streets and held races every Sunday. News reports mentioned other courses at "Madison" and "Nevada [City]." Stakes were usually arranged by competitors. Spectators flush with gold dust wagered money like water. Johnny Grant of Deer Lodge* was a participant. He announced in the November 1864 *Montana Post* that he would race his three-year-old colt, Limber Bill (sometimes recorded as "Limber Belle") at 400 yards against "any three year old in this territory" for stakes of $3,000 to $5,000.[27]

_____

* See chapter 4.

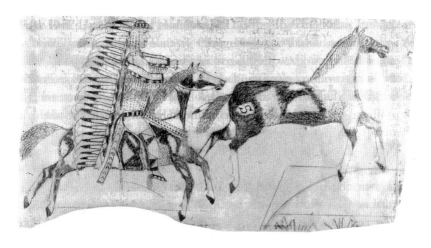

The Apsáalooke people were known for their excellent horses. *Elk Head* [Hidatsa] *Steals a Horse from the Crows Branded S.* Ledger drawing, circa 1883–85. *MHS X1937.01.02.*

The Saga of Billy Bay

The most famous racehorse in Virginia City was Billy Bay. Described as a "Kentucky Thoroughbred," he might be the first named Thoroughbred in Montana, though there is no documentation of his ancestry—nor when he arrived. By 1863, the horse was owned by fur trader Malcolm Clarke. Like Alexander Culbertson, Clarke married into the Blackfeet tribe; in his case, he had two "Piegan" (i.e., Piikani, Blackfeet) wives.

Clarke obtained Billy Bay from the Blackfeet, who "captured" the horse "in the neighborhood of the Great Salt Lake"—Oregon Trail country. As noted in chapter 1, many good "blooded horses" were brought along that route—and at times got new owners. Thus, Billy Bay's Thoroughbred ancestry is possible but unverified.

Billy Bay was a champion at intertribal races, where stakes included "money, pelts, and other valuables."[28] Later reports claimed he was everything from black to buckskin, but his name probably reflected his color, a rich, dark bay—often seen in Thoroughbreds.

When Clarke met a freight hauler named Jack Slade and sold Billy Bay to Slade's beautiful wife, Maria Virginia Slade, the horse's story became part of Montana's history.

Jack Slade had a "Jekyll and Hyde" personality, activated by alcohol. Described by Thomas Dimsdale, "Those who saw him in his natural state

Horses raced down the streets of Virginia City. Wallace Street, 1869. *MHS Photo Archives 956-314.*

only, would pronounce him to be a kind husband, a most hospitable host and a courteous gentleman; on the contrary, those who met him when maddened with liquor and surrounded by a gang of armed roughs, would pronounce him a fiend incarnate."[29]

Slade had worked for the Overland Stage Company throughout the 1850s, guarding freight shipments and developing a reputation for brutality. He encouraged a legend that he murdered twenty-six men, recounted by Mark Twain in *Roughing It*. In reality, he may have killed only one—a fellow named Jules Beni (or Reni), who probably needed killing. Slade kept Beni's ears as a souvenir.

Slade's reputation initially led to promotions; he built the stage stop of Virginia Dale (possibly named for his wife) in northern Colorado. But once settled in one spot, his drinking was a problem. The company ignored his jaunts to Denver, where he got drunk and shot up saloons, but when Slade did the same at a local military outpost, his employer could no longer turn a blind eye. His tenure at Virginia Dale ended.

The Slades arrived in Montana in 1863 and came to Virginia City. They soon settled near the Madison River, where Jack built a stone house and hoped to set up a toll road. Along the way, they picked up two racehorses. One was Billy Bay; the other, possibly named Copperbottom (after a famed racehorse of an earlier era), was Jack's. The pair became avid competitors in the Sunday races. Virginia Slade, a brilliant rider and excellent dancer, was popular and well liked.

Jack Slade was more controversial. Initially a supporter of the Vigilantes, he became their problem child. He would come to town, get drunk with friends, and wreak havoc. He trashed saloons. He once rode his horse into the mercantile and pitched supplies out the door. Another time, he led his horse into a saloon, grabbed a bottle of alcohol, and attempted to force the animal to drink it. One day, Slade dumped a large canister of milk over the head of the delivery driver, and another time he burst into a theater, speaking to the women there with the "most insulting language."[30]

Slade was arrested several times, but with plenty of money from hauling freight, he was repeatedly freed after he offered a tearful apology, sobered up, and paid generously for damages.

But by March 1864, matters had come to a head. Having hanged Henry Plummer's gang that January, the Vigilantes now had to keep the peace—and Slade's alcoholism was out of control. His finances depleted, he offered to pay for one round of trouble with his most precious possession—Beni's desiccated ears. When the Vigilantes issued a warrant for Slade's arrest, he responded by ripping it up. When warned to get out of town, he instead put a gun to the head of the local judge, Alexander Davis. This sealed his fate. Though Slade had not—yet—murdered anyone in Montana, the Vigilantes put out a call. An armed mob formed from the mines up and down Alder Gulch. At least two hundred strong, they arrested Slade at gunpoint. Slade was promptly taken to a nearby corral with a crossbeam across tall gateposts. There, a noose dangled.

Slade had many friends, and when the death sentence was pronounced, someone raced to tell Virginia. She was at their home on the Madison River, an estimated twelve miles away. Hearing that Slade was to be hanged, Virginia immediately mounted Billy Bay and galloped for town.

She probably was armed: Slade's legend included a tale that he was kidnapped by a band of thieves who planned to kill him. He begged to be allowed to say goodbye to his beloved wife. His captors agreed, and when Virginia arrived, she insisted on seeing Slade alone. Having concealed multiple firearms under her skirt, she passed him his weapons. The pair shot their way out of the situation, leapt double on Virginia's horse and galloped away.

No doubt the Vigilantes feared the Slades would try to repeat history. Slade's hanging was the Vigilantes' most controversial execution of the period, and the situation was tense. Even as Slade stood on a box and the hangman's noose was put over his head, he screamed, "For God's sake, let me see my dear wife!" Eyewitness accounts agree that Slade tearfully begged for mercy. Later accounts claimed the Vigilantes feared Virginia's "feminine wiles" would sway the crowd to sympathy, but the men on the scene were probably more worried that her charisma and skill with firearms could inspire Slade's friends to help her take on the mob.

A large hill lay between the Slade's home and Virginia City, and as observers saw her in the far distance, cresting the hill on her champion racehorse, the command "Men, do your duty" rang out. The box Slade stood on was kicked away, and he died almost instantly.

"X" Beidler, one of the Vigilante committee, quickly gathered a crew, cut Slade down, and "packed him off" to the Virginia City Hotel. When Virginia arrived, her horse forgotten, she threw herself over his body and later was found "sobbing and moaning, bowed over a stark form shrouded in a blanket."[31]

Refusing to have him buried in the town, Virginia obtained a zinc-lined coffin, and—ironically—preserving his body in alcohol, arranged to ship his remains to his childhood home in Illinois. Running out of money, she got him as far as Salt Lake City, where he was buried. After a short-lived marriage to Slade's friend Jim Kiscadden, Virginia left the territory.

BUT WHAT OF BILLY BAY? Hyperbole and horse stories pair like bread with butter, so there are multiple tales of his fate. The most improbable is a 1941 tale that his name was Yellowhammer and that he collapsed and died of exhaustion at the scene of Slade's hanging. Because such a dramatic collapse would have been noted by eyewitness accounts, this probably did not happen. Further, Billy Bay was born in an era where horses were ridden many miles daily. Exhaustion or lameness was possible, immediate death unlikely.

He may have appeared on November 16, 1870, at a sixty-mile race around Olin's track at Deer Lodge. The $2,000 match was between Valiton and Talbot's horse, six-year-old Lizard, and a ten-year-old horse alternately named Billy Bay or Billy Boy, owned by C.C. Thornton. Lizard won in a time of four hours and twenty-eight minutes, and his supporters "took him from saloon to saloon to celebrate." Slade's Billy Bay would have been at least ten years old in 1870, so it is possible this was the same horse.[32]

Another tale comes from 1890. A thirty-year-old horse named Bob, a decrepit "dull buckskin" who pulled a wagon through the streets of Helena, was said to be "the animal…on which [Virginia Slade] swiftly galloped." This horse was once owned by Dan Flowerree, a rancher and racing enthusiast. This fate is unlikely, but not impossible: an old bay horse with a dry, bleached-out coat might look vaguely buckskin, and horses can live to be over thirty.[33]

The final legend is that the ghosts of Billy Bay and Virginia Slade haunt the hills northeast of Virginia City. On some nights, the sound of hoofbeats punctuates the dark, followed by wails of grief as a woman on a lathered horse gallops by, her long hair and skirts flowing in the wind.[34]

VIRGINIA CITY'S RACING CONTINUED after the Slades departed. In 1865, a match between Monte's Wild Charley and Foster's Crepin Horse began innocently enough, with each side putting up $250 for a six-hundred-yard contest on August 20. That match proved inconclusive when Crepin's rider decided to "foolishly lash" the horse, which bolted sideways to evade his rider, and yet was only beaten by a half length. Foster claimed foul, and the match was reset for August 27 at $300 each.

The *Montana Post* covered the rivalry with great enthusiasm. In the final matchup, the footing was slippery, putting the unshod Crepin at a disadvantage. Foster offered to sweeten the pot by another $50 if the match was postponed again, but to no avail. Wild Charley won, and the *Montana Post* declared, "At any rate, the question of the relative speed of the two horses may now be considered definitely settled."[35]

When the gold played out, Virginia City faded. Dethroned as territorial capital in favor of Helena, it is now the Madison County seat. With a series of territorial laws passed between 1872 and 1885, towns gained the authority to ban horse racing in the streets and outlawed racing on Sundays. Horse racing moved to better footing; the Madison County fairgrounds were built at Twin Bridges.* Today, Wallace Street is State Highway 287.

---

* See chapter 12

4

DEER LODGE

From Racetrack to Ranching

The Deer Lodge Valley, part of a major Native trade route, hosted intertribal meet-ups and competition. Today, Interstate 90 winds through the area. At exit 195—"Racetrack"—modern travelers may glance about, seeing only a small cluster of buildings over on the frontage road, and drive on, idly wondering what sort of racetrack was there.

Racetrack was named for a flat straightaway used for match races. Local historians think it was roughly where Quinlan Road is today. Other racing flats in the area were along the Albee bench and west of the Blackfoot River near Garrison. Powell County was one of the earliest centers of white settlement in Montana and a hotbed of organized horse racing.

Johnny Grant

Each cowpuncher owned one or more fine saddle horses, often a thoroughbred, on which he lavished his affections....Horse racing was one of his favorite sports.
—*Granville Stuart*[36]

The first livestock arrived in Montana in the 1840s with missionaries and fur traders. Settlers traveling the Oregon Trail, though well south of Montana, were another source. A major stop was Fort Hall, a Hudson Bay Company outpost near present-day Pocatello, Idaho. Travelers stopped

C.M. Russell. *A Race for the Wagons*, 1926. *MHS X1952.01.33.*

there to rest and resupply. Animals that were thin, lame, and unable to travel on were left behind, sometimes traded for local stock. This was Shoshone country, and horses were plentiful.

Richard Grant, who managed Fort Hall, saw profit in this influx of trail-worn livestock. He traded pioneers two trail-worn animals for one that was fat and healthy. Cattle allowed a year to eat and recover from their journey were traded to the next year's migrant trains. The best animals were kept, then reproduced, and his herds grew.

Richard's teenage son Johnny came to the frontier to live with his father about 1847. Young Johnny Grant had a good eye for horses. In 1849 he obtained a "valuable blood horse" from passing immigrants and was infuriated when his father claimed the animal. Father and son continued to clash, and by 1850, Johnny had struck out on his own, trading, trapping, and, like his father, buying stock from pioneer trains. He soon adopted his father's two-for-one tactic, improving his stock by keeping the best animals.

As cattle herds grew, so did the need for pasture. Montana's Beaverhead Valley had lush grasslands, and the Grants drove cattle north to fatten up. The trade route through the Deer Lodge Valley offered another profitable market, and Johnny Grant wintered there in 1857–58. He settled permanently in 1859. He established good trading—and family—relations with the many tribes that traveled through the area. Grant was polygamous for much of his life; one of his wives, Quarra, of the Lemhi Shoshone, was the sister of the famed chief Tendoy.

In 1853, a year when Johnny admitted "we spent most of our time in horse racing and gambling," he owned a "Thoroughbred Indian Horse" that he named "Cream." Like Virginia Slade's Billy Bay, Cream's pedigree is unknown, but he was never defeated and could race over distance: he won a seven-horse match race at one mile, 300 yards. Cream may have preceded Billy Bay to Montana: Grant sold Cream while still in Idaho, but joyfully explained that he bought the horse back in 1860 when Cream, by then an aged horse, recognized him during a chance encounter and whinnied in greeting.[37]

Grant was in the right place at the right time when the 1862 Grasshopper Creek strike launched Montana's gold rush. He owned many horses and over one thousand head of good-quality cattle. Miners needed food and transportation. Grant supplied both.

New arrivals also presented more opportunities for horse racing. As noted in chapter 3, Grant advertised for race challengers, running for stakes in the four figures. Flush with cash, he spent money as fast as he earned it.

When Grant raced, he preferred riding bareback with a horsehair rope, a setup he considered more comfortable and easier on the horse. Two of his racehorses were specialists: John ran at a thousand yards. A sprinter, Sam, was described as a "quarterhorse." Another "fine blood colt" of Grant's was bad-tempered and resold "to the Crows" (the Apsáalooke), who, he said, "always can break in horses." At Fort Benton the next year, the colt was tamed, but his new owners refused to sell at any price, saying, "This horse just plays with the buffalo."[38]

Kohrs and Bielenberg: Gold on the Hoof

The cattle interests of the territory are annually increasing, which makes [an] *increased demand for* [horses]…*An excellent horse for this purpose may be had by infusing thoroughbred blood into our common stock.*
—Rocky Mountain Husbandman, *December 11, 1879*

When Conrad Kohrs met Johnny Grant, it was an ideal situation for both men.

Kohrs, born in Holstein and trained as a butcher, reached America in the 1850s. In 1862, he came to Montana, seeking gold and hoping to strike it rich. When offered $25 a month to run a butcher shop in Bannack and keep the books, Kohrs decided a steady job beat the vagaries of prospecting, discovered he had a head for business—and became rich.

By the fall of 1862, miners' demand for steaks, sausage, and tallow candles was so high that Kohrs went out to buy cattle nearly full time, hiring another butcher to process meat. He went into business for himself in 1863, followed the miners from Bannack to Alder Gulch, and set up shop near Virginia City. There he became a cattle broker, delivering goods on the hoof to multiple butchers.

Grant sold cattle to Kohrs and willingly extended credit. The two men developed a firm friendship. In November 1863, carrying $5,000 in gold dust to pay a debt to Grant, Kohrs covered sixty miles from Virginia City to Grant's place in six hours, evading highwaymen all the way. Grant, impressed by the brave and honest man, sold more cattle to Kohrs at bargain prices. In doing so, Grant kick-started Kohrs's beef empire. Kohrs, more careful with money than Grant, eventually became the cattle king of Montana.

The horseman of the family was Kohrs's younger half-brother John Bielenberg, who came to Montana in 1864. The two men were partners

Conrad Kohrs (*right*) circa 1905. *L.A. Huffman, courtesy Allen.*

in the livestock business. In 1866, when Grant decided that Montana was getting too civilized for his tastes, Kohrs bought out his ranch. Today it is the Grant-Kohrs Ranch National Historic Site.

Kohrs knew that horses able to cover Montana's vast distances were key to his business, but his horse management skills fell short. In his 1863 ride to Grant's place, the price was paid by Kohrs's "good horse," Grey Billy. Kohrs admitted with sorrow that he lacked the knowledge to properly care for the horse after such hard use and ruined the animal. He did the same to another by traveling 480 miles in six days.

Though the historic record is silent on the matter, it is likely that Bielenberg provided necessary expertise. By 1865, Kohrs understood that to travel quickly, it was wiser to keep many well-cared-for horses to avoid damaging any single animal from overuse. He took twelve good saddle horses and stationed them at various places so he could travel quickly by relay. He enjoyed beating the stagecoach from Virginia City to Helena.

In 1868, Kohrs and his new bride, Augusta, attended the 1868 Helena Territorial Fair "at Cody's ground near the present site of Kessler's Brewery." There, John Bielenberg entered a trotter named Sorrel George, "who bolted and lost the race."[39]

Bielenberg was also reputed to be an excellent rider. A lithograph of the Kohrs and Bielenberg operation in M.A. Leeson's *History of Montana* shows a mustachioed man with an excellent seat astride their prize stallion Regent; the resemblance to Bielenberg is unmistakable.[40]

Kohrs's horses, 1885. Regent under saddle, Strideaway to the left. *Leeson M.A.*, History of Montana.

As gold played out, Kohrs drove cattle to the railheads in southern Wyoming to ship east. He added grazing land throughout Montana, starting in the Sun River area in 1869, moving into eastern Montana by the late 1870s. To manage his cattle (28,000 head at one point), Kohrs and his cowhands needed hundreds of good, fleet-footed horses, and Kohrs got serious about breeding his own.

"Blooded" Horses

In 1870, Kohrs advertised a "Thoroughbred horse" at stud but without details. Eight years later, he traveled to visit family in Iowa, and there he purchased two stallions, the "trotter" Strideaway and the Thoroughbred Regent. Some sources identify Regent as the first Thoroughbred with "papers"—a documented pedigree—to arrive in Montana, in part on account of some sources listing him as an 1876 purchase. That said, another Thoroughbred, Cariboo, a son of the great stallion Lexington, was purchased in New York by Charles Williams of Helena, shipped to Montana in August 1876, and entered in a race. Most likely, Cariboo beat Regent to Montana.[41]

Regent's son Montana Regent was his best-known offspring. Regent has Thoroughbred descendants today and also appears in Quarter Horse, Paint, Appaloosa, and Warmblood pedigrees. His most interesting descendant was the gelding Halston, winner of the Irish Grand National steeplechase in 1920 and 1922. Information on Strideaway is harder to pin down; multiple horses of the era had the same name.[42]

Kohrs met Marcus Daly in 1877. A decade later, as Daly got heavily into racehorses, Kohrs visited Hamilton and was impressed with the Bitter Root Stock Farm, noting Daly's covered track.* In 1893, Daly wanted to buy Kohrs's trotting team Ben and Button, a pair of Morgans that Kohrs considered the best he'd ever owned. Bielenberg was attached to the team, but pragmatism prevailed. They sold to Daly at an "expensive" price— $700.[43]

---

* See chapter 8.

From Willow Run to Kentucky

Along with Grant and Bielenberg, Samuel Larabie was another horse aficionado in the area. Larabie went into business with Robert Donnell and William Andrews Clark, opening a bank in Deer Lodge in 1869. Clark moved to Butte to open another bank in 1877. There, Clark accepted mining claims in lieu of loan payments and became one of Butte's "Copper Kings." Larabie, more cautious, remained in Deer Lodge and took horses as loan collateral. He was comfortably wealthy and invested his money in race horses.

Larabie purchased some "Kentucky horses" in 1875. These appear to have been trotters. He owned two colts, Superior (foaled 1875) and Assignee (foaled 1876), both grandsons of Rysdyk's Hambletonian, foundation sire of the Standardbred. Superior raced and won at the Helena fair in 1878.

Larabie's interest in breeding harness horses was short-lived. In 1878, his "time being too much engaged to give the business the attention it requires," he sold Superior and Assignee to James Harper of Bozeman and thirty-six head of "mostly pedigreed" horses to George Harvey of Clancy. In 1879, he sold Harvey the promising young stallion Mambrino Diamond and sold "five valuable blooded brood mares" to other people, apparently the last of his harness racing stock.[44]

About 1880, Larabie started breeding Thoroughbreds at his Willow Run Stock Farm. A few years later, he went into partnership with Augustus Eastin of Lexington, Kentucky. The Eastin & Larabie horses were bred and started in Montana, then shipped to Kentucky to race. It was an odd but successful partnership. The men apparently only met in person twice, communicating mostly via letter and telegraph.

Larabie's champion, Montana Regent, was foaled in 1883. After Montana Regent went east and won several races in Kentucky and Tennessee, Eastin & Larabie sold him in 1887 for $10,000. The buyer was James Murphy, who trained Thoroughbreds for James Ben Ali Haggin.[*] However, in this case, Haggin never was listed as the colt's owner. After a month of speculation, the papers reported Montana Regent's owner was a brash and wealthy Colorado mine owner, John D. Morrisey. Morrisey retired the horse to stud in 1888.[45]

Eastin & Larabie's partnership produced other champions, including Poet Scout, winner of the Suburban Handicap; Ben Holladay, three-time

---

[*] Haggin was a business partner of Marcus Daly's. See chapters 7 and 8.

winner of the Municipal Handicap; and Kinley Mack, winner of the 1900 Suburban and Brooklyn Handicaps. When Eastin retired from the turf in 1901, the partnership sold its Kentucky holdings and horses to Haggin for an estimated $120,000 to $150,000. Larabie kept some horses, but he is seldom mentioned in Montana's racing news after 1900. His brother, Charles X. Larabie, kept trotting horses over in Madison County and is discussed in chapter 12.

Powell County Races

The Deer Lodge area had several racecourses. "Olin's Course," owned by blacksmith Giles Olin, was the most popular. Built east of town and now covered by a residential neighborhood, it was a one-mile oval boasting 440-yard straightaways. It was the site of the first race meet in Powell County—second in the territory after Helena's Territorial Fair of 1868. Olin went to great expense to develop the track, booths, judges' stand, and spectator seating. To recoup his costs, he charged admission.

"Derby Day of the Valley" was held on August 5, 1869. The premiere race was a six-hundred-yard dash with a $2,000 purse. The entrants were both mares: Lady Lightfoot of Butte and the oddly named Tin Cup Joe from nearby Pioneer City ("for gracious sake, change that name," begged the press).[46] Each owner deposited $500 against forfeit. On race day, one thousand spectators arrived, some from Helena and Missoula. Betting was heavy.

Unfortunately, the event was a fiasco. No one clarified which direction the horses would run, and unable to agree, both owners withdrew. The ensuing mess "created a bad impression among visitors," though "a number of scrub races afforded some amusement in lieu of the great sport anticipated." Olin himself was "the worst aggrieved," having put his own reputation on the line. Nonetheless, Olin overcame his frustration, and his course hosted racing for many years.[47]

The Deer Lodge Fair and Racing Association formed in 1886, with the idea of adding a county fair to the existing race meet. The group purchased land from Nick Bielenberg (another half brother of Kohrs's), put up stands and held races the next year. News reports are scattered, but the town organized races annually, or close to it, until about 1916. Then, probably because of Montana's 1915 gambling ban, there was a gap until racing revived in 1926.

Horse racing, Deer Lodge, 1909. *Courtesy Hinton.*

In 1938, the meet emphasized its professional standards and, by 1947, had added a set of gateless starting stalls. In the post-1965 regulatory era, the Horse Racing Commission granted dates to the Tri-County Fair in Deer Lodge from 1966 to 1968.[48] After that, organized meets ended, with reasons unclear, but some of the track footprint at the Powell County Fairgrounds remains visible in aerial imagery today.

MONTANA'S DERBY HORSE

Spokane

The colt named Spokane won the Kentucky Derby,
set a record for the mile-and-a-half, the colt named Spokane was born running.
—Sherman Alexie[49]

Montana's only Kentucky Derby winner to date, Spokane, was foaled in 1886. Although he never raced in Montana and left the state as a two-year-old, his tale is a key part of Montana's racing lore. His Kentucky Derby win in 1889 announced Montana's arrival on the national racing scene and challenged statehood itself as the biggest news story of the year. Recounting Spokane's history requires wading through a morass of tall tales, some expounded in breathless hyperbole at the time of his 1889 Derby victory, others springing up long after his death. But the stories behind the legends are as compelling as any myth.

NOAH ARMSTRONG

Canadian-born Noah Armstrong first visited Montana in 1863. He declared himself a Montana pioneer but often resided in Minnesota with his wife, Hannah, and their three children. In 1873, at age fifty, he brought his family to Glendale, Montana. There his children married and had children of their own.

The most profitable of Armstrong's many mining claims was the Hecla lode in the Pioneer Mountains. In 1875, Armstrong and his business partners built a smelter at Glendale to process ore. The Hecla Consolidated Mining Company incorporated in 1877. Processing an assortment of metals, but primarily silver, Glendale boomed to over one thousand people. The company was once valued at over $1.5 million in 1880s dollars.* Glendale declined after the collapse of the silver market in the Panic of 1893. Today, it is a ghost town.

Noah Armstrong. *Wikimedia Commons.*

Armstrong managed Hecla until 1879. After that, he diversified his business interests into railroads—and racehorses. After the loss of three grandchildren to a diphtheria epidemic in 1883 and then Hannah's death in 1885, Armstrong left Glendale and focused his passion on one of his remaining loves: the turf.

In Glendale, like many small mining towns, horse racing on the main streets was a common form of entertainment. But Armstrong set his sights higher: In May 1883, a horse he owned and stabled back east, Lord Raglan, ran third in the Kentucky Derby.[50]

DONCASTER RANCH

In 1882, Armstrong bought a ranch in Madison County just north of Twin Bridges. Sellers were his son Charles and daughter-in-law Elizabeth, who inherited the property from her parents. Buying up adjoining land until he owned 4,000 acres, he built a horse farm, calling it Doncaster Ranch.

Accounts of Armstrong's life do not explain why Armstrong had a passion for the sport of kings, but he clearly had a vision. Some histories mention in passing that the ranch was named after a "favorite" or "famous" horse, but "Doncaster" had special meaning in the racing community.

Doncaster Racecourse in England hosts the classic St Leger horse race, first run in 1776. In Armstrong's time, the racehorse Doncaster won the

---

* About $38 million today.

1873 Epsom Derby. In 1880, Doncaster's most famous son, Bend Or, also conquered Epsom. Armstrong was said to have admired the great stallion. So did other Montanans: a local horse probably added to historians' confusion. In 1880, W.H. Raymond of Sweetwater Creek (discussed in chapter 12) named a foal Doncaster. That Standardbred became a winner on Montana's harness racing circuit, though not until 1883.

The Round Barn

Armstrong believed the altitude of Montana could produce horses with the lung capacity and endurance to be world-class racers. Bunchgrass grown in the Jefferson River Valley was claimed to be superior to the bluegrass of Kentucky for building strong bone. But knowing the harsh Montana climate, as soon as Armstrong bought the ranch, he started building a state-of-the-art barn. Still standing today, renovated into a privately run event center, the Doncaster Round Barn is in the National Register of Historic Places.

Round barns were a modern design in the 1880s, promoted by agricultural colleges for efficiency and lower cost. Armstrong valued the design's purported wind resistance and self-supporting roof, allowing a more open interior.

The Doncaster Round Barn is one hundred feet in diameter at ground level and three stories tall, tiered like a wedding cake. The interior further demonstrated Armstrong's modern thinking and concern for his animals' care. The walls were weather-tight. The first floor had twenty-four box stalls around the perimeter, each with a window. The walls between the stalls were solid for four feet, then gave way to "railings"—open bars. The design, Armstrong said, gave "each horse a chance to see his neighbors for about halfway around the building….This promotion of neighborly companionship greatly [relieved] the monotony of indoor horse life."[51] Exterior doors opened to a paddock for each horse, with fence lines fanning out over a total of 2.5 acres.*

Each stall also opened to an internal track about 20 feet wide. In winter, this dirt corridor, about 220 feet in circumference (a diameter roughly

---

* The Round Barn's features were sometimes exaggerated, and the NRHP application repeats two: 1) the indoor track was not a quarter mile around—measuring the barn and use of π provides the estimate given here; 2) the outside paddocks encompassed 2.5 acres total, not per horse (which would require over 60 acres).

Doncaster Round Barn. *Wahler.*

similar to a modern 70-foot round pen), allowed horses to train and exercise indoors. When winter weather went from average to dreadful, the track sheltered extra horses normally kept outdoors.

In the central hub was the tack room, veterinary stalls, a circular staircase, and a hay and grain "elevator." At the core was a well pipe that drew water to an 11,000-gallon cistern on the third floor. A windmill on top of the barn pumped water from the well to the cistern, piped from there into each horse's stall.

The second floor was feed storage. It was reported to hold up to 50 tons of hay and contain grain bins built to store 12,000 bushels. Sloped chutes above each stall allowed feed to be pushed down to the horses. In aerial imagery, another part of the ranch's racing history is still visible: a strip of greener grass across undeveloped hay land outlines an oval around the barn—the training track.

In this barn, the mare Interpose foaled a chestnut colt in 1886. Armstrong was visiting Spokane Falls, Washington Territory (now the city of Spokane), at the time. Receiving a letter from his ranch foreman announcing the foal's birth, he decided to name the little fellow Spokane. He told the press after Spokane's 1889 win that the horse's name not only honored the community of Spokane Falls, but "secondly," he said, "because of an old Indian tradition of that locality that very much interested me."[52]

This "old tradition" is part of Spokane's story.

Horse Slaughter Camp

Washington Territory was created in 1853. Before long, territorial governor Isaac Stevens pressured the Yakama* Nation and other tribes into signing the Treaty of 1855, ceding millions of acres, but promised them two years to relocate. Twelve days later, Stevens authorized access by settlers and prospectors. Kamiakin, leader of the Yakama, declared the treaty void, and the Yakima/Coeur d'Alene Wars began.

By 1858, the Spokane, Palouse and other inland Northwest tribes joined the fray. Their primary concern was the Mullan Road, planned to connect Fort Benton to Fort Walla Walla. After Native forces defeated the U.S. Army at the Battle of Pine Creek, Colonel George Wright left Fort Walla Walla with orders to "win decisively." With howitzers and seven hundred troops, he did, at the Battle of Four Lakes and then at Spokane Plains.

The tribes, fearing their greatest wealth—their horses—would be captured, fled. Troops under Captain Erasmus Keyes caught up and captured about one thousand horses. Most belonged to the Palouse people, led by their chief, Tilcoax.

Isaac Stevens (1818–1862).
Wikimedia Commons.

* The Yakama Nation uses this spelling today; "Yakima" is used for geographic names and historic events.

Near present-day Liberty Lake, Washington, on September 8, 1858, Wright ordered his troops to destroy the entire herd. First they lassoed horses individually, shooting adults and killing foals with blows to their heads. By September 10, "to avoid the slow process of killing them separately, the companies were ordered to fire volleys into the corral." Keyes wrote, "It was a cruel sight to see so many noble beasts shot down. They were all sleek, glossy and fat, and as I love a horse, I fancied I saw in their beautiful faces an appeal for mercy."[53] The military documented 690 horses killed and 130 kept for future use, though other accounts put the number destroyed as high as 900.

The carcasses were left to rot. Wright reported, "A blow has been struck that they will never forget." For over fifty years, bleached bones covered such a wide area that the Coeur d'Alene (Schitsu'umsh) people called the valley "white lake." Other names were "Wright's boneyard" and "Horse Slaughter Camp."

Wright then ordered a scorched-earth policy. His troops burned lodges, destroyed winter supplies, and killed livestock. By October, he had forced "peace" on the Native people of the Inland Northwest by guaranteeing starvation.[54]

The Legend

A number of stories arose from the tragedy. Spokane–Coeur d'Alene writer Sherman Alexie opened his poem "Horses" with this version:

1,000 ponies, the United States Cavalry stole 1,000 ponies from the Spokane Indians, shot 1,000 ponies & only 1 survived, shot 1,000 ponies & left them as monuments, left 1,000 ponies falling into dust, fallen, shot 1,000 ponies and only 1 survived.[55]

In Alexie's poem, the survivor was a mare that fled to Montana and gave birth to Spokane, "born running from the United States Cavalry, born running into the Kentucky Derby."

Susan Nardinger, in her book *Spirit Horse of the Rockies*, recounted a legend that Tilcoax had a vision that the rust-red blood of the slaughtered horses rose from the ground, merging into the heavens in the form of a chestnut stallion. The Creator told Tilcoax the spirit of the murdered animals would be reborn in a fleet-footed colt who would redeem the losses of his people.[56]

A Nashville reporter recounted a similar tale in 1889: a wounded warrior had a vision that the spirits of the dead horses rose to the clouds, blending into a single horse. A voice told the warrior, "The spirit horse will return with the speed, the endurance, and the pluck of all the horses dead on the battle field. He will enter into the body of a colt, and that colt will be called 'Spokane', and will go forth to conquer all the horses of the earth." With Spokane's Kentucky Derby win, the reporter concluded, "The prophecy is fulfilled."[57]

It is unclear if the spirit horse story existed prior to Spokane's win. A Spokane Falls resident claimed he overheard Armstrong in 1886 saying he would name the colt "Spokane" to commemorate his visit. But Armstrong picked up local lore: he explained to reporters that the word "Spokane" meant "Children of the Sun." His cryptic reference to an "old Indian tradition" creates a reasonable hypothesis that Armstrong heard a "spirit horse" legend, however much it changed in retelling.

Armstrong certainly saw Horse Slaughter Camp. The boneyard was impossible to miss; it was located near present-day Interstate 90 and the Spokane River Centennial Trail. He no doubt heard the story—perhaps with sympathy. Armstrong's descendants showed support for twentieth-century Native causes, particularly his great-granddaughter, anthropologist Harriet Turner (1920–2015). She became an honorary member of the Snoqualmie tribe for helping that nation regain federal recognition in the 1990s.[58]

Spokane in Myth and Fact

Spokane's own story requires much unsnarling of fact from fiction. In 1885, Armstrong visited the Meadows Farm of General Richard Rowett in Carlinville, Illinois. There he spent $1,000 to purchase a "three in one package": the mare Interpose, her suckling filly, and a foal in utero.[59]

Interpose was in foal to Hyder Ali, an excellent stallion owned by Meadows farm.* Armstrong shipped the mare to Montana, where Spokane was foaled. After Rowett's death, Hyder Ali also went to Montana: James Ben Ali Haggin bought the stallion, then sold him to Marcus Daly, who brought the aged stallion to his Bitter Root Stock Farm in 1890.

---

* Some sources claim Hyder Ali was a "half-Arabian." While Thoroughbreds have Arabian ancestors, Hyder Ali's pedigree is a who's who of Thoroughbred breeding. His sire was Leamington, a four-time leading sire in North America. His dam was a daughter of the great Lexington.

Spokane, 1889 Kentucky Derby winner. *TBHAM.*

Spokane was a good-looking colt that matured to be 16 hands tall. Registered as a chestnut, there are scattered references to him being "roan." He may have had minor body white: some Thoroughbreds have small scattered white spots called "Birdcatcher ticks"; others have light sprinkling of white hairs on their barrel and flanks, called "rabicano." Spokane's pedigree contains horses with these traits.

There are no photographs of Spokane and few artist's renderings. One is a color oil by artist Henry Stull. Stull was a poor equestrian painter—his animals tend to be disproportioned—but he was meticulous with color and markings. Stull painted Spokane as a chestnut, with a blaze and white hind legs, ridden by a jockey wearing Armstrong's silks of blue and dark gold.

Many tall tales about Spokane are recounted as truth. The most notorious—and persistent—is a sensationalistic 1951 account of Spokane's origins written by Howard Wade for the *National Police Gazette*—a girlie magazine "not renowned for the accuracy of its sources."[60]

The tabloid account claimed Interpose escaped and ran wild with mustangs for seven years, then was captured and bred to Hyder Ali at

Old-style "pancake" racing saddle.
MHS, 1996.19.01.

Doncaster Ranch. Not stopping there, Wade declared that she fled to the wild again, leaping a fence—while pregnant—and then foaled Spokane in the wilderness under the stars. Next came a dramatic tale of young Spokane barely escaping a ravenous mountain lion, which raked its claws across the flanks of the colt, scarring Spokane for life. Wade concluded his vignette by stating that Spokane was captured off the range and it took six men to subdue him.

Though tabloid nonsense from beginning to end, the mountain lion story survives; this author heard it repeated by NBC's sportscasters during the live broadcast of the 2018 Kentucky Derby.

In reality, Spokane was started under saddle in Montana by a teenage ranch hand named Joe Redfern. Redfern later recounted that the colt was athletic but easy to train, started "without spur" and "with pancake saddle" (cowboy slang for an English saddle). The colt shipped east in the spring of 1888. Armstrong placed Spokane with a trainer in Tennessee, John Rodegap. The colt's first race was July 5, 1888, where he finished fourth. Rodegap raced him five times total that year, winning twice. Described by Redfern as a bit lazy, Spokane was a closer: he hung back early, then poured on speed at the end.

THE DERBY

The May 9, 1889 Kentucky Derby was Spokane's second start as a three-year-old. The money was on Proctor Knott, the two-year-old champion and fan favorite, named after a popular Kentucky politician. Yet the track handicapper quietly gave Spokane 118 pounds to Proctor Knott's 115. By all accounts, Armstrong did not boast that his colt could beat Proctor Knott. Instead, he told Spokane's jockey, the experienced Tom Kiley, to try for second.

In the race, Proctor Knott was rank, false-started twice, but once underway opened up a five-length lead before bolting toward the outside fence. Spokane, under Kiley, stayed steady on the rail. Spokane took the lead at the sixteenth pole. Proctor Knott struggled back, and the two horses hit the wire almost at the same time.

After a lengthy discussion among the racing officials, Spokane was declared the winner by a "short neck." Here, another Montana thread enters the story: the lead judge was none other than the man who developed Churchill Downs and began the Kentucky Derby: "Colonel" Meriwether Lewis Clark Jr., grandson of William Clark. Clark's decision granting the Derby to Spokane was questioned, but he was centered at the judge's stand with his eye on the line. Controversy did not particularly bother Clark. He was a reformer who promoted parimutuel betting and developed rules for racing still used today. He stood firm in the face of a stunned crowd, and the result was official.[61]

Spokane set a Derby record of 2:34-1/2 for the mile and a half distance. The race was shortened to a mile and a quarter in 1896, and thus his record still stands. Spokane was also the first horse bred "west of Nashville" to win.[62]

Kentuckians could not believe their favorite was defeated by a Rocky Mountain upstart. They cast about for reasons: the jockey was weak, the start was bad, the timer was off, the judges were blind. But the most far-fetched tale claimed a magic potion was at work: supposedly, Spokane was born so puny he should have been shot. But, "a medicine man of the Flathead tribe" harvested white flowers at sunrise and brewed them into a concoction that gave the colt his power and strength.[63] Another version of the account said that dried flowers were sent with Spokane to Kentucky, where a groom administered the tonic. But the only verified "secret recipe" is that Spokane spent his first two years breathing Montana air and eating fodder grown in Montana soil.

The victory launched a press frenzy. Illinois, Tennessee, Washington, and Montana all claimed Spokane as their own. Armstrong firmly identified him as a Montana colt, much to the delight of the western press, which promoted Montana as horse-breeding country. Spokane proved his win was not a fluke. Five days later, he defeated Proctor Knott in the Clark Handicap, this time winning by two lengths. He shipped to Chicago in June.

The citizens of Spokane Falls were equally ecstatic. Creating a subscription pool with a goal of $500 to custom tailor a blue velvet horse blanket and hood with ornate embroidered gold lettering and trim, they reportedly raised $5,000. Presented in Chicago on June 21, 1889, Spokane was paraded on the track at all his subsequent races wearing the outfit, secured with a gold surcingle. The people from Spokane Falls who delivered the blanket also

Spokane's blanket and hood, 1889. Model horse, Toledo Display Horse Company, circa 1892–1915. *"Riders Under the Big Sky,"* 1995–1996. *Horse, X66.20, MHS. Blanket, Northwest Museum of Arts and Culture.*

attended his races, going through the stands to hand out flyers promoting their community and the soon-to-be state of Washington.

Spokane won the American Derby at Chicago's Washington Park by a length, again defeating Proctor Knott, who came in last. His win in Chicago completed what was the "triple crown" of the time; it led the sports section of the June 23 *Chicago Sunday Tribune.*

Tragedy and Retirement

The American Derby was Spokane's last win. Proctor Knott finally got his revenge and won their next meeting. Spokane, losing condition, seemed "off" in his remaining 1889 races.

The rest of Spokane's life is complicated. That autumn, tragedy struck. While Spokane was laying down in his stall, a stable hand poked him with a pitchfork to make him get up. It is unknown if this blow came from impatience, malice, or ignorance. The incident became a legend that Spokane had been "killed by an enraged stable hand." It nearly ended his career. When jabbed, the colt scrambled to his feet in a panic and, in the process, tore a tendon and possibly wrenched his back.

Spokane did not race again until June 1890. He then ran four races in a month, finishing second twice, and was retired that July. Spokane's racing record was 17:5-4-2.

The final years of Spokane's life are as legend-laden as his birth. Some sources assert he had fertility problems, though records show him as a sire of nine or ten recorded offspring, several of whom raced, and one, Spirituelle, was a stakes winner. The stallion moved around Kentucky, standing at stud in several different stables. In 1897, Spokane was advertised at stud at Maxwelton Stock Farm. It is unknown how long Armstrong kept an ownership interest in Spokane. He sold all his Montana properties during the 1890s and moved to Seattle, where he died in 1907.

The final mention of Spokane in the newspapers of his time was when he sold on November 29, 1898, for $170. His purchaser was W.H. May and Sons. The *Louisville Courier-Journal* commented, "The ingratitude that men who own racehorses show to the animals which served them so well is an old story." Other accounts claim he limped to the block and sold "amid laughs."[64]

After this sale, Spokane disappears from the historic record. But tall tales abound. Most revolve around the gratifying but unverified notion that Spokane somehow returned to Montana, usually by rail, even to Madison County, perhaps greeted by parades and a brass band. Other sagas claim his train wrecked. Some say he got sick in Miles City and was pulled off the train. In some accounts, he returned to health; in others he died. One old-timer said as a little boy, in 1914 or so, he got "old Spokane" as a gift and the horse lived to be thirty. The problem with that story is that the teller claimed the horse had one white hind leg, not two.

It is implausible but not impossible that Spokane returned to the Big Sky. Nardinger stated she wondered if W.H. May was an agent for Marcus Daly, who had owned Hyder Ali. There are clues: Daly's 1897 purchase of Hamburg was via a confidential agent and Daly's involvement not initially disclosed. In 1898, W.H. May & Sons nominated horses for stakes races in Butte and Anaconda. Given multiple rumors that Spokane returned to Montana on a train, perhaps the horse returned to the West, but his fate remains unknown.[65]

The winner of the implausibility stakes was a story in a 1988 Spokane Chamber of Commerce newsletter; it claimed Spokane was made into a taxidermy mount.[66] The writers apparently were confused by a life-sized plaster model horse commissioned by T.C. Power that stood for many years at the original Power-Townsend store in Helena's Steamboat Block. Today, that battered chestnut steed resides in a Montana Historical Society storage warehouse. A similar model (except bay, not chestnut) painted with Spokane's distinctive blaze served as a saddle mannequin at DeVore's Saddlery in Helena until that business closed in 2007. It then moved across the street to Bert & Ernie's Restaurant.

Spokane's fate is unknown, but his place in Montana history is secure.

HISTORIC HELENA

When the Queen City Reigned

The most ideal spot in the state for racing.
—Edgar Brown, 1964[67]

In 1868, Helena hosted the first organized race meet in Montana Territory. Ambitious from the start, "Queen City" promoters built a one-mile track in 1870—five years before the 1875 founding of Churchill Downs and the first Kentucky Derby. As racecourses came and went across Montana, other one-mile tracks gave way to half-mile "bullrings." But Helena's track survived for 130 years before the homestretch fell to development, the last mile oval in a multistate region.

Helena racing went through three stages: Privately organized fairs sponsored races from 1868 until 1896. Helena rehabilitated its track and hosted the "official" state fair with legislative approval from 1903 through 1932; then private groups held small meets into the late 1930s. A third wave of privately organized racing ran from 1967 to 1999. A valiant battle to save the track occupied the early 2000s, ended by the courts in 2007.

The Fashion Course

When Helena's promoters organized the first territorial fair in 1868, the mining town was only four years old. In July 1864, some tired prospectors had taken one last chance at striking it rich—and succeeded. Word spread

Helena hosted the first territorial fair. *Two Dollars on the Nose*, Robert F. Morgan, acrylic, 2002. *Courtesy Lewis and Clark County Fairgrounds Foundation.*

quickly that the "Four Georgians" found gold, and on October 30, 1864, the "Last Chance" mining camp became a town named Helena.

As in other gold rush towns, informal horse races were common, such as when Dan Flowerree won $400 for a 400-yard race in 1867. What was different is that he won at "the race track on Ten Mile."[68] The "race track on Ten Mile" was probably Madam Coady's. She ran a private club, the Two Mile House, near Tenmile Creek. Coady (or Cody) invited the "Ladies and Gentlemen of Montana" to dine at "the Favorite Resort of Pleasure-Seekers" featuring "the finest liquors and choicest cigars in Montana." Her one-mile "Circular Race Course," also known as the Fashion Course, advertised horse training and boarding.[69]

By 1868, city promoters wanted Helena to get respectable. They organized the Montana Agricultural, Mechanical and Mineral Association to host a territorial fair. Horse racing, of course, was a critical component. Madam Coady's track was a perfect location.

The exact location of Coady's is an unsolved local mystery. Researcher Kennon Baird placed it roughly between present-day Country Club

Avenue and Highway 12. Conrad Kohrs described it as near Kessler's Brewery. Given that a mile oval encloses roughly 40 acres of unbroken terrain, these clues suggest it could have been near present-day Spring Meadow Lake (which did not exist in the 1860s) or today's Archie Bray Foundation.[70]

The association raised $5,000, leased Coady's racetrack, and built necessary structures. It advertised $10,000 in purse money for a week of racing, $200 for a single race. On October 5, 1868, "some fine running animals" drew visitors from a wide area. Using the Fashion Course again in 1869, the association invited "all horses in the territory."[71]

MONTANA'S FIRST AND FINEST FAIRGROUNDS

Racecourses in America date to 1665, but the first "modern" racetrack opened at Saratoga in 1864. Helena's public track was constructed just six years later—the same year as the East Coast's Monmouth Park and Pimlico.

In 1870, promoters formed the Montana Mineral & Agricultural Association. They raised money from a stock offering, bought 83 acres, and immediately set to constructing a track and assorted buildings. On September 24, 1870, the grounds were finished, just in time for the start of the territorial fair on September 28. The *Helena Daily Herald* declared the one-mile racetrack the "finest in the territory," noting with pride the quarter-mile homestretch: "almost perfectly straight." Horses arrived from as far away as Salt Lake City, but the largest purse, $400, went to a local: Hugh Kirkendall's Nellie.[72]

In 1875, Helena became the territorial capital of Montana. Located near the Mullan Road, Helena survived the decline of gold mining by becoming a financial center. Its central location brought railroads; the Northern Pacific arrived in 1883. By 1889, the city was said to be home to fifty millionaires.

Racing kept pace with Helena's growth. On September 27, 1876, the *Helena Weekly Herald* reported three thousand people at the track. That day, the "Fair Association" stallions' race offered a $1,500 purse. The auction pool was $6,000, and outside betting was estimated at $10,000. After three one-mile heats, the winner was Charles Williams's six-year-old bay, Cariboo, newly arrived from New York. Possibly the first Thoroughbred with documentable pedigree to arrive in Montana, Cariboo raced again October 4 and won a two-mile dash.[73]

In 1877, Samuel Larabie came over from Deer Lodge with his racehorses and their Kentucky trainers. Williams returned with Cariboo. Throughout the 1880s, the fair was part of an organized racing circuit that included Butte, Bozeman, Deer Lodge, and, after 1888, the Anaconda Driving Park. The association granted a fifty-foot easement to the Montana Central Railroad, allowing construction of a rail spur and siding at the fairgrounds, making it easier and safer to ship in horses and other stock.

Trotting races, the "common man's sport," were more popular than running races prior to 1900. At Helena's meets, Silas Harvey's Red Cliff Farm in Clancy produced many harness winners. Harvey came to Montana in 1867 to oversee the Diamond City Mining Company. In 1870, he brought "blooded" horses into Montana. Most were Standardbreds of the Mambrino-Clay lines. While he died of consumption in 1878 at only fifty-three years old, his widow, Frances, and their children, particularly son George, continued the family business. They bought Larabie's stallion Mambrino Diamond in 1879 and operated Red Cliff Farm until 1888.

Helena's Hugh "Kirk" Kirkendall dominated Helena's racing scene for twenty years. He bred from the best local stock; his champion harness racing mare, Dollie, was a daughter of Mambrino Diamond. He also ran Thoroughbreds. In 1895, he was described as "among the most successful horsemen and breeders in Montana."[74]

Statehood

Montana became a state on November 8, 1889. Helena's territorial fair became the state fair in 1890, though state government was not involved. A private association put $12,000 in improvements to the fairgrounds, re-grading the track until it was "as smooth as a billiard table."[75]

Local legend holds that "carloads of imported Kentucky earth" were added to the track. But no research to date has verified the story. Some versions claim Marcus Daly arranged the shipment, which may have originated with a story that Daly brought in Kentucky soil to add to his private track in Hamilton. It is doubtful that he would have done so for Helena, locked in a battle with Anaconda—Daly's company town—for the permanent location of the state capital.

The early 1890s saw horses from Spokane and Denver shipped to Montana. With purses fattened by mining wealth, a trotter could earn more money in Montana than back east. The 1890 meet in Helena offered $15,000 in purses.* In 1891, runners and trotters shipped in from California, Idaho, Oregon, Nevada, and Kansas City. From Butte, W.A. Clark sent horses to race in Helena. Clark, not the passionate horseman Daly was, nonetheless had business connections with Samuel Larabie and an apparent desire to compete against Daly on every front—including horse racing.

Helena's citizens fretted about a growing seedy element, and some people opposed racing altogether. In 1890, the *Helena Daily Herald* snarked, "These fairs should be patronized more generally by our people interested in things other than horse racing." Noting the source of most of the spectators and cash, race supporters snarked back: "Those who criticize this strain are the very ones responsible for this condition of things."[76]

The Panic of 1893 threw the economy—and Helena racing—into turmoil. Fair organizers borrowed against the property to fund events until 1896. That year they went broke, and state fair racing ended until 1903. The land sold, and the facility fell into disrepair.

Nationally, the 1890s saw increased racing regulation. The American Jockey Club formed in 1894, "to establish racing on such a footing that it may command the interests as well as the confidence and favorable opinion of the public."[77] Meanwhile, the Montana legislature passed several reform statutes in 1895. It—again—banned racing on Sundays (a perpetual exercise in futility) and authorized a three-year prison sentence for anyone attempting to enter a "ringer" in a horse race. As the economy rebounded, state and national racing reform helped launch Montana's first golden age of racing.

Revival

A festival of their society at its apex, acclaimed by the age's chief envoys of money and power.[78]

Helena racing's golden age began when a local group bought the fairgrounds and transferred ownership to the State of Montana. The legislature authorized funds for an official state fair and gave Helena the nod to host it. The 1903 state fair hosted twenty thousand visitors, arriving on local streetcars and trains from out of town. That year, the racing circuit included Helena, Butte, Anaconda, Billings, Great Falls, Missoula, Kalispell, and Bozeman.

---

* About $417,000 in 2017 dollars.

A 1911 state fair postcard. *MHS Photo Archives. PC 001-HELE.MontStFair1911.*

Women's relay competition, further discussed in chapter 13, was a popular new event in 1903. As the decade progressed, Thoroughbred "running races" became more popular than harness racing as the car replaced the horse.

In 1906, the grandstands were rebuilt to hold five thousand people. George Klotz of Butte ably managed the race meet. The year 1909 saw the track's finest moment when President William H. Taft came to Montana and visited the state fair. In 1914, the final year with legal betting before the 1915 ban, fairgoers saw 334 horses entered and $455,000 wagered.[79]

GEORGE COONEY (1866–1942) WAS a well-known member of Helena's racing community in the early twentieth century. His gelding Jack o' Lantern won the Montana Derby in 1907. In 1910, when told that California horses were coming to Montana for the season, Cooney just smiled and said, "Bring 'em on."[80] Over the years, he shipped horses as far away as Tijuana, where purses were high and betting was wide open.

Cooney's most famous horse was his homebred High Low, who won in Helena then left the state. In 1919, Montana fans eagerly followed High Low's career as he ran at Oriental Park in Havana, Cuba, then in Kentucky at Churchill Downs and Lexington. Cooney's local stock continued to shine as well. In 1925, Just Right broke a fifty-two-year-old world record, running 2-3/4 miles in 4:50-3/5. In 1937, Cooney was still in the game: at Great Falls, Gretna B won the North Montana State Fair Derby. The same day, Half Saint set a track record at five furlongs.

TROUBLED TIMES

In 1915, the Montana legislature abolished gambling on horse races.* After repeated attempts, legalized parimutuel betting returned in 1929. But in between, drought and post–World War I economic downturns led the state to eliminate funding for Helena's fair, and it was canceled in 1926. Private donors rallied, and Helena's state fair had its final run from 1927 until 1932.

Attendance rebounded with the return of legal wagering. In 1930, the meet drew 350 horses and twenty-five thousand spectators. But in spite

---

* See chapter 7.

of successful race meets, plus the 1931 revival of racing in Great Falls,* Helena's state fair ended after 1932. The official reason given was that people could not afford fair admission because of the Great Depression. Racing continued without the fair; the Lewis and Clark Racing Association hosted small meets through 1939. The state fair title transferred to the North Montana Fair in Great Falls by the end of the decade.

Helena's track and grounds took several hits in the 1930s. The first hit was literal: the October 1935 Helena earthquake. This 6.2-magnitude temblor liquefied the alluvial soil under the fairgrounds. The ground shook like Jello in a bowl, destroying structures made of brick or stone and killing a transient sleeping in the horticulture building.

Next, in November 1937, a fire swept through the fairgrounds, destroying more buildings, including a barn and the home of "Mother" Berry, whose story is told in chapter 13. George Cooney had racehorses in training at the grounds, but those barns were saved and his horses unharmed.

The fairgrounds hosted rodeos and stock car racing in the 1940s and 1950s. The track was used for O-Mok-See relays and informal races. In 1958, a group of local citizens began renovations. With tax support from the county and a lease from the state, the first Last Chance Stampede Rodeo was held in 1961. But Helena still lacked parimutuel horse racing.[81]

The Longest Run

In 1964, the Montana Quarter Horse Association, led by Edgar Brown of Jefferson City, sought to revive racing. Brown and other horsemen advocated for a state commission to regulate meets. Soon after, the 1965 legislature authorized the Montana Horse Racing Commission (later Montana Board of Horse Racing). The commission had authority to license track personnel and regulate races. Improved governance launched Montana's second golden age of racing.

Horse racing returned to Helena in 1967, beginning Helena's longest run, with meets held twenty-eight of the next thirty-two years. Races were sponsored by the Capital City Horse Racing Association (CCHRA). Founders included president Sheldon J. "Skip" Score and vice president/ treasurer Bev Tomaskie. CCHRA started with a three-day summer meet and steadily added more days over the next decade.

* See chapter 15.

Montana's new 1972 Constitution allowed gambling "by acts of the legislature or by the people through initiative or referendum." Parimutuel gambling was immediately approved, giving horse racing a wagering monopoly. Statewide, racing days grew: in 1973, CCHRA added a second Helena meet in May.

With parimutuel takeout flowing into local coffers, larger cities wanted longer meets—and in Montana's short racing season, they sought the same prime summer dates. This competition was the first gray cloud on the racing horizon, with Helena at the center of the mêlée.

Trouble began in 1975 with overlapping dates between Great Falls and Helena. Horses could run at both tracks when management cooperated. But spectators couldn't be in two places at once—parimutuel handle dropped in both locations. The next year, many horse people choose to stay at Great Falls, the larger city with the longer meet. Spectators followed. In Helena, the CCHRA went under.

In 1977, Last Chance Racing (LCR) organized, led by businessman Tom McHugh with Ron Leland as treasurer. The new group hustled to get good horses and sold season passes to the spring and summer meets. In spite of a successful season, LCR had a problem: director of racing William Hedge. "Retired" at age forty-eight, Hedge was "known to play poker and carry around large sums of money." That winter, Hedge left town and took the meet's profits with him. He returned after an arrest warrant was issued. A small amount of money was actually his salary, and Hedge repaid most of the remaining cash.[82]

In spite of endless spats between towns over conflicting race days, the 1980s marked the peak years for horse racing across Montana. In 1987, Helena ran twenty-one days and handle topped $1.8 million. Some years, the race meet saw seven hundred horses. However, trouble was on the horizon.

In 1988, Last Chance Racing scheduled three meets from May to September. But over-optimistic new leadership exceeded their budget and overlooked looming problems: legalization of video poker was eating into racetrack handle, plus a 1985 lawsuit brought by an injured exercise rider settled in August 1988. LCR had to pay part of the settlement. The year closed out with a record-setting twenty-four racing days, but handle was down. Facing a double whammy of less income plus the settlement, the September meet had to be cancelled. In debt, LCR was refused race dates for 1989, and folded.

Statewide, multiple lawsuits by injured track workers caught the eye of Montana's workers' compensation. Changes to work comp laws and skyrocketing insurance costs soon caused as much trouble for racetracks as did video gambling. But the 1970s and '80s were truly Helena's—and Montana's—second golden age of racing.

No Such Thing as One Job

I always liked fast horses.
—John Tomaskie, 2018[83]

John and Beverly Tomsakie were racehorse owners of Montana racing's second golden age. Unlike the wealthy turf kings of the nineteenth century, the Tomaskies were "working folks." John ran heavy equipment for the city; Bev was a telephone operator. They came home to a small horse farm and five children. "There's no such thing as having one job in this family," explained John.[84]

Successful at O-Mok-See relays, John and Bev started racing their fastest Quarter Horses in the late 1960s. Racing had to pay the bills, so they did most work themselves. Bev, a jockey-sized woman, conditioned five or more horses each year, starting in January. Like many owner-trainers, she took in a few outside horses to help with the expenses.

Tomaskie's homebred Quarter Horse filly Born a Deck won the 1970 Helena Derby and a hefty purse. The win kick-started big dreams: John promised Bev, "I'm going to build you a barn so you don't have to exercise these horses on Mount Helena when it's 30 below zero." Their new indoor riding arena was the biggest in Helena at the time. "Born a Deck built that barn," John said, his eyes twinkling, "she was a good carpenter."[85]

They soon realized that Thoroughbred racing offered more races and bigger purses. The Tomaskies' first Thoroughbred champion was Montskaia (31:12-2-7). The 1977 California-bred bay ran in Southern California until laid up by a bowed tendon. Bev bought him at a Hollywood Park sale, declaring to John, "That bow is high, I can take care of it." She doctored and rested Montskaia for a year. He debuted at Great Falls in 1982 and retired in 1987. Under Bev's eye, he "earned a paycheck"—finishing in the top four—in over 80 percent of his races. Montskaia set a number of track records in the '80s. Six still stood a decade later.[86]

When Montskaia retired, the Tomaskies began attending the Keeneland yearling sales in Kentucky. Each fall, they watched high-rollers spend

Bev Tomaskie holds Montskaia. Helena, 1986. *Courtesy Tomaskie.*

millions, but their budget was $6,000. John bid carefully, noting, "experiments are expensive." Then in 1993, a dark bay colt walked into the ring. "I couldn't stop at six," John said. At $11,500, the gavel dropped and the Tomaskies owned a grandson of Triple Crown winner Seattle Slew.[87]

Super Ciel (69:15-12-7) took the Northwest by storm. In 1994, he won the Spokane Futurity at Playfair in Washington and the Budweiser $100,000 Futurity at Billings. In 1995, he conquered Playfair again in the Spokane Derby, winning by eleven lengths. He won Helena's Montana Stakes in 1996.[88]

From there he went to western Washington. Super Ciel did too well: he was claimed from the Tomaskies at Emerald Downs in 1998. He went to California with new owners and raced two more years. During his California sojourn, his jockeys read like a hall of fame roster: Russell Baze in San Francisco, Laffit Pincay Jr. and a not-yet-famous Victor Espinoza in Los Angeles.[89] After retirement in 2000, "We brought him home," Bev said. In 2018, at age twenty-six, Super Ciel grazed in the Tomaskies' pasture in the Helena Valley.

GAMBLING ON THE FUTURE

Montana's Constitution helped racing after 1972 but also triggered its decline. Video poker became legal in 1985, and after laws expanded it in 1987, gambling money flowed to taverns instead of tracks. The voter-approved lottery in 1986 also drew wagering dollars. Statewide racing handle, which peaked at $11.8 million in 1984, fell to $4.8 million by 1994. The problem was aptly described by John Tomaskie: "When the poker machines take [people's] money, they ain't got any money left to bet on the horses."[90]

The racing industry, caught flat-footed, was not able to tap gaming tax revenue to offset losses. Simulcast wagering was authorized in 1989, which helped live racing, but horses on the track competed with screens at the tavern for the public's attention—and concession dollar.

In 1991, veterinarian and state senator Jack "Doc" Rea introduced a bill to transfer some revenue from video gaming to the Board of Horse Racing. The committee hearing brought dozens of people in support. Steve Meloy of the Montana Department of Commerce, a former executive secretary of the Montana Board of Horse Racing, explained:

> The enabling legislation which created horseracing under the pari-mutuel system enacted in 1965 was predicated on the agricultural and economic impact on the state of Montana. It was not a gambling enactment nor was it considered a gaming bill. The only reason this bill is before you today is because of the adverse effects expanded gaming pursuits seem to be having on an agricultural and economically diverse industry.[91]

Unfortunately, opposed by the well-established video gaming industry, the bill was tabled and died. The 1990s were a tumultuous period, as horse racing struggled to stay alive.

Final Countdown

In 1990, a new group formed, led by Skip Score. They created "Helena Downs" and ran races in 1990 and 1991. Score recruited veteran racing secretary Holly Burrows to organize the meet. But the Helena fairgrounds were falling apart. With barns crumbling and mill levies failing at the ballot box, no races ran in 1992. A private nonprofit, Fairgrounds Users Inc., stepped in. The group, led by President Gib Goodman, raised $1.5 million to fix crumbling roads, repair water lines and conduct critical maintenance.

Queen City Racing (QCR) resurrected the Helena meet in 1993. Excitement built: Bobbie Gruel started writing a horse racing column in the Helena *Independent Record*, following in the footsteps of longtime race reporter "Ray the Railbird" Anderson. Leadership included veterinarian Russ Bloom and, later, Patty Rambo. But the Board of Horse Racing stopped allowing overlapping meets, and Helena could only get dates for May—often cold and rainy in Montana. Attendance was poor. After rain held the 1996 meet to only three days, QCR was out of money.

In 1997, a county mill levy finally passed. Lewis and Clark County took over management from the Fairgrounds Users. QCR started fundraising. By 1999, the organization had enough funds to claim its rainy springtime dates and run a modest four-day meet.

But just when things were looking up, the fatal blow struck: county engineers condemned the 1906 grandstands—the roof was in danger of collapse. The county deemed rehabilitation too expensive and, in spite of objections, demolished the historic structure. The 2000 race meet was canceled. In 2001, the county refused to front costs for QCR to rent temporary infrastructure, and racing was suspended again.

With no racing, local government officials began eying the track infield for development. In response, Helena's respected historic preservation community sought a National Register of Historic Places designation. A local group of racing enthusiasts formed Save the Track Foundation.

Skijoring, Helena backstretch, January 2018. *Wahler.*

78

All was for naught. In 2005, the fair board and county commissioners approved new construction that put an exhibition hall and parking lot in the infield. Save the Track sued. In 2007, the court sided with the county. By 2008, buildings were up and the finish line was paved over, concluding a 130-year saga.[92]

> *Sometime horse racing will return—it always has.*
> *—Ray the Railbird, 1992*[93]

Over 130 years, dedicated enthusiasts time and again resurrected Helena racing. It remains possible that it could return. The current fairgrounds still has open space, or perhaps the next Fashion Course has yet to be built. A remnant of the old track is still used: In the winter, the backstretch hosts skijoring, a timed sport likened to water skiing on snow. Snow is shaped into hills and jumps on either side of the straightaway. As an intrepid skier grasps a tow rope, a horse and rider run a straight line as the skier slaloms back and forth over a course of jumps and hills.

7

BUTTE AND ANACONDA

The Highest Highs and the Lowest Lows

All men are equal on and under the turf.
—*Marcus Daly (quoting Lord George Bentinck)*[94]

Copper, buried within the "Richest Hill on Earth," made Butte the largest city in Montana by the 1880s. That decade, Marcus Daly, one of Montana's "Copper Kings," built the Washoe Smelter and a new town named Anaconda. From there, Butte and Anaconda, quite literally, electrified America.

While Spokane's 1889 Kentucky Derby win gave birth to Montana's first golden age of horse racing, Butte nurtured the turf to maturity—even though "not a blade" of grass would grow in the Mining City. As railroads arrived, the Butte and Anaconda racetracks drew hundreds of horses from across the United States. The rails also brought fresh-cut hay from the lush Bitterroot Valley to feed them. Telegraph wires sent racing results to the *Daily Racing Form*, where they were published nationally. Fans attended by the thousands.

Then the Montana legislature banned gambling.

BUTTE'S RACING ROOTS

There are few reports of racing in Silver Bow County before the late 1870s, but Butte horses traveled to nearby meets. One was Lady Lightfoot, mentioned in chapter 4, who was at Deer Lodge in 1869.

Butte's organized racing began in 1877 when Lee Mantle built a track. In 1878, H.G. Valiton leased it, holding a meet with rules "securing perfect square play." Purse money of $2,500 enticed Larabie to bring horses from Deer Lodge, while Williams in Helena readied Cariboo. Trotting and running races went off during a freezing-cold second week of October. In subsequent years, papers promoted both July and October races, organized by the West Side Racing Association. On the Fourth of July in 1881, horses ran for $1,200 in purses, and that year the autumn races moved to September.[95]

The "West Side Racing Association" moniker is confusing, as the track was on the flats—then east of Butte. That said, it probably referred to Butte being west of the Continental Divide, contrasted with Bozeman's Eastern Montana Racing Association, east of the Divide.

The association built a grandstand in 1886 that seated two thousand. That year also brought the "Paris mutuals"—parimutuel—system of betting, considered a more honest system than wagering through a bookie. Articles of incorporation in 1888 listed stockholders W.A. Clark, M.J. Connell, Marcus Daly, Henry L. Frank, and John Noyes.[96]

Another small track was built in 1888 by Gordon and Ritchie at the original Columbia Gardens. A few scattered races were reported there, but it had a seedy reputation and never challenged the West Side. When W.A. Clark purchased and redeveloped the property in 1899, he eliminated the track.

Marcus Daly

Old Marcus—'e's crazy about harses [sic].[97]

No one had a greater influence on Montana horse racing than Marcus Daly (1841–1900). Daly left his Irish homeland at age fifteen. Arriving in New York in 1856, he traveled to California to make his fortune, then went to Nevada and the Comstock Lode. He arrived in Butte in 1876 to manage a silver mine called the Alice. In 1880, he bought the Anaconda mine. Seeing great potential in copper but needing capital, he partnered with three California businessmen (and fellow horse aficionados): James Ben Ali Haggin, George Hearst, and Lloyd Tevis. Together they formed the Anaconda Copper Mining Company.

Newspapers mention Daly at the Butte races in 1886, when he had hired harness trainer C.B. Jeffries away from W.H. Raymond.* In 1887, Daly brought "the best horses on the track" from his stables in Anaconda, and in 1888, he moved his horses to his Bitter Root Stock Farm near Hamilton.† Conrad Kohrs said it best: "Up to 1893 and 1894, John Bielenberg's colts had always been fortunate enough to beat the colts of Marcus Daly, but after 1894, we were not so successful."[98]

Daly's love of horses stands in vivid contrast to his rival copper king, W.A. Clark. Clark was notable by his absence at the Butte races, and the *Daily Racing Form* later dismissed his racing stable as symptomatic of an obsession to vanquish Daly.[99] Motives aside, Clark left details to others—his son Charles handled the turf.

"BEAUTIFUL" BOB WADE

Romanticized accounts claim that in 1890, Butte's racing fans had to "hike on foot the dusty two miles from the center of the camp to the race track," but this is nonsense. With Silver Bow County's population over twenty-three thousand, Butte was hardly a "camp." Awash in copper, 1890 was when Butte's Electric Motor Company put up wires for streetcars, bringing thousands of working people to the track. Better-heeled spectators arrived in carriages and horse-drawn cabs.[100]

Miners working for Daly got paid days off to attend the races. Taverns on the grounds sold beer for a nickel. Shots of whisky were technically twelve and a half cents each, though no one ordered just one.

Bob Wade was a horse of uncertain part-Thoroughbred ancestry, registered with the Jockey Club for racing purposes. Today, he is considered a Quarter Horse. At Butte on August 20, 1890, the four-year-old gelding set a world record for the quarter mile (440 yards) of :21-1/4 seconds. It stood for sixty-eight years.[101]

The season featured three top sprinters: Bob Wade was the "beautiful bay," owned by A.H. Sutton of Walla Walla, Washington. His competitors were Nettie S, the "gray mare of Anaconda," owned by Barker & Parrott; and Cyclone, "the great California chestnut," owned by A.D. Hitchcock. The *Anaconda Standard* explained, "All around the circuit they have been

---

* See chapter 12 for more on Raymond.
† See chapter 8.

rivals and their owners desired the question of supremacy settled."[102] A three-horse match race was squeezed into the Butte schedule.

Cyclone held the world record for three furlongs (660 yards), but Bob Wade had defeated Cyclone in the past. Nettie S had run 440 in a blazing :21-3/4, only a quarter of a second off the former record.

When the race went off, Bob Wade had a bad start, but at 220 yards he came nose to nose with Nettie S as Cyclone faded. Unleashing a final kick, Bob Wade surged to the front, winning by a head. The three timers conferred. One had :21 flat on his stopwatch, the second had :21-1/4, and the third, "a little premature" with his thumb, got :21-3/4. They put up :21-1/4, a new world record, and telegraph wires hummed with the news.[103]

Sutton was deluged with offers for Bob Wade but turned them all down. Even W.A. Clark failed to buy the gelding. Bob Wade ran again twice more in Butte and, on August 28, set a track record at 600 yards. After that, the horse was sold and went to the West Coast.

Bob Wade campaigned in eight different states. He entered seventy-six races between 1890 and 1892, winning thirty-three. His last reported win was at East St. Louis on October 29, 1892. His last reported race was a half-mile contest on April 5, 1894, in Madison, Illinois, where the eight-year-old finished well back in the pack. No further records of his fate have been located.

His quarter-mile record stood until 1958. That year, under modern conditions, Red Jones ran a quarter mile in :21-1/5 at Cranwood Race Course in Ohio. The 440-yard record as of 2018, set in 2009 by First Moonflash at Sunland Park, New Mexico, is :20.274.[104]

The Reign of Butte

The bands played, the horses pranced and flashed like light, the sweating toil of thousands of men within the earth was forgotten.[105]

Daly purchased Butte's track in 1896 and made it a showplace. That year, Butte raced forty-eight days and Red S tied the world record for three furlongs. Daly built a three-story grandstand and thirty-two barns, plus seven cook houses to feed workers. By the time he was finished, the Butte Jockey Club hosted a restaurant, two bars, and a separate building for betting.

Butte Jockey Club track and grandstands, July 4, 1914. *Todd Photographic Company, LOC.*

Local history states that "Daly withdrew from active participation" and "the race track came under new management."[106] But this misstates Daly's role: he actually hired a top professional to run his meets.

Ed Tipton of Kentucky, later co-founder of the Fasig-Tipton Thoroughbred Sales Company, designed and managed the Butte track for Daly. Tipton arranged special railroad rates that attracted horses from Chicago and other distant places. He banned bookies; betting was via auction pools and parimutuels. Fans wagered $6 million* between 1896 and 1898.

In November 1900, Daly died. Conrad Kohrs noted, "The strain of political activities affected his [Daly's] health and they were the cause of calling him to an early death."[107] Daly's passing did not end racing. If anything, Butte's passion increased, as the *Anaconda Standard* wryly noted in 1901:

> *Horse, horse, horse! That is all one hears in Butte these days....The hotel lobbies are full of people talking horse; the street corners get next to the latest dope; business men remark that this year's meeting ought to be a crackajack; ladies wonder if such and such a horse will be here again this year, for, oh, he was just the handsomest horse they ever saw. The small boy awaits with eagerness...the race meet in Butte....They all have the fever; the disease is epidemic; there is no cure for it.[108]*

---

* $6 million in 1898 is over $155 million in 2017 dollars.

ATOKA

After Daly's untimely passing, trains loaded with racehorses continued to roll into Montana. The Butte meet expanded to sixty days; nearby Anaconda ran thirty. On August 14, 1902, a horse named Judge Thomas set a world record for three and a half furlongs.

By 1906, a circuit of Butte, Anaconda, and Helena offered a combined $125,000 in purse money. That year, Butte fans saw 750 horses on the grounds and another world record broken—twice at the same meet—by the same horse.

Atoka was a six-year-old chestnut gelding owned by Stokes and Spargur. Spargur did double duty as his jockey. On August 23, 1906, Atoka broke the world record for three furlongs, winning by a nose over the horse Billy Mayhan in :33-3/4. Third by a head was Sam F, "a throat-latch away." The finish "made every one of the thousand spectators stand up and cheer…for the race belonged to any of the three leaders until the last jump was made."[109]

On September 6, Atoka vanquished Sam F a second time, again closing fast in the final yards. Sam F's owner, E.W. Meredith, sought a rematch. Each owner put up $250 and agreed to "catchweights"—no assigned handicap. On September 7, Sam F. went off carrying 79 pounds to 123 for Atoka. Sam F started fast and was two lengths ahead at the turn. Then Atoka opened up and blazed past Sam F in the final forty yards, winning by two lengths in :33-1/2, breaking his own record. Spargur savored the victory for decades—and the official record stood for thirty-two years.

Butte jockeys, 1905. *Fogarty photo, MHS Photo Archives PAc 95-06.6.*

In 1938, Galley Slave ran :32-4/5 on a straightaway at Santa Anita. Around a curve, as Atoka ran, the record held until 1967 when Jim J ran :32-3/5 in a timed workout at Aqueduct in New York.[110]

THE "SLOUGH OF DESPOND"

*All good citizens should combine to take temptation out of the path
of the youth and wage earners of this state.
—Walter Laidlaw (on gambling in New York)*[111]

As the twentieth century dawned, gambling was denounced as a moral vice. New York's 1908 Hart-Agnew law banned betting in that state, and by 1911, every New York racetrack had closed. In 1913, an appellate court revived racing in the Empire State by deciding that Hart-Agnew only applied to bookmakers, not to individuals betting "among themselves"— thus legalizing parimutuel wagering.

In spite of the lessons offered by this East Coast drama, Montana walked the same path—in its own fashion.

Montana's 1889 Constitution banned fraud-laden "lotteries and gift enterprises," but race betting was mostly ignored. State law required proper identification of racehorses and banned ringers. Other statutes required tax assessments on "blooded" stallions, let towns restrict racing in the streets, and tried to prevent racing on Sundays.

Trouble arrived in 1909. The Montana legislature outlawed off-track "poolroom" wagering, allowing bets only within an "inclosed [sic] racetrack or fair-grounds." It also restricted racing to thirty days per year in "any County of the first class." This hit Butte's sixty-day meet; Silver Bow was the only "county of the first class." The same statute limited all other counties to fourteen racing days each. That provision only impacted Deer Lodge County,* where Anaconda ran thirty days.[112]

Butte's poolrooms fought back. A telegraph office went in upstairs from the M&M Saloon, connected by a back staircase. Down in the M&M, Ed Sylvester set up a blackboard and recorded race results as they came in via a separate telegraph line.

Someone tipped off law enforcement. When the sheriff arrived, Sylvester claimed the races were announced for entertainment, denying the M&M took wagers. Upstairs, the telegraph manager, Harry Rose, produced customers' "business messages" such as "Glorio first at track odds 20.00." He claimed ignorance of activities in the bar. The problem was a horse named Intrinsic—whose name appeared both on telegrams and the chalkboard at the M&M. Sylvester and Rose were arrested.

Juries convicted both men. They appealed. When the Montana Supreme Court upheld their convictions, Sylvester paid his fine—then started other clandestine wagering operations. Rose skipped town.[113]

In 1911, the racing crowd tested the thirty-day limit with meets in two locations. The Butte Driving Club graded a rough oval "on the boulevard" south of town. It staged fifteen days of racing, with "a trivial amount" of daily wagers. Then the Butte Jockey Club began its regular meet.

Seventeen days in, William Gemmell, secretary of Butte's Jockey Club, made a wager. Silver Bow County Attorney Thomas Walker witnessed the

---

* Readers outside Montana might be justifiably confused that the town of Deer Lodge is the county seat of Powell County, while Anaconda is the county seat of Deer Lodge County.

bet, declared it day thirty-two for wagering in the county, and had Gemmell arrested. Later asked if he also had wagered, Walker replied, "If I did not, it was something unusual."[114]

District Judge Michael Donlan acquitted Gemmell, stating the law meant thirty days per track. The Montana Supreme Court disagreed, and in 1912, it firmly declared that thirty days meant thirty days for the entire county, period. Gemmell's case was remanded. Judge Donlan acquitted Gemmell again, this time declaring that the Butte Driving Club meet was illegal (thus its fifteen days didn't count) because the track, inadequately fenced, was not really "inclosed."[115]

Then the legislature dropped the hammer. In 1915, Montana banned gambling on "any contest of speed or skill or endurance of animal or beast." Horse racing remained legal, as were "jackpot" purses pooled from entry fees.[116]

Without legal wagering, the Butte Jockey Club folded. In 1916, the land was platted into residential lots and sold. Today, Grant, Marcia, Howard, and Garfield Streets in Butte's "Racetrack" neighborhood roughly border the site. East Middle School occupies land once graced by some of the finest Thoroughbreds in America. One structure remains: a house on Howard Street, said to have been the "ticket house." A memorial to the grand track is at Racetrack Park on Farragut Avenue.

In 1917, 1919, and 1921, the legislature tried and failed to legalize parimutuel wagering. When Governor Sam Stewart vetoed the 1919 bill, the *Daily Racing Form* ranted about the Montana situation:

> *If fairs can be made to succeed without the element of wholesome entertainment provided by horse racing, I hope to live to see it done, but I question if the enthusiasm developed by ping pong, parlor croquet, popgun and spit ball contests, drop the handkerchief, button, button, who's got the button? [,] lemonade, popcorn, and no smoking allowed on the grounds, will ever take the place of the most popular of outdoor entertainment.*[117]

South of town, the Butte Driving Club bought new land on Harrison Avenue and laid out a modest track. There, racing aficionados held meets during the 1920s. Montana's racing press dubbed this period the "slough of despond."[118]

Helena tried a different approach: getting around the anti-wagering statute legally. It introduced the "Florida Plan," a parimutuel system in all but name. The system—including machines to perform necessary

Racetrack Park commemorates a once-bustling showplace. *Wahler.*

calculations—arrived in 1925. People purchased "shares" in a racehorse, then paid an "entry fee" of $2 for "their" horse to run a race. The "co-owners" of the winning horse then split the "jackpot."

Helena attorney Edmond Toomey—counsel to the governor—brought a "friendly test suit" of the Florida Plan. At the 1925 state fair, he paid $2 to "enter" a horse named Florence Fryer. After the horse lost, he sued the fair board, arguing that his loss came from betting on an illegal game.

In *Toomey v. Penwell*, decided in 1926, a unanimous Montana Supreme Court ruled in favor of the fair board and the Florida Plan, stating, "Horse-racing, as such, is not now and, so far as we know, never has been, prohibited in this state. Neither is it unlawful to conduct a horse-race for 'a purse, prize, premium, stake, or sweep-stakes.'"[119] A crack opened in Montana's anti-gambling law.

CANADIAN BOYS

While lawyers wrangled in Helena, a fifteen-year-old boy from Edmonton, Alberta, arrived in Butte. Johnny Pollard's parents entrusted him to a guardian who was supposed to help Pollard apprentice as a jockey, but the man abandoned him.

Homeless and penniless, Pollard found Butte's "bullpen" track in 1925. He galloped horses in morning workouts and rode a few races. He never won in Butte, but it may have been where he picked up his racing nickname, "Red"—for his hair color. Pollard left town in 1926, traveling from Canada to Tijuana. Along the way, he finally started winning.

In his travels, Pollard befriended another Canadian jockey who gained experience in Montana: George Woolf from Cardston, in southern Alberta. Some accounts say Pollard gave Woolf his nickname, "Iceman." As a boy, Woolf lived in Babb, on the Blackfeet Reservation, where it was said he rode match races when he was six. He also may have ridden Indian Relay and at Montana fair meets. State newspapers gladly called him "Woolf of Montana" as he found fame.

In 1936, Red Pollard met up with Seabiscuit. Pollard became Seabiscuit's regular rider as the horse became a newsreel hero and "the people's champion." When Pollard was injured, Woolf piloted Seabiscuit to win the 1938 "match of the century" against Triple Crown winner War Admiral.[120]

A third Canadian on his way up, Johnny Longden, rode in Butte as racing revived in 1929.

1929 RECOVERY

With the 1926 *Toomey* decision, anti-gambling laws were in shambles. "Co-ownership" plans spread from fair to fair as fast as calculating equipment could be brought into the state. In 1929, the Montana legislature legalized parimutuel wagering. The statute used *Toomey*'s wording, not saying "parimutuel," but everyone knew racing was back on.[121]

R. James Speers, a Canadian entrepreneur from Winnipeg, immediately developed Marcus Daly Park just outside of Butte, near where the airport is today. (This might have been the Butte Driving Club track.) Speers hauled in modern technology, including a starting barrier and an electric odds board.

Great excitement accompanied the 1929 meet. Celebrities visited: writer Will James was in town. Lon Spargur came by and told stories of Atoka. Johnny Longden—a fast-rising star of the Calgary track who later won the 1943 Triple Crown on Count Fleet—arrived by express train to ride in the Musselshell Handicap. (He lost.) Races ran twenty-five days, and five hundred horses graced the grounds. Eight thousand fans attended the final day.

Horse racing at Marcus Daly Race Park, 1929. *MHS Photo Archives PAc 2001-14.3.*

Unfortunately, the Stock Market crashed that October, and the Great Depression put the brakes on Speers's ambitions. He ran a fifteen-day meet in 1930 but could not pull off a meet in 1931. Walter Hill, son of railroad magnate James J. Hill, bought the property a few years later. Managed by Abe Cohen, the facility held one more meet in 1936. Soon after it concluded, a fire of mysterious origin destroyed the grandstands and clubhouse, and Butte's racing era ended.[122]

Anaconda Racing

If Chicago owners think of shipping here stop them unless they have good horses. Short distance low-class sprinters will not do. They are coming in by the hundreds.
—Ed Tipton, Anaconda, Montana, June 7, 1897[123]

In 1883–84, Marcus Daly built the Washoe Smelter and founded the town of Anaconda, which became his home base. Horse racing followed. Daly teamed up with Standardbred breeder Morgan Evans and graded a racetrack east of town in 1886. It is not clear where this track was, as it was only used while a bigger project developed: Daly's Anaconda Driving Park opened on the town's west side in 1888.

The original grandstand seated one thousand people in front of a one-mile oval, with a bar and dining room beneath the stands. Daly's great trotting stallion Prodigal and his pacing mare Yolo Maid both graced the track. Challengers included W.H. Raymond's Belmont Park stable from Madison County.

Racing permeated Anaconda. A cable car ran from the town to the track. Turf and Daly's on Main Street ran a bookmaking operation where patrons, including Daly himself, wired bets to the coasts. A telegraph operator called the big races as they came in, especially when Daly's horses were running.

Daly's favorite Thoroughbred, Tammany, was a local celebrity. On July 2, 1892, the telegraph announced Tammany won the Lawrence Realization Stakes at Sheepshead Bay on Coney Island. Residents decked everything from dog collars to flagpoles with Daly's copper and Irish green stable colors, put out Fourth of July decorations early, and threw a party. The *Anaconda Standard* commented the next day, "If some of the participants are a little worse for wear this morning, the occasion certainly justifies the performance."[124]

Daly expanded the Anaconda track in 1896, building a two-story grandstand with seating for two thousand. It was a banner year for harness

The Anaconda grandstands. Undated, circa 1896–1911. *MHS Photo Archives 940-401.*

Right: Tammany Mosaic, E.R. Newcomb, artist. *Courtesy Daly.*

Below: Main entry, Montana Hotel, Anaconda. *Al Huntsman, Photographer. Historic American Buildings Survey, LOC.*

racers. Kirkendall brought his string from Helena to challenge Daly, Frank Higgins of Missoula brought his mare Antrima, and all faced off against horses from as far away as Calgary and Kansas City.

Daly's Thoroughbreds also visited Anaconda. Fans saw Ogden win in 1896 before he shipped east to make his name on the national scene. They saw Scottish Chieftain return from his 1897 Belmont Stakes victory to dominate Montana racing in 1898.*

---

* These horses are discussed further in chapter 8.

At Daly's Montana Hotel, he commissioned a $3,000 mosaic image of Tammany, set into the floor of the hotel bar. Artist E.R. Newcomb of Chicago created the four-foot-square hardwood inlay, said to contain one thousand individual pieces. It was so precious to Daly that anyone who stepped on it had to buy a round of drinks for the house.

Decades after Daly's death, bartenders such as Louis Minter kept the legend alive and the mosaic in pristine condition. But as the hotel deteriorated in the 1970s, legend faded to a rumor that stepping on it was merely "bad luck." The hotel sold in 1976 to a developer who sold off valuables piecemeal and partially demolished the structure. When the mosaic was torn from the floor, the Daly estate quickly snapped it up. It survives today, in storage at the Daly mansion in Hamilton.[125]

After 1900, the Driving Park became the county fairgrounds. In August 1911, the iconic grandstands burned down. Arson was suspected, as the blaze started in multiple places at once. Prevailing winds saved the stables, and bleachers were hastily constructed so racing could continue that year. When gambling was banned in 1915, the track closed. In 1922, the Anaconda Company repurposed the track into athletic fields. In 1949, the entire property opened to development and is now the Second Western Addition. Streets named Hamburg, Ogden, and Tammany honor Daly's greatest horses.

Parimutuel racing never returned. Some records mention the "Marcus Daly Race Track"—Speers's track in Butte—mistakenly placing it in Anaconda. Another track was proposed at Gregson (near Fairmont Hot Springs), but it did not come to fruition.

The Anaconda Saddle Club built a 3/8-mile oval in 1945–46, but no races were reported. Sprints and relays were popular at O-Mok-Sees in the 1950s, so the track may have been used for such events, but ultimately it was abandoned. A faint footprint remains visible in aerial photos of the grounds.[126]

DALY'S DOMAIN

Hamilton and the Bitter Root Stock Farm

The awful work thrown upon me by my business would kill me but for the fact that now and then I can run up to the Bitter Root and see the colts. That place has cost me a lot of money, but it is worth it to me when I stop to think of the relief it furnishes.
—Marcus Daly[127]

Marcus Daly was king of the Montana turf. In a bright but too-brief decade, his Bitter Root Stock Farm was one of America's finest racehorse operations. Daly's copper, green, and silver racing colors graced tracks from California to New York. Had Daly lived to see his plans come to fruition, his name might now be listed among America's most notable breeders.

Daly also opened his private racetracks to the public to host Hamilton's Ravalli County Fair, starting a strong tradition of local horse racing that lasted one hundred years.

HAMILTON'S ROOTS

The sheltered Bitterroot Valley was the ancestral home of the Salish, visited by Lewis and Clark in 1805. St. Mary's Mission, founded in 1841 near present-day Stevensville, was the first white settlement in Montana. Later,

John Owen built Fort Owen, and in 1856, he mentioned a man named Bonaparte trying to set up a match race with some Nez Perce.[128]

In 1855, at Council Grove—near present-day Missoula—Isaac Stevens negotiated the Hellgate Treaty with the Salish, Kootenai, and Pend d'Oreille (Qlispém, Kalispel), using it to clear the way for the Mullan Road and white settlement. Chief Victor (Xʷelx̣λ̓cin) signed the Hellgate Treaty, believing Isaac Stevens's statements that the Bitterroot would remain in Salish hands. But with rich soil well suited to agriculture, the Bitterroot drew farmers and ranchers. In 1864, they named the community around Fort Owen "Stevensville." In 1872, Victor's son, Charlot (Słm̓x̣e Q̓ʷox̣qeys), refused to sign the Garfield Agreement and leave the Bitterroot, insisting the Hellgate Treaty reserved land for his people. Nonetheless, the government opened all "unoccupied" land to settlement in 1883. Charlot and his people remained until forced to leave in 1891.[129]

In 1886, Marcus Daly bought the Anthony Chaffin homestead as a summer residence for his family. He named it Riverside and purchased surrounding land until he owned 22,000 acres. In 1888, Daly brought "a large force of carpenters" from Butte and started building horse barns. He moved in his racehorses from Anaconda and "over 20 [box]car loads" of Thoroughbreds, Standardbreds, and draft horses from California. The ranch held over 1,200 horses at its peak.[130]

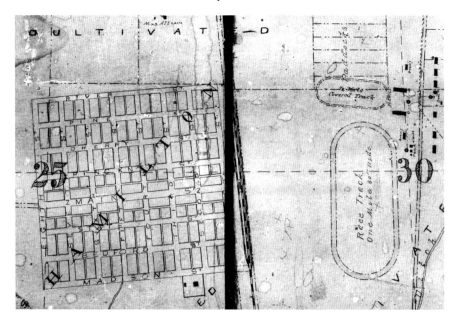

Thoroughbred division, Bitter Root Stock Farm map, 1890. *RCM.*

Meanwhile, the Anaconda Company needed vast amounts of timber. Daly started a mill near the Bitterroot River and platted the town of Hamilton in 1890 for his workers. By 1892, he finished the "Big Mill," which churned out thirty-five million board feet a year. He negotiated a favorable route for the railroad. Ravalli County was created in 1893, and Hamilton grew beyond a company town to become the economic hub of the Bitterroot.

Daly's Passion

Some accounts assert that Daly got into racing due to the influence of his Anaconda Company partners, in particular James Ben Ali Haggin, who had "a love of horses bred in the bone." His 40,000-acre Rancho del Paso in California was one of the largest horse breeding operations in the world. Haggin later purchased the Elmendorf farm in his native state of Kentucky.[131]

Anaconda partner George Hearst (father of newspaper magnate William Randolph Hearst) also owned a racing stable and built the Bay View Park racecourse in San Francisco. Less obvious in enthusiasm was Lloyd Tevis, president of Wells Fargo & Company. But he was Haggin's silent partner in Rancho del Paso, and the society press later described Tevis's family, saying, "They are not *of* the horsey set. They *are* the horsey set."[132] Today, the "Tevis Cup" goes to the winner of the famed 100-mile Western States Endurance Ride.*

Daly probably received advice from these men, but his equine passion suggests origins in childhood. Ireland is a horse-mad nation with racecourses across the country, some within reach of Daly's birthplace in County Caven. Even a poor boy would have seen Ireland's magnificent horses. Daly himself said little about his youth, though legends abound, including one claiming his family were once horse trainers. Another unverified story is that Daly was a stable hand at a racing barn on Long Island when he first came to America.[133]

In any case, Daly's interest was personal: he spared no expense for the finest care of his animals and annotated his annual catalogue with savvy insights about individual horses. His pedigree knowledge, eye for conformation, desire to improve his stock, and hands-on involvement all showed interest far beyond that of a wealthy dilettante.

---

* The "Haggin Cup" goes to the best-conditioned top-ten-finishing horse in the same event.

Bitter Root Stock Farm

There would never be a place in horsedom like the Daly Bitter Root farm.
—Montana Standard, *March 29, 1929*

Daly built the Bitter Root Stock Farm into a state-of-the-art facility. The "trotting department," north of his home mansion, had an outdoor three-quarter-mile training track and a covered indoor track consisting of a quarter-mile-long straightaway with "a curved end" to allow horses to turn around.[134]

Even more impressive was the Thoroughbred department. It sat east of what today is Highway 93 and Hamilton's downtown. A mile oval training track sat between present-day Daly Avenue and Kurtz Lane. Today's East Main/Marcus Street crosses what was the final turn. According to local historian Ada Powell, Daly imported a boxcar of Kentucky soil to supplement the footing.

The marvel of the Thoroughbred department was a half-mile covered track. Shown on the 1890 stock farm map and in an 1892 landscape painting by Henry Cross (now displayed at University of Montana's Mansfield Library in Missoula), the covered oval allowed racehorses to be conditioned during Montana's winters. An estimated 400,000 board

Stock farm "trotting department" and covered training track. *DA-03.025 RCM.*

feet of lumber went into its construction.[135] That said, its engineering was flawed; after Daly's death, a section collapsed, and the rest of the structure was torn down. In contrast, the trotting department's runway-style building housed county fair exhibits in 1912.

The showplace was the stallion barn: Tammany's Castle. On September 29, 1893, Tammany defeated the great eastern champion Lamplighter at Guttenberg racetrack in New Jersey. Daly had declared that if Tammany won, he'd "build him a castle" at his farm in the Bitterroot.

Completed in 1895, the steam-heated brick building had cork floors in the stalls. Twin cupolas graced the roofline, and two flags flew over the structure: One was an American flag and the other a copper and green banner for the Daly Stables. Ada Powell located evidence the walls of Tammany's stall may have been covered with carpeting. Legend claims the wall cover was velvet and fresh flowers were placed near his stall daily. "The Castle" stands today, converted to a private home with the exterior façade nearly unchanged.

The horses' well-being came first. The Stock Farm included an on-site veterinary hospital developed by Dr. E.W. Hagyard of Hagyard and Sons Veterinary Hospital in Lexington, Kentucky. Sparing no expense, Daly commissioned several specially appointed railcars to haul his horses to distant tracks in comfort.[136]

Tammany Castle, now a private residence. *Wahler.*

Leading the Thoroughbred department was Sam Lucas, a Kentuckian who had previously trained for Woodburn Farm and for August Belmont. Lucas came to work for Daly in 1890. Lucas was well liked in Hamilton and returned the sentiment. Following Daly's death, Lucas returned east, but he renewed his Montana connections in 1905 when he passed through Montana with a shipment of eastern racehorses bound for Japan. He later retired to Butte. Lucas said if Daly lived longer, the stable "would have conquered the world of turfdom."[137]

On the East Coast, Daly's lead trainer was Matt Byrnes. Byrnes trained for Haggin, then took on Daly's string in 1891. Byrnes guided most of Daly's champions, with the notable exception of Hamburg, discussed below. Byrnes frequently teamed up with jockey Ed "Snapper" Garrison for the biggest races. Daly's horses often won with the come-from-behind closing rush that became labeled a "Garrison Finish." After Daly's death in 1900, Byrnes bought his own breeding farm in New Jersey.

THE HORSES

I am satisfied that in the Bitter Root valley,
the ideal conditions for successful horse breeding are found.
—Marcus Daly, 1896 Stock Farm Catalogue

Daly spent over $1 million buying racehorses (a conservative estimate*), not counting what he spent to build and manage the Stock Farm. His initial investments were in harness racers. Daly's lead Standardbred stallion was Prodigal. Lightly raced, the stallion trotted a standard mile in 2:16, hitched to an old-style high-wheeled sulky. The harness stable raced mostly in Montana and on the West Coast, though the Prodigal-sired China Silk won the 1896 Kentucky Trotting Stakes Futurity.

Daly's fame came from his Thoroughbreds—by 1889, he had "running horses" at his stables. Daly also purchased a small farm in the United Kingdom, Aperfield Court. Described as Daly's "recruiting station," carefully selected mares were bred to the best English stallions and then shipped to Montana. He also imported a few stallions, notably the "plain but substantial" Inverness, who sired Scottish Chieftain, winner of the 1897 Belmont Stakes. In 1896, with Tammany unproven at stud and Hamburg yet to be purchased, Daly designated Inverness as "best on place."[138]

---

* Over $30 million today.

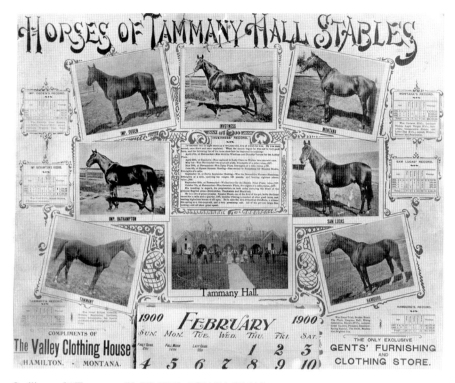

Stallions of "Tammany Hall," 1900. *RCM DA-02.010.*

Tammany

Daly was king of the Montana turf, and Tammany (14:9-1-2) was king of the Stock Farm. Foaled in 1889 at the Belle Meade Stud in Tennessee, Tammany sold to Daly as a yearling. The pretty chestnut had distinctive markings, including irregular hind socks and a blaze that resembled a backward question mark. He was reputed to have an exceptionally gentle disposition: one story maintains that when the stable's puppies wandered into his stall or paddock, Tammany picked them up by the nape of their necks and carried them around, unharmed.[139]

As a two-year-old, Tammany went east to train with Byrnes and won the Great Eclipse Stakes. As a three-year-old, he won four major stakes races in New York and New Jersey. He was later declared 1892 Horse of the Year.

As a four-year-old, Tammany had hoof problems and missed some of 1893's top contests, but he healed up and raced in the fall. As noted

Tammany (*left*) and Hamburg (*right*) at Tammany Castle, circa 1898–1900. *MHS Photo Archives 955-285.*

previously, he won his most notable race that September, the match race against Lamplighter. Tammany earned $113,290 in his career.*

The "Castle" was still a vision when Daly retired Tammany. The chestnut had to settle for his old spot in Daly's existing stables when he arrived home on October 10, 1893. Nonetheless, Tammany's "old" stall was paneled in hardwood, and the barn was steam-heated, with hot and cold running water. Daly declared, "I could put the horses in the house and move out to the barn and I would still get the best of the deal." It was fortunate such stabling was available; Tammany caught a cold on the train, and then an early cold snap hit Montana (Havre saw -13° F). Tammany developed pneumonia, and Daly's veterinarians struggled to save him while Daly panicked. But by October 30, Tammany was out of the woods and went on to sire dozens of offspring at the Stock Farm.[140]

---

* Over $3.1 million today.

Tammany's alter ego was Montana (24:6-3-6). The Haggin-bred stallion was Daly's first major winner. He had a respectable record that included a remarkable "Garrison Finish" win at 40–1 odds in the 1892 Suburban Handicap, then considered one of America's most important races. But Montana was vicious. "Big and common—mean…Don't like him," grumbled Daly in a scrawled annotation to his 1896 catalogue.

Montana would attack anyone who came near him. Matt Byrnes related that when they stabled at a vermin-infested barn, Montana dispatched the rats himself, grabbing them with a snap of his teeth. In retirement, the rangy bay once got too close to Tammany and attacked, tearing skin off the chestnut favorite. Photos show Montana as a thin horse, unhappy even at the haven of the Stock Farm.[141]

Ogden and the Chieftain

Ogden (28:15-8-1) solidified Daly's credentials as a horse breeder. The dark bay colt was foaled in England in 1894. He was imported with his dam, Oriole, noted by Daly as "the best of the imported mares."[142]

The colt grew slowly. He stayed home in 1886 when other two-year-olds shipped east in the spring. Ogden started racing at Butte and Anaconda. He struggled until July—then got Daly's attention by winning three races in a row. Though Byrnes was unimpressed, Daly shipped the colt to New York anyway, along with Ogden's Montana crew, trainer John Campbell and jockey "Doc" Turberville (or Turbiville). Daly entered Ogden in the Futurity Stakes, then one of America's most prestigious races for two-year-olds. He won by a length and a half, beating agemate Scottish Chieftain.

In 1897, Ogden finished dead last in the Belmont Stakes and Byrnes sent him home. Returning in 1898, he had a respectable season, then retired to stud. When seven-year-old Ogden sold to William Lakeland in January 1901, he raced again, winning multiple handicaps as the season progressed. He retired a second time after John Madden purchased him that December.

Scottish Chieftain is famous for winning the Belmont Stakes, but he did not impress Daly. "Good, but needs selling," Daly commented. After losing to Ogden in 1896, the son of Inverness entered the 1897 Belmont as Ogden's "rabbit." But the pair traded places: "The Chieftain" fought off two horses of August Belmont Jr. and won. The Montana press was delighted, as the colt was born and raised in Montana, "a genuine product of the Bitterroot

Ogden. Henry Stull, oil on canvas, 1896. *MHS X1969-51-01.*

ozone and bunch grass."[143] He and Spokane remain the only two Montana-raised horses to have won any of the Triple Crown classic races.*

Scottish Chieftain failed to win further eastern races, and Daly brought him home. He ran and won several times in Montana in 1898. Still unimpressed, Daly sold him in 1899, along with fifty broodmares, to "Mr. Montgomery," a breeder in Monida.

HAMBURG

Daly and Byrnes disagreed on the virtues of Hamburg (21:16-3-2), considered the greatest horse Daly ever owned. Trainer John Madden had purchased Hamburg as a weanling for $1,200. The powerful, flashy bay colt was a challenge to train and had an enormous appetite. But once Hamburg

---

* Alysheba, 1987 Derby and Preakness winner, had Montana connections. Pamela Scharbauer, his co-owner, lived in Missoula. But the horse never spent time in Montana.

figured out his job and had all he could eat, he was unstoppable. As a two-year-old in 1897, he won twelve of sixteen starts under stunningly high imposts ranging up to 135 pounds.

Hamburg made Madden's career. That December, the sports press was abuzz when he sold Hamburg for a record-breaking $40,001. The buyer's agent, trainer William "Billy" Lakeland, initially stayed mum as to the buyer while the newspapers whipped themselves into a froth of speculation. Asked if Daly had purchased the colt, Matt Byrnes scoffed, "I wouldn't have had him for I don't believe he is the great horse now that people credit him with being."[144]

Byrnes had to eat crow when Daly's ownership came to light, and the colt stayed in training with Lakeland. Madden took his profits and bought his dream farm in Lexington, Kentucky, which he named Hamburg Place in honor of the horse. Legend holds that Madden later grumbled, "That colt is worth a gold mine and I sold him for a paltry $40,001."[145]

As a three-year-old, Hamburg lost the Belmont Stakes before Lakeland realized the colt's enormous appetite combined with hard workouts was his secret to success. Hamburg won thereafter, earned back almost his entire purchase price and is listed as 1898 Horse of the Year. With handicaps up to 140 pounds, Hamburg was often jockeyed by Tod Sloan, famous for revolutionizing race riding with what was initially derided

Young Marcus Daly II with Hamburg, circa 1898–1900. *Courtesy Daly.*

as a "monkey seat"—riding crouched over the withers with very short stirrups—now standard today. "Hamburg was the only great horse I ever rode," said Sloan.[146]

At the 1898 Lawrence Realization Stakes, Hamburg defeated Plaudit, that year's Kentucky Derby winner. Later, Hamburg led gate to wire in the 2-1/4-mile Brighton Cup before retiring with career earnings of $60,380.

DALY'S LEGACY

It seemed like a day of mourning, a time when the entire population of the city stood sorrowed, bowed at the funeral of their brightest hopes. The grand beauties were leaving the valley.[147]

After Daly's death in 1900, his horses were sold. Trotting stock, coach horses, draft horses, and even Shetland ponies were auctioned at Butte and on the West Coast. Many of the Thoroughbreds shipped east. As Daly's special railcars departed Hamilton for the last time, the townspeople sadly watched them go.

Fasig-Tipton ran multiple sales of Daly stock in 1901, bringing in $728,755 to the estate.[148] The *New York Times* described the first of these sales, held at Madison Square Garden, as "one of the most important, if not actually the greatest sale of thoroughbred racing stock ever held in America."[149] Hamburg, Tammany, Ogden, Inverness, and four other stallions all went to the block. So did ninety-eight mares and many young racehorses in training.

On January 30, 1901, the three-day sale began. A capacity crowd of seven thousand gathered, "the most singular that has attended a horse sale in New York, and would have done credit to the [National] horse show on a fashionable night."[150]

First in the ring was Hamburg. The crowd cheered madly as the stallion circled calmly among the tumult. A fierce bidding war erupted immediately between agents for two of the most powerful Thoroughbred breeders in America, W.C. Whitney and—no surprise—James Ben Ali Haggin.

Whitney had two agents. One was a sleeper: Hamburg's former owner, John Madden, who opened the bidding at $40,000. Haggin's agent bid a cautious $41,000. Then Whitney's trainer J.W. Rogers threw down the gauntlet with $45,000. Bids flew in thousand-dollar increments, double-teaming Haggin to $58,000. Then Madden bid $60,000.* Haggin was done. The gavel dropped, and Madden announced he had been bidding for Whitney.[151]

Hamburg sired over two dozen stakes winners. He was North America's leading sire in 1905. In 1915, his granddaughter Regret became the first filly to win the Kentucky Derby.

The top-selling mare, sold to James Keene for $10,000, was Pastorella, an English import. In 1905, she foaled Colin, a great racer undefeated in fifteen starts.

Ogden sold for $4,200 to Lakeland, who raced him that season and then sold him to Madden. Madden kept Ogden at Hamburg Place until the stallion's death in 1923. Ogden had a significant impact in the breeding shed: his progeny won over $1 million at the track. His best son may have been Sir Martin, exported to England, where he won the 1910 Coronation Cup. Ogden's other great son, The Finn, won the 1915 Belmont. The Finn sired Zev, who won the 1923 Derby and Belmont, and Flying Ebony, who won the 1925 Derby.[152]

Tammany, age twelve, sold to M. Murphy of Pittsburg, Pennsylvania, for $4,000. He produced a 1902 foal, Bonnie Sue, out of one of Murphy's mares, but has no later progeny of record. His ultimate fate is unknown.[153]

The final Daly-connected Thoroughbred of fame was Sysonby (15:14-0-1). Daly booked Sysonby's dam, Optime, to Epsom Derby winner Melton for a spring 1901 breeding. Though Daly died in November 1900, his instructions were carried out. Optime, in foal with Sysonby, shipped to America and was purchased by James Keene. In two years of racing, Sysonby's only defeat was to Hamburg's daughter Artful. Sysonby died tragically in 1906 of an undetermined skin disease that caused bleeding sores and sepsis. The beloved champion was buried in New York at Sheepshead Bay, with four thousand people paying their respects. Keene later had the skeleton exhumed and mounted in racing stride by the American Museum of Natural History in New York City.[154]

Daly's will specified one stallion, Senator Grady, be pensioned at the Stock Farm. It is unclear why. Senator Grady was Tammany's less-successful sibling—both were sons of Iroquois. After an impressive two-year-old season, Senator Grady took on an unusually strong class of three-year-olds in 1894, hitting the board but not winning the major races. In retirement, ranch hands entered him in two 1909 Fourth of July races at Hamilton. The eighteen-year-old won one sprint and was third in another.

---

* Roughly $1.8 million in 2017 dollars

Daly's widow, Margaret, was furious, but the horse seemed none the worse for wear.[155]

Horse breeding returned to the Stock Farm with Countess Margit Sigray Bessenyey (1910–1984), Daly's Hungarian-born granddaughter. Taking over the property in the 1950s, she brought Hungarian Warmblood and Shagya Arab sport horses to the ranch. Upon her death in 1984, her herd dispersed and the property passed to her stepson, Francis Bessenyey. Much of the land sold to settle the estate. One area is now an exclusive subdivision known as The Stock Farm. The mansion and about 47 acres around it are owned by the State of Montana and managed by the Daly Mansion Preservation Trust.

HAMILTON RACING

Marcus Daly's racing empire put the Bitterroot on the map, but local residents raced before and after Daly's time. Stevensville hosted mule races in 1866 and a four-hundred-yard horse race in 1869.[156] Newspapers announced races at Victor, Darby, and Corvallis. By the mid-1890s, Daly opened his one-mile oval to the public. He put up grandstands, and local residents held a county fair in 1895. Daly paraded his stallions for the crowd's delight, but race competition was mostly local.

The Ravalli County Fair and Racing Association organized meets for many years. Fourth of July races ran at the mile oval after Daly's death until Ravalli County purchased the current fairgrounds site on the northeast side of town in 1913. The Bitter Root Stock Farm Corporation sold just under 38 acres to the county for $9,750. Contrary to widespread community belief, the property was neither a gift from Margaret Daly, nor did the deed prohibit the sale of alcohol. Fair organizers scrambled to grade a half-mile oval in time for the fair in October; exhibits in 1913 were displayed under large tents. By 1915, even without gambling, the fair was touted as "The Great Ravalli County Fair" and offered four days of racing.[157]

The Stock Farm corporation deeded some of the area around the mile oval to the county in 1929. That deed carried a stipulation that the land was to be used only for athletic purposes, and American Legion Park is there today.[158]

Hamilton apparently had a gap without racing, linked to the onset of the Great Depression. But in 1937, news reports proudly announced

Top: Daly enjoyed exhibiting his horses in Montana. Tammany, Ogden, and Hamburg, with riders in Daly's silks, circa 1899–1900. *Powell*, Copper, Green, and Silver.

Bottom: Trotting race in Hamilton, circa 1905. *RCM*.

the county repaired its fairgrounds and track, reviving its fair and races. Thereafter, the Ravalli County Fair hosted three or four days of races annually. In the second golden age of the 1970s and '80s, the "Marcus Daly Triple Crown" was awarded if a horse won three specified races in Kalispell, Missoula, and Hamilton.

The Ravalli County Fair's last year of racing was 1996. Hamilton succumbed to the same problems as other small meets in the 1990s: rising

Bobbie's Protest wins the Dale Mahlum Feature, Hamilton 1991. Toni Hinton, trainer (*left*); Jim Johnson (*right*); Robin Biegler, jockey. *Courtesy Hinton.*

insurance costs and decreased parimutuel handle. But the Bitterroot remains horse country. Graded stakes–winning trainer Greg Tracy has a stable in Victor, and one of Montana's favorite jockeys, Holly Gervais, is a Ravalli County native.[*] Today, the fairgrounds hosts horse shows and rodeos. Part of the track footprint remains visible. In theory, racing could someday return to the Bitterroot.

---

[*] See chapter 13.

GALLOPING IN THE GALLATIN

Bozeman and the Beaumont

O rganized horse racing in Bozeman dates to the 1870s, but Gallatin County's brightest years centered in nearby Belgrade during the 1950s and 1960s. In between, Bozeman was the birthplace of William "Smokey" Saunders, a Triple Crown–winning jockey. In 1954, Lloyd Shelhamer Jr. and his wife, the former Jane Ringling, built and operated the Beaumont Club, the most glamorous and modern racetrack in Montana. The racetrack struggled while Shelhamer realized that the real money was in supporting multiple tracks with parimutuel equipment. Starting with a portable odds board he hauled to county fairs, he founded United Tote, which became a publicly traded company worth millions.

EARLY BOZEMAN

When Lewis and Clark reached the headwaters of the Missouri River in 1805, they named the easternmost tributary for Secretary of the Treasury Albert Gallatin. The Blackfeet claimed the area, but local lore described it as neutral ground, called the "valley of flowers." The Siksika name for Gallatin region, Ahkoto waktaɪ Sakum, translates to "many-come-together country," said to refer to the joining of rivers at

Three Forks.[159] But multiple tribes came together as well—the Gallatin Valley was the shortest route between the Missouri headwaters and the Yellowstone River.

Whether neutral territory or not, there are no known reports of intertribal gatherings with horse races. Dominance of the Blackfeet kept most whites out of the area until the gold rush hit western Montana.

In 1863, John Bozeman and John Jacobs scouted a route off the Oregon Trail from Wyoming to Montana, later called the Bozeman Trail. On August 9, 1864, Bozeman led a migrant train to the lush Gallatin Valley. Though he was the last of three competing explorers to bring in settlers, the charismatic Bozeman was first to organize a town. Settlers urged the community be named for him.

Once established, Bozeman became the largest city in the agricultural region and soon hosted a county fair. In July 1871, local promoters raised $3,000 to purchase 80 acres. The *Bozeman Avant-Courier* ran a notice in November announcing four days of running and trotting races with $1,000 in purse money.

These were probably not the first horse races in the Gallatin Valley. Race organizers knew the local competition: trotter Yankee Notions was banned from the half-mile dash, and organizers assigned a handicap of 108 pounds to the runners Midnight Belle and Buckskin. Following

Cheyenne match race—horses visible at right. "Beef issue day at the agency," Lame Deer, 1901. *L.A. Huffman, courtesy Allen.*

the meet, a "thoroughbred" horse named Ginger was raffled off as a fundraiser for the Eastern Montana Agricultural and Mechanical Association.[160]

In 1878, the association purchased another plot of land on the north side of town, laid out a track, and planned races for the next year. Also that year, Bozeman's James Harper bought Samuel Larabie's Hambletonian grandsons Superior and Assignee.

East of the Bozeman Hill, the *Avant-Courier* reported an 1872 "Indian race" held following an annuity distribution at Fort Parker. This outpost, east of present-day Livingston, housed the first Crow Indian Agency from 1869 until 1875. This is the first mention of horse racing in Park County and an example of how horse races traditionally accompanied Native gatherings. Livingston ran organized meets by 1905.

Bozeman held regular race meets between 1884 and 1894. As the twentieth century dawned, Bozeman joined Montana racing's first golden age, part of a state circuit from at least 1901 through 1908. Records are unclear if there was racing between 1909 and 1922; the 1926 Gallatin County Fair promoted itself as the "Fourth Annual." That fair sponsored trotting, pacing, and running races. Renamed the "Inter-mountain Fair" in 1927, organizers added relay races and a "boys and girls pony race."[161] Evidence of organized horse racing in Bozeman extends into the 1940s. Maps of Bozeman in 1961 show a half-mile oval covering a substantial portion of the current fairgrounds. Today, the area is now used for parking and assorted buildings, with a ball field nearby.

A 1935 STORY IN the Montana Newspaper Association Inserts (MNAI) suggested the Three Forks area may have hosted Montana's first steeplechase meet. "The Inserts" are not known for their accuracy, and "facts can be mixed." But with that caveat, the story goes like this:

Sometime in the 1880s, investors from England bought land near Willow Creek. They arrived with a number of fine Thoroughbred fox hunters. The bored young men of the group set up a steeplechase course and organized races with considerable betting involved. On one occasion, according to the MNAI story, an old cowboy put up his disreputable-looking sorrel in a four-mile match race against a Thoroughbred, then, bringing in a ringer, came away with substantial winnings.[162]

Judge's stand, Bozeman 1903. In the stand (*left to right*): unidentified, Nelson "Bud" Story Jr., Albert "A.C." Roecher and R.D. Steel. *MOR, x83.13.117.*

TWENTIETH-CENTURY BOZEMAN

Bozeman has a major claim to American racing history: William "Smokey" Saunders. The Canadian Horse Racing Hall of Fame jockey, who rode Omaha to the Triple Crown in 1935, was born in Bozeman in 1915. He moved to Calgary with his parents when he was eight. He exercised horses on Canadian tracks but returned to Bozeman to live with his uncle, Guy Saunders, and attend high school. He also rode "half-milers" on Montana's "kerosene circuit"—the smallest meets.

In 1932, Saunders went to work for L.T. Whitehill, a California-based trainer, winning his first race on April 4 at Tanforan racetrack in Northern California. Later, Saunders headed east, where he was tapped by the famed trainer "Sunny Jim" Fitzsimmons to ride Omaha for the Belair Stud. [163]

In August 1940, Bozeman's race meet offered parimutuel wagering on everything, including the five-entry pony race for children. The biggest money was the jackpot-added "Dude Ranch Special," where the Hart Ranch and the Lazy K Bar worked out a local rivalry, entering two horses each. In a "Stock Horse" race, Brownie was entered by his owner, a teenager named Lloyd Shelhamer.

Shelhamer (1923–2010), raised near Wilsall, was said to have so loved his first pair of cowboy boots that he slept in them. Growing up, he broke horses his family owned for sale to the U.S. cavalry. Shelhamer graduated from Bozeman High School in 1941 and entered the military during World War II.

His equestrian background placed him with the Army Veterinary Corps at the famed Fort Robinson, Nebraska remount center. There, he served under Colonel Floyd Sager. The two men stayed in touch over the years. Sager ultimately became the resident veterinarian at Kentucky's famous Claiborne Farm.[164]

Returning home from the war, Shelhamer rodeoed. In 1950, he married the former Jane Ringling. Her family owned the Ringling Bros. and Barnum & Bailey Circus, plus a substantial amount of Montana land. The couple raised six children. Age and responsibility moved Shelhamer from the rodeo arena and into raising racehorses—and he began thinking of creative ways to support his family.[165] In the racing world of the early 1950s, parimutuel meets in Montana were down to three: Billings, Great Falls, and Shelby. Finding few tracks to run his horses, Shelhamer built his own.

"Beautiful Mountain View"

Belgrade, Montana, was founded in 1883 when the Northern Pacific Railroad arrived and farmers of the fertile "Gallatin Empire" needed a place to ship their crops. The small town became a crossroads; U.S. Highway

"Beautiful mountain view," Beaumont Club, circa 1961. *GHM.*

10 paralleled the railroad and doubled as Main Street. Gallatin Field airport was sited to the northeast, and to the west, Jackrabbit Lane offered a shortcut to Yellowstone National Park.

In 1953, Lloyd and Jane Shelhamer purchased the Hacienda, a roadhouse with acreage, near the intersection of Jackrabbit Lane and Highway 10. They renamed it the Beaumont, for "beautiful mountain view." Shelhamer invested $250,000, creating the first dedicated racetrack since the Butte Jockey Club. He excavated a half-mile oval and built horse barns. Promoting the facility as offering "Kentucky Derby–style racing," he got an electrically operated starting gate and installed a photo-finish camera. He built a covered grandstand that held 1,500 people. The roadhouse became a modern nightclub and restaurant. Insisting that nothing prevent patrons in the clubhouse from watching the races, Shelhamer installed 160 feet of glass windows.[166]

The Beaumont Club opened Memorial Day weekend, 1954. It was a hit: 170 horses arrived from as far away as California, Arizona, the Dakotas, and Wisconsin. Running races through the Fourth of July, the Beaumont averaged 2,500 visitors a week, and on the third weekend of June, 4,500 people attended. The clubhouse, open from 8:00 a.m. until 2:00 a.m., featured two bars and a restaurant. It offered a wine list

Beaumont Club beer, circa 1955–66. *MHS, 1983.60.04a.*

featuring European vintages, and its "surf and turf" menu included lobster thermidor, Chateaubriand beef—and frogs' legs. Evening entertainment featured bands from Las Vegas.[167]

That winter, Shelhamer brought cutter racing to Montana. In the 1950s, racing cutters were often home-crafted half-barrel "chariots" welded onto runners, pulled over snow by two-horse teams. Not the most stable design ever concocted, and advertising for "chills, thrills, and spills" was accurate. In February 1955, the Beaumont meet was a prep for the national cutter racing championships in Jackson Hole, Wyoming, and drew twenty-five teams. Shelhamer even entered his own horses, R No-Gough and Dutch S.[168]

Shelhamer needed one more thing for his modern track: an electronic tote board. As early as the 1930s, electric equipment displayed racing odds in real time, gathering data from multiple betting windows. But the 1954 Beaumont meet had odds put up on a chalkboard, with old-style preprinted parimutuel tickets. Shelhamer went to Chicago and bought a used Totalizator.[169]

The electric tote board debuted in 1955. That year, the newly formed American Quarter Horse Association (AQHA) evaluated the track and approved the summer meet. This allowed the Beaumont's Quarter Horse races to become part of a horse's official record. Horses ran in front of a large, enthusiastic crowd. In the 1960s, Quarter Horse numbers were strong, especially the years when Billings and Great Falls ran Thoroughbred-only meets. In August 1964, the track hosted a race with one of the largest purses ever offered in the state up to that time—$70,000.[170]

UNITED TOTE

Finding it a challenge to keep the Beaumont profitable with races only offered a few weeks each year, Shelhamer looked for outside revenue. He found it at other tracks. Montana race meets were expanding, and everyone wanted wagering. With a mobile tote board and a team who could calculate payouts, Shelhamer and his staff began to travel from track to track. He managed some of the smaller meets, at times even called races. In 1957, he founded United Tote. The company grew along with Montana racing.

By 1966, the newly formed Montana Horse Racing Commission approved dates for fifteen tracks, and many used Shelhamer's equipment and expertise. United Tote expanded beyond Montana to ten other states. Under fire in 1969 and again in 1973 for using antiquated equipment that produced inaccurate payouts, Shelhamer had to update his operations. To do so, the company started manufacturing and leasing equipment. By 1979, Shelhamer's children became active in the company, and United Tote went "high tech," becoming the first Totalizator corporation to computerize its systems.

The Shelhamer family took United Tote public in 1984, and by 1986, annual earnings were close to $10 million. At that time, United Tote controlled 65 percent of the market for parimutuel equipment. In 1994, Shelhamer retired to his ranch in Shepherd, north of Billings. United Tote is still in business today, now a wholly owned subsidiary of Churchill Downs, Incorporated.[171]

THE PALOMINO

In the early 1960s, the Beaumont was home base for a Quarter Horse named Robert Beaver. Owned by Tom H. Tucker, "Beaver" was Appendix registered; his sire was a Thoroughbred.[172] The flashy golden palomino started his racing career as a stallion in hopes he would prove outstanding. But good looks couldn't overcome a bad disposition and a mediocre race record. So, Beaver went to the vet, and when gelded, he got serious about running.

At the Beaumont in 1963, he won his first race. From then on, Beaver mastered 350-to-400-yard straightaways, becoming "a good honest horse" who hit the board more often than not. Ultimately, as purse money for Quarter Horses at the Beaumont declined, the Tucker family moved into racing Thoroughbreds. Beaver retired from racing and had a brief stint as a barrel racer but disliked making tight turns, so it was not a successful second career. He sold to a rancher near Dillon and became a ranch horse.[173]

Robert Beaver's career illustrated how Shelhamer struggled to keep the Beaumont running. The supper club did well, United Tote profited, but the racing side had trouble. Race purses were low—and racehorse people could not survive on $100 a race, split between the top four finishers, jockeys, trainers, and owners. Low purses led to fewer entries, which led to fewer spectators and reduced betting handle, a vicious spiral to the bottom.[174]

Robert Beaver in the winner's circle, Beaumont Club, 1963. (*Left to right from fence*) Tom P. Tucker, Millie Hubber, Tom H. Tucker, Arlee Tucker, and jockey Allen Avery. *Courtesy Tom P. Tucker.*

Abandoned Beaumont clubhouse, circa 1976. *Florence Shoebridge, GHM.*

Shelhamer sold the club and the track in 1967. While the supper club periodically remained open under different ownership, the land was sold and subdivided. Belgrade today has Triple Crown Road, Quinella Street, Show Place, and Secretariat Street near the local high school. These streets outline the general vicinity of the Beaumont track. Businesses on West Main Street are built on land that once housed the clubhouse and parking lot.

Today, Gallatin County is a popular tourist destination. But before interstates came through Montana, racing fans had to travel long distances on two-lane highways to get to the track; Gallatin County alone lacked the population to support it year-round. Shelhamer later said he was ahead of his times; had he started the facility twenty years later, it might have succeeded as a resort-style destination. He could have been right: he later owned Sunland Park, a successful track in New Mexico.

For just over a decade, Beaumont thrived, reviving Montana racing's glamorous past. With a more favorable legal climate on the horizon, Shelhamer's showplace track and support of small county fair meets helped launch Montana racing's second golden age.

10

THE PHOENIX

Determined Missoula

Has it been one night since the crowds filled the spot
And the betting was lively and the horses were hot
And winners posed in glorious delight—
Has it been 50 years or just one night?
—*"The Last Goodbye," Phyllis Tryon, 1995*[175]

FIVE VALLEYS

The Indians and Some of our men amused themselves in running races on foot as
well as with their horses.
—*William Clark, July 2, 1806*[176]

Missoula's Five Valleys were a trading hub for Native people. A trail known as "the road to the buffalo" ran east through Hellgate Canyon. The area was probably a distribution point for some of the first horses brought into Montana.

The first written account of a horse race in Montana was in present-day Missoula County. As noted in chapter 1, on July 2, 1806, at Traveler's Rest, Lewis and Clark each journaled about horse races held by their Nez Perce guides.

By 1860, Christopher Higgins and Frank Worden, along with their young clerk, Frank Woody, had a trading post along the Mullen Road called

Traveler's Rest, Lolo, site of Montana's first documented horse racing. *LOC.*

Deposit Dancer and winning connections, Missoula 2003. Trainer Jody Lacey, owners Clancy and Jan Ibach. *Courtesy WMTC.*

Hellgate Village. Finding a market selling lumber and flour to settlers, they set up "Missoula Mills" on the Clark Fork River. Today, this area is downtown Missoula.

By 1866, the thriving town was the county seat. In 1871, the town's first schoolteacher grumbled about horse races running on the Sabbath—probably match races in the streets and on the outskirts of town. Two years later, the Higgins Avenue bridge was completed, improving access to the south side of the Clark Fork, and there begins the history of modern horse racing in Missoula.[177]

Early Races

The Western Montana Agricultural, Mechanical, and Mineral Association formed in December 1874. Investors included Higgins and his commercial rival, R.A. Eddy. In 1875, the group purchased 85 acres, roughly southwest of the present-day fairgrounds, and graded a one-mile oval. Local entrepreneur John Rankin financed eight barns, a saloon, and a restaurant. The first county fair in Missoula opened in 1876, hosting horse racing, a flower show, and an exhibit of agricultural implements.

The group reformed in 1878 as the Western Montana Fair Association with Worden, Higgins, Eddy, and others each putting up $50 in startup funds. Horse races ran annually even when a smallpox outbreak limited other gatherings. The group disbanded after the 1883 fair and the land was sold.

Without a fair, horse racing continued—in the streets. During the winter, the police blocked off Higgins and Main every Sunday for "horse racing and sleigh races." Frank Higgins—lawyer, legislator, mayor, and ultimately Montana's lieutenant governor—was an eager race participant; his "game little mare" Antrima was a frequent winner. She also trotted at tracks across Montana and was described by the *Anaconda Standard* as a "star in the 2:30 class."[178]

The Northside Track

The Missoula County Fair and Racing Association formed in 1889. Organizers included Frank Higgins and A.B. Hammond (founder of the Bonner Mill and Eddy's partner in the Missoula Mercantile). John Higgins

MISSOULA COUNTY

Fair & Racing Ass'n

Fourth of July.

___

GRAND ATTRACTIONS

At the Grounds of the Missoula County Fair and Racing Association.

FIVE SPLENDID RACES.

First Race--Running, 3-8 Mile, Purse . . . $100
Second Race--Running, 1 1-16 Mile, Purse . . . 150.
Third Race--Trotting, Missoula county horses that have never before started in a race, Purse . . . 100
Fourth Race--Trotting, Free-for-all, Misoula county, Purse 150
Fifth Race--Trotting and Pacing, Free-for-all, Purse . 250

In the Trotting Races for Missoula county horses Daly's stable barred.

Entries to close July 2, at 6 o'clock p. m.

The regular Fall meeting of this Association and commencement of the Montana circuit will begin July 14 and end July 19. For further particulars, address,

JNO. L. SLOANE, Secretary.

Fourth of July races, Missoula, circa 1890. *From the* Missoula Weekly Gazette.

sold the association some property north of the Clark Fork River, west of what is now North Reserve Street. They invested $20,000 in land, infrastructure—and a track. Horses raced that September, with a hot air balloon hired to draw additional spectators.[179]

Newspapers announced a Fourth of July meet in 1890. The 1891 races offered $10,000 in purse money* and concluded with fireworks. But the next year, the association was in debt, stockholders were spatting, the racing manager quit, and the organization dissolved. The property sold at a sheriff's sale.

The track's closure created a public nuisance. By 1893, parents of small children complained about the hazards created by horses—once again—racing down the streets. They begged the city to exercise its authority. Not wanting to be unreasonable, they suggested designating just one street in town for "fast driving."[180]

In 1895, the northside track was resurrected. It was a good location; the nearby rail line allowed horses to ship in from distant areas. Prisoners from the local jail built a better road. It is unclear if the earlier infrastructure was still standing, but by fair time, the property had a one-mile racetrack and a two-story grandstand.

Missoula's population grew nearly 200 percent between 1900 and 1910, reflected in the popularity of the fair.† In 1905, bleachers for another one thousand spectators were added alongside the grandstand. One day in 1906, five thousand people attended the races. Fairs and horse races were held until the land was sold in 1908. Today, the area is occupied by a KOA campground.[181]

___

* About $278,000 in 2017 dollars
† In 1900, the county census stood at 13,964, growing to 23,596 by 1910. The city of Missoula grew from 4,366 to 12,896 in the same period.

A New Fairgrounds

A 1903 law allowed counties to spend public funds on fairs. When the northside track closed, the public wanted a new fairgrounds. The county commissioners announced they would purchase land, the voters supported a 1912 bond issue by a 2:1 margin, and the county closed on a parcel where the current fairgrounds sits today. At the time, the land was well outside of the city limits.

The first thing built was the racetrack. A one-mile oval was envisioned but required almost 40 acres, leaving no room for other buildings. A half-mile oval, covering 13 acres, went in. Organized racing returned to Missoula in 1914, though the Missoula Ministerial Association got an injunction banning the sale of liquor.

Racing continued even after Montana's 1915 gambling ban. The fair was canceled in 1917–18 because of World War I. Money woes led to another gap in 1921–22. But Missoula County held a fair and races most

Western Montana Fairgrounds, 1937. *United States Forest Service.*

other years. After the 1926 Montana Supreme Court *Toomey* decision, the meet grew rapidly. By 1928, horse numbers tripled from previous years. The 1936 races drew the biggest crowds in the history of the fair to that date, and in 1937, fair organizers bought a new, modern starting gate.

On August 21, 1941, disaster struck. A fire broke out in the east end of the grandstands. Three thousand spectators evacuated safely, but the grandstands and five other buildings burned, including a horse barn. There is no mention of horses lost, though the blaze killed all the poultry on exhibit. Local volunteers and WPA workers banded together, cleared the debris and installed temporary bleachers, and the fair went on. Afterward, with America's entry into World War II in December 1941, Missoula's fair—and racing—ended for over a decade.[182]

In 1951, the county began to revive the fair, funding reconstruction with a mill levy. By 1954, the fair restarted—with horse racing. But horsemen pointed out that the track surface was in miserable shape; it had been used for stock car racing. With profits from a successful first year, fair organizers hauled in over one thousand yards of dirt to renovate the footing.[183] Thereafter, the fair hosted annual horse races for over fifty years.

ORGANIZERS OF HORSE ACTIVITIES at the fairgrounds in the mid-twentieth century included Roy and Ruth Rodenberger, multitaskers before the word was ever coined: Roy doubled as an event announcer and fair board member, and Ruth, a horsewoman who participated in racing, horse

Jet Jester, morning exercise, Ken Mathews up. Missoula, 1987. *Courtesy Hinton.*

showing, and barrel racing, supported the needs of horses and horse owners at public events.[184]

Missoula endured a second fairground fire, more tragic than the first. On August 24, 1967, a blaze destroyed barn no. 2, killing twenty-five horses. The fire was probably kindled by smoldering sparks from a fireworks display. A night watchman called in the blaze while people desperately tried to free the horses as flames engulfed the barn. Many horses were trapped, some padlocked into their stalls (probably to prevent theft). Other barns successfully evacuated. The *Missoulian* reported the fire was "scattering dozens of other horses throughout the city."[185]

One owner was treated and released at the hospital; another burned his hands trying to push a horse trailer out of the way. No human lives were lost, but Roy Rodenberger sadly tallied the horse fatalities a few days later: twenty-one show horses, including a mare and foal, and at least four racehorses. As before, the resilient fair went on, though the lawsuit brought by some of the horse owners lasted until the Montana Supreme Court decided the matter in 1973.[186]

The Horse-Training Lawyer

Larry Elison (1932–2017), a native of Idaho, first visited Montana with his father's racing stable in 1948. He was a jockey as a boy, but grew too tall to make riding his profession, so he started training. At his father's urging, Elison became a lawyer. Moving to Missoula when he was hired by the University of Montana's School of Law in 1962, Elison found his perfect job: when the academic year ended, he and his family spent their summers at the track.[187]

Elison wanted racing to grow—in honest and legal ways. He welcomed the 1965 creation of the Montana Horse Racing Commission and new laws passed that year to govern parimutuel wagering.[188] He also had a personal dream: a privately financed racetrack.

In 1966, Elison teamed up with other racing enthusiasts and formed Montana Meadows, Inc. They envisioned a million-dollar facility with the latest technology, a glassed-in clubhouse, and an infield lake. The group purchased land west of Missoula near the "Wye," where U.S. Highway 93 joined U.S. 10. In November 1966, even as Lloyd Shelhamer closed the Beaumont in Belgrade,* Montana Meadows broke ground, graded a parking

---

* See chapter 9.

Montana Meadows' promising beginning, circa 1966. Larry Elison (*right*). *Courtesy Elison.*

lot and one-mile oval, and began foundations for horse barns. The goal was to be ready to race in the summer of 1967.[189]

Unfortunately, the stock offering did not draw enough investors. In retrospect, Elison believed the corporation should have put the buildings on hold, thrown up simple bleachers, stabled horses at the fairgrounds, and run races with the funds they had; investors follow success. Instead, the corporation had to sell the land.[190] The area is largely built over today, but excavation lines remain visible in aerial photographs. Street names memorialize the project: Racetrack Drive and Grandstand Drive trace the original roads to the track. Derby Drive and Futurity Drive pass near the boundaries of the original plat.

Elison became legal counsel to the Governor's Office in 1973 and shifted focus back to his own horses. His best winner was Le Cherro, co-owned with then-future state supreme court justice Frank Morrison. Le Cherro was a granddaughter of Bold Ruler (Secretariat's sire), and she won the 1978 "Marcus Daly Triple Crown"—races in Kalispell, Missoula, and Hamilton. She later raced in California at Bay Meadows and Golden Gate Fields, becoming a multiple stakes winner.[191]

Montana Meadows mile oval track, still visible in 2003 aerial imagery. G: planned location of grandstands, B: barn area, P: parking. *USGS data via Google Earth, annotations by author from diagram by Tom P. Tucker.*

In the 1990s, Elison formed partnerships to purchase horses at the Keeneland auctions and bring them west. Most promising was Salapache, whom he nominated for the 1992 Kentucky Derby. But during a winter workout at Bay Meadows, the colt bowed a tendon and was retired to stud.[192] Passionate about horse racing his entire life, Elison also continued to teach law and became a leading expert on Montana's 1972 Constitution.

Elison versus Shelhamer

While Elison's idea for a dedicated racetrack failed, his other goals—for regulatory protection and to see Montana's seasonally dictated racing expand—succeeded. His goal of 130 annual racing days was reached several times during the 1980s, topped by 143 racing days in 1984.[193]

Elison joined the Montana Horse Racing Commission in 1969. He was part of a "tough new commission" appointed by newly elected Governor Forrest Anderson to "shape up operations."

Nationally, 1969 saw two major issues in racing: licensing of women[*] and litigation surrounding 1968 Kentucky Derby winner Dancer's Image, disqualified after testing positive for phenylbutazone ("Bute"). Montana wrestled with similar issues, but Elison's biggest headache was the way things had always been done—and there he crossed swords with Lloyd Shelhamer.

Shelhamer's United Tote provided parimutuel equipment across Montana. Shelhamer was a hero to many local fair boards. But reports showed United Tote's antiquated equipment had frequent mechanical failures and calculation errors. Posted odds sometimes changed after races started, and payout tallies were off by hundreds of dollars—some bettors received larger or smaller winnings than they should have.

AmTote, a competing company that ran parimutuels at Great Falls and Billings, did not have these problems. As rumors flew, the commission asked the county fairs to "hold off on contracting" with Shelhamer while the matter was investigated, then set up a hearing in January 1970.

At the hearing, Shelhamer brought three lawyers, Roy Rodenberger, and several other supporters. Shelhamer's contingent faced off against Elison and the commission in a five-hour "free for all." The commissioners outlined the problems of United Tote, only to be questioned on their own financial dealings and accused of trying to put Shelhamer out of business. At one point, someone demanded the entire commission resign. After defending the commission, Elison hit back. "We've been rocking the boat," he said. "It's quite apparent the boat is not wanting to be rocked in any regard."[194]

Ultimately, Elison laid down the law: The commission was "most certainly" going to regulate horse racing. But the unspoken problem was that the rules governing Montana parimutuels were inadequate. Elison could only conclude the investigation by stating that fairs now had the information they needed to "make their own decisions" about which parimutuel contractor to hire.[195]

The commission's annual report, issued a month later, suggested updated regulations to avoid future problems. Chair Norman Kalbfleisch wrote, "The Commission has encouraged forceful and honest control of racing for the protection of the public."[196] Elison drafted new rules. Shelhamer stayed in business, falling under fire again in 1973, but ultimately improved his operations.

---

* See chapter 13.

Flying Catman

One of Missoula's crowd favorites was Flying Catman (35:5-11-4). The 2001 California-bred bay gelding, a grandson of Storm Cat, was a closer. At Portland Meadows' mile oval in 2003, he'd start slow, close in the homestretch, but never timed his move quite right. "Late rally," "finished well" read the charts. He hit the board in most of his races, but never won. By 2004, "Catman" was a hot mess. Losing weight, he finished a tired fifth three races in a row and was sold.

His new owner was Toni Hinton. She worked to bring him back to form. "We fed him all the alfalfa he would eat," she said. After a two-month break, Catman had a test run at the Crooked River Roundup, near Bend, Oregon. Refreshed, he finished second, only a half-length behind the winner.

Then Catman arrived in Montana. Hinton formed Silent Stables, the ownership group that raced Catman for the rest of his career. The August 2004 Thoroughbred Maiden Derby at the Western Montana Fair was his first stakes race. On the half-mile oval, under the hands of jockey Shannon Wippert, Catman's signature style finally worked. Last out of the gate, he

Flying Catman in retirement, 2018. *Wahler.*

gained slowly down the backstretch but then slingshotted off the final turn, poured it on heading for home, and won by a neck. The track suited him; his come-from-behind style thrilled the crowds.

Catman began winning, often by his favorite margin—a neck. Silent Stables had all the excitement it could handle. "He'd about give you a heart attack," said Hinton. Catman ran three years in Montana and Alberta. His lifestyle was typical for a racehorse on the northern plains, where the racing season is short. In the summer, several races each month were "paid workouts" and covered the feed bills. Winters were time off. His trainers, the Berkrams, kept him in shape with indoor riding and pasture turnout.

Catman figured out racing. Once in front, he'd stare down the opposition and stay there. But on an off day, he phoned in the race, not knowing or caring that a snarky "No threat" went on the charts. Overall, he finished fourth or better—earning purse money—in two-thirds of his races.[197]

The 2006 Missoula race meet ran on a shoestring, and Catman paid the price. Race organizers feared the footing was breaking down. They protested that too many trucks were driving across the track. Dirt surfaces, pulverized and eroded by time, are easily packed hard by vehicles crossing at the infield access gaps. A galloping racehorse can be injured while passing over unexpected hardpack.

On the first day of the meet, Catman went off as the favorite in the third race. Along the backstretch, he began his gradual rally. But as he accelerated, he passed the backside gap—the trouble spot. Something felt off, and jockey Fernando Gamez pulled him up. Limping from the track, Catman had a bowed tendon—and a bad one. His racing career was over.

Luckily, his story was a rehoming success instead of a tragedy. Buyers sought retired racehorses at the track after meets, and Hinton put out word Catman was available. But the average buyer wanted a healthy horse, not a lame one, so Hinton had to screen out "sketchy" shoppers.

Her caution was warranted. In 2003, news broke that 1986 Kentucky Derby winner Ferdinand met his end in a slaughterhouse. Montana horses risked a similar fate. One scam was to gather a truckload of horses "free to a good home" and send them north to sell by the pound. Calgary, Alberta, had a well-known horsemeat export company. Hinton wasn't going to let that happen to Catman.[198]

Ferdinand's tragic end inspired a rescue and rehoming movement. In Missoula, a young woman named Rebecca Donnelly incorporated a horse rescue. She contacted Hinton. A dollar changed hands, and Rebecca had a handsome Thoroughbred with a halter, some powdered Bute, and a set of leg wraps. Catman went to rest and rehab with Rebecca's mom, Marylynn, who had horse property in Helena. After Catman healed up, Marylynn kept him as a trail horse.

Twelve years later, Catman still grazed in Marylynn's Helena valley pasture and supervised "the brats"—a small group of young horses. A little slower, his love of the chase remained. He circled other horses in the field, tempting them to run. If they ignored him, he took the direct approach and nipped them in the rear. Then he chased the pack before once again closing with a burst of speed to pass them all.

The Last Goodbye

Like a phoenix rising from the ashes, Missoula horse racing repeatedly declined and revived. The peak was the 1986 race meet, running twelve days with a record-setting handle of almost $900,000. But expanded gaming depressed Missoula racing—as it did everywhere—and the Western Montana Fair settled for a six-day meet in the 1990s. Parimutuel handle stabilized at about $500,000 annually.[199]

The Western Montana Turf Club formed in 1999. The founders included Toni Hinton, Jim Johnson, Karen Miller, and Joy Billingsley. Reese Halvorson became treasurer a year later. With support from Missoula's director of racing, Gary Koepplin, they gathered race sponsorships and organized events for fans, including handicapping clinics and a hat contest on "Montana Derby Day." They built a VIP club and sponsored the "horse-o-scope" tip sheet—a historic part of the Helena and Missoula newspapers, started in 1972 by Gene Robertson and later written by Don Hinton. With the Turf Club's efforts, the 2002 meet was the biggest since 1986: it ran ten days with handle over $700,000.[200]

But the grandstands were iffy, the barns were falling apart, and the restrooms were antiquated. Upgrades to crumbling infrastructure were an expense only Missoula County could authorize. At the same time, advance-deposit wagering (ADW) on the internet took a toll on state simulcast revenues.* On paper, the races lost money. Expenses kept rising, and facilities aged. Changes to the law removed jockeys from the Workers' Compensation system, and tracks had to buy private coverage, costing thousands of dollars per day.

---

*Montana began regulating ADW in 2008.

Missoula paddock, circa 2004. *Courtesy WMTC.*

The county commissioners held a hearing in 2006 to decide whether to pull the plug. Supporters said that races brought more spectators to the fair and increased admissions should count on racing's balance sheet. Race spectators also spent money between races: the Sons of Norway pleaded their case, explaining that 30 percent of their sales of "Vikings"—a fair staple of battered, deep-fried meat on a stick—came from racing fans.

"Dat Hat" contest winner, Missoula, 2003. *Courtesy WMTC.*

Bruce Micklus was a key supporter. Owner of Missoula's iconic independent music store Rockin' Rudy's, Micklus was a racehorse owner and called races at the meet. He pointed out value-added benefits of racing: visitors spent thousands of dollars on gasoline, restaurants, hotels, and supplies. The county commission decided to keep racing another year, but with no money for upgrades.[201]

After 2006, lacking funds for repairs and upfront expenses, Missoula had no races until a brief revival in 2010, when a private organization managed to pull together a two-day meet.

What ultimately ended racing at the Western Montana Fair was changing times. The 47-acre fairgrounds, always cramped for space, became surrounded by the city of Missoula, bordered by a tangled maze of busy streets. A new strategic plan envisioned activities deemed more attractive to city-dwellers, such as hockey games and concerts. The track infield was eyed as a parking lot.

The Missoula and Helena track battles had similarities. In both cases, the track footprint stayed in diagrams shown to the public, but a written narrative said otherwise. Both urged historic preservation and questioned the cost of building a new indoor event center. Both to no avail.

Missoula racetrack bulldozed, May 2018. *Tom Bauer, Missoulian.*

In 2013, the Missoula County Commissioners voted unanimously to end horse racing. The spreadsheets created an untenable political situation for elected officials who needed to justify use of taxpayer dollars. The opposition to racing was led by Commissioner Jean Curtiss, who had argued that the track encumbered over half the fairgrounds, preventing long-term development.

At the end, racing supporters in the community tried to save the track by setting up a meet. Support came from both political parties: racehorse breeder, former legislator, and past Board of Horse Racing chair Dale Mahlum was a Republican. Racing fan, lawyer, and State Representative Kim Dudik was a Democrat. The MBOHR agreed to reserve dates for a 2016 Missoula meet and provide a $30,000 match. The Turf Club lined up sponsors. But the county commissioners would not change their position.[202] Ultimately the bulldozers tore out the track the spring of 2018.

Missoula racing survived both long gaps and multiple moves. Racing could rise again with a new track. One possibility is a private, dedicated facility like Elison envisioned. Another possibility is a new fairgrounds built outside of town. If Missoula revived horse racing, there is currently no other track between Kennewick, Washington, and Great Falls. The highways in between, roughly paralleling the historic Mullan Road, could draw racing fans to Missoula from a wide area.

11

BILLINGS

Running under the Rims

Billings was founded in 1882 when the Northern Pacific Railroad platted a townsite about two miles from the Yellowstone River. Named for Frederick Billings, president of the Northern Pacific, the new town sprang up nearly overnight—like magic—hence Billings's nickname, "The Magic City." The nearby town of Coulson, founded in 1877 on the banks of the Yellowstone, was soon abandoned in favor of the new site.

Records indicate that the Apsáalooke (Crow) people, noted for their love of horses and racing, traded furs at Coulson and held horse races there. Trade goods and money were freely wagered between whites and Native people. A 1953 history claimed, with only slight exaggeration, that goods were "piled high on the open prairie."[203]

The first fairs in Billings began in 1892, sponsored by the Yellowstone Fair Association, a private organization started by I.D. O'Donnell, a founder of the Billings Sugar Company. Horse races were run from the outset, and at the 1892 meet, photographers attempted to capture exciting finishes, producing blurred images of horses in motion. The track was on a 20-acre plot of land with a one-thousand-seat grandstand for spectators. Today this area is North Park, and one of the exhibition buildings, converted to a private residence, still stands at the corner of Sixth Avenue and North Twenty-Second Street.[204]

The North Park location hosted fairs and racing until 1915, but the Magic City was growing and the fair needed a new home. A 1912 map shows

This house near North Park held exhibits at Billings's first fairgrounds. *Wahler.*

Aerial view, Midland Empire Fairgrounds, circa 1935–45. *Reich Postcard Collection, 2011-1529-093, YCM.*

North Park surrounded by residential streets, and a boundary line labeled "fairgrounds," today's MetraPark, was already drawn. A bond issue was approved by the voters in April 1916, promptly launching the construction of the iconic exposition building that stood until 1969. The name "Midland Empire" was proposed for the new event: Billings was midway between Minneapolis and Spokane and midway between Denver and Canada. In September 1916, the first Midland Empire Fair opened.[205]

SACRIFICE CLIFF

One horse is inextricably linked with MetraPark, though few realize this. Prior to white settlement, the Apsáalooke called the fertile Yellowstone river bottom area Ammalapashkuua, "the place where we cut wood." According to journalist Roger Clawson, who was adopted into the Crow tribe, a smallpox epidemic swept through the area prior to white settlement. Such events were not uncommon. Previously unknown European diseases passed along trade routes, arriving long before settlers.[206]

Sandstone bluffs behind the Billings racetrack, possibly the original "Sacrifice Cliff." Billings, 1977. *From the* Billings Gazette.

A young hunter returned home and fell into despair upon discovering his sweetheart had died while he was away. He entered into a pact with his best friend to join the young woman in the afterlife. Asking an elderly woman to bear witness, the pair, riding double on a white horse, galloped over a cliff and plunged to their deaths. Suicide was a known survivor response to the tragedies of epidemics.[207]

Other versions of the tale claim the sacrificial deaths stopped the epidemic itself. Non-Native accounts sensationalized and greatly exaggerated the story to involve many horses and dozens of warriors. Today, the name Sacrifice Cliff describes an area of the dramatic South Rims overlooking the Yellowstone River. But according to Clawson, the actual Sacrifice Cliff is the sandstone bluff behind the final turn of the racetrack. Part of it was blasted away during construction of MetraPark Arena, but the cliffs behind the track remain.[208]

THE MIDLAND EMPIRE

The 1915 gambling ban threw the Montana turf into the "slough of despond," but in 1916, Billings put up small purses and raced anyway. In 1917, Billings hosted four days of racing with harness events sanctioned by the American Trotting Association. To replace betting and draw interest, organizers added women's relay and motorcycle races. Making the best of things, promoters boasted that "half a hundred blooded horses"—in other words, fifty—attended the meet.

In spite of Prohibition and the gambling ban, racing in Billings remained popular through the 1920s. In 1928, the fair added the "co-ownership" system of betting that the *Toomey* decision allowed. Spectators had more reasons to attend—measured in greenbacks. That year, seventy-five thousand people attended the fair. Among the competitors present was Helena's colorful trainer "Mother Berry," with her favorite racehorse, Rosa Lockwood. When Berry returned to Billings with Rosa Lockwood in 1931, the eight-year-old mare was a longshot. Finishing second, her $2.00 place tickets paid bettors $22.40.[209]

"Indian racing" was a particular draw in Billings, in part due to the city's proximity to the Crow Reservation, noted for excellent horses.* One contestant was an Apsáalooke teenager named Frank Takes the Gun.

_____
* See chapter 16.

Horses on the homestretch, Midland Empire Fair, 1936. *Harry Fitton Collection, 036-72-369-21, YCM.*

Horses break from the starting gate, Billings, 1947. *PCM*

Starting in 1924, when he was about fifteen years old, and again in 1925, 1927, and 1931, the papers reported that he hit the board in both Indian Relay and regular races at the Midland Empire Fair.

Takes the Gun became a leader within the Crow Nation and president of the Native American Church. He lobbied the state and federal government on various issues related to water rights on the Big Horn River and religious use of peyote. Today, Takes the Gun is also remembered for the support and inspiration he gave his grandson, modern-day hip-hop artist and Apsáalooke dancer Christian Parrish Takes the Gun, known professionally as "Supaman."[210]

Although the Midland Empire Fair was canceled in 1933 because of the Great Depression, race promoters pulled together a small independent meet, warning that "purses won't be the best." Records from 1930 through the 1950s are scattered, but Billings ran horses throughout the period. Billings rebuilt the grandstands in 1950, and by 1954 Billings ran six days of racing.

RACING'S PEAK

When the regulatory era began in 1965, the Midland Empire Fair raced seven days a year. From there, Billings boomed. In the 1980s, Billings offered over thirty days of racing every year. It was the largest meet in the state, peaking at forty days in 1984. No other track had run that many days annually since Butte's golden era. Research to date indicates that MetraPark's Budweiser $100,000 Futurity (won by Super Ciel in 1994*) was the state's richest horse race.

Norm Amundson worked as a racing secretary and track announcer from 1964 until 1978, when Billings was consistently the leading track in Montana for both racing days and parimutuel handle. Much of the success in Yellowstone County was credited to Amundson. A nephew of Lloyd Shelhamer's, he began announcing races at Beaumont Downs when he was fifteen years old. In 1971, he won the Rocky Mountain Association of Fairs "Man of the Year" award in the horse racing division. After his Montana years, he worked at Playfair in Spokane and went on to various track positions in several states, including a twenty-year stint at Sunland Park.[211]

In the 1970s, prominent jockeys at the Billings track included Val Brinkerhoff, who went on to train horses on the highly competitive

---

* See chapter 6.

Billings jockeys, 1977. Val Brinkerhoff (*second from left*) is now a trainer in southern California. *From the* Billings Gazette.

Southern California circuit. Eastern Montana's own Suzy Wilson, one of the first women to be licensed in Montana,* was repeatedly featured in the *Billings Gazette*.[212]

The year 1989 was special. The great hall of fame jockey William "Willie the Shoe" Shoemaker retired with a farewell tour riding at tracks across America. Montana landed on Shoemaker's bucket list twice: he rode horses in both Billings and Great Falls. At MetraPark on August 13, Shoemaker signed autographs for over two hours. Then he rode seasoned handicap horses Great Pal and The Right Gift, winning both races in front of a crowd estimated at ten thousand. The Turf Club threw him a party afterward. The charming, fifty-seven-year-old, four-foot, eleven-inch jockey still wasn't tired and wanted to go out dancing. Tom P. Tucker, then the director of racing at MetraPark, remembered, "We didn't stay out too late, but he really had a good time in Billings."[213]

One of the top jockeys at MetraPark was Kym Espy (née Powell). She was named the leading rider in Billings twice, the first time in 1996, when she was the first woman to earn the title. Records show that from 1989 to

* See chapter 13.

"YELLOWSTONE EXHIBITION FUTURITY TRIALS"-Division III
YELLOWSTONE EXHIBITION   AUGUST 13, 1983   ESTRA LITA   BILL & JEAN BARRETT------------owner
KUIDI------------------------------place   RACE 5   BILL BARRETT-----------------trainer
THE PRIZE FOX-----------------------show   6½ furlongs 1:24.2   JESS DAVIDSON---------------------up

Estra Lita wins in Billings, 1983. *Courtesy Barrett.*

2011, she rode Thoroughbreds, Quarter Horses, and other breeds in more than 5,000 races, with over 600 wins and lifetime earnings topping $2 million. What makes this remarkable is that she earned it mostly at tracks in Montana, eastern Washington, and Alberta, riding daily in nearly every race on the card. The bigger tracks she conquered included Sunland Park in New Mexico and Canterbury Downs in Minnesota. But Billings was her home.[214]

THE STRUGGLE TO SURVIVE

Like the rest of Montana, racing in Billings began a slow decline in the 1990s. In 1983, MetraPark reported the largest one-year handle in the history of the state: $5,583,831 from thirty-nine days of racing. But expanded gambling hit hard: In 1990, thirty-two days of racing brought in only $2,649,136. In contrast, handle for thirty-three days in 1982 was $5,063,825.[215]

Crowds remained enthusiastic as popular local sportscaster Bernie Lustig called races. Yet the meet dropped to sixteen days by 1996, partly from declining handle, but also because the Board of Horse Racing stopped awarding overlapping days. Racing regrouped in 1997 and became Yellowstone Downs. Amundson came back to help. Ben Carlson, a successful master plumber and businessman who loved horse racing, became racing director, and Jim Espy was president of the organization.

By 2000, the meet was down to ten days, and handle was $700,092. It was a reduced but sustainable model for the decade. In 2005, Billings claimed a world record for Montana tracks, nearly one hundred years after Atoka's record in Butte. On September 17, the Quarter Horse filly Eyes of Dawn ran 300 yards in :14.909. She was ridden by Bobby Webb, owned by Ray and Wendy Norgaard of Arlee, and trained by Mike Taylor.[216]

Attendance in 2011, the last year of racing in Billings (as of 2019), averaged over 3,900 people per day, and the betting handle remained close to the $700,000 average. Racing ended that year with the potential to continue.

Yellowstone Downs applied for 2012 dates, but although MetraPark management was supportive, statewide problems tanked the meet. That year, the Montana Board of Horse Racing had temporarily suspended all simulcasting and had no revenue for local tracks. The complex situation included problems with a simulcast contractor on top of a significant financial deficit. Yellowstone Downs could not independently secure $140,000 in startup funds. In 2014, it tried again, but there was still no state financial support. Race supporters threw in the towel.[217]

Jockey Jim Beeson prepares to exercise a horse. Billings, 2011. *James Woodcock*, Billings Gazette.

Indian Relay has kept some tracks from being bulldozed, and Billings was no exception. The track hosted the Indian Relay National Championships from 2015 through 2017.[218]

There was no official decision to end horse racing in Billings, but organizers drifted away, and an empty infield, as always, is tempting space for development. Construction projects are slowly eating into the track footprint, and equipment has been sold off. MetraPark kept facilities for horse shows and rodeos, but the track was slated to be torn out.

Yet, horses ran in Billings consistently from 1892 until 2011 with few significant breaks. Billings once hosted the largest and longest race meets in Montana, making the Magic City a logical place to revitalize its turf.

12

THE "BUSHY-BUSH"

Rural Montana Racing

We were family.
—*Sue Resch, 2018*

The major racing cities of Montana have run meets bringing in hundreds of horses and millions in wagering handle. Nonetheless, located far from the major racing centers of California, New York, Kentucky, or Florida, they are called "bush" tracks.

Throughout Montana history, there was an even smaller circuit: small county fairs running horses for a weekend or two, with results seldom reported outside the weekly newspaper. In the 1930s, these small tracks were called the "kerosene circuit." In the 1970s, jockey Suzy Wilson dubbed them "the bushy-bush."[219]

Race conditions met local interest, equipment was primitive, rules were loose, and family pride was the largest stake. For the most part, youth riders and women could race against men. Until the post-1965 regulatory era, horses did not always need papers and pedigrees to compete.

In Montana's early years, there weren't even tracks—as noted throughout this book, match races ran along any flat straightaway—prairies and dirt streets were perfect. In 1868, the Phillipsburg stringer for the *Montana Post* boasted, "Horse racing is the order of the day lately—two races a day and on Sunday, four. If anyone thinks they can beat 'Dick of the Bed Rock' on horse racing, let them come."[220]

Havre match race, Fourth of July, circa 1912. *Overholser.*

Details from small-town meets are a challenge to uncover precisely because horse racing was so ubiquitous. Unlike the larger communities, where races had the whole town talking "horse, horse, horse!" unless something spectacular occurred, small-town results were reported in passing, if at all.

Yet racing was everywhere. The photo on page 163, circa 1900, shows a women's relay in Big Timber. Other photos from Sweet Grass County captured horses trotting in harness races. Local papers eagerly advertised upcoming races. White Sulphur Springs, ambitiously dubbed "Montana's Saratoga," set up a track and hosted a race meet in 1876. Dillon, in Beaverhead County, ran races on the coattails of the large Butte meet in 1896.

Local tracks offered a place for young horses and new jockeys to test their potential. Into the late twentieth century, a horse winning at small tracks could remain eligible to run in "maiden" races at the major fairs. Jockeys like Suzy Wilson could be a "seasoned three-year veteran" and still qualify for the lighter weight allowance that accompanied an apprentice bug.

There were multiple circuits. The Hi-Line saw meets in Glasgow, Dodson, Havre, Chinook, and Shelby. In 1965, when the newly formed Montana Horse Racing Commission began formally approving meets, the eastern

Montana circuit started the racing season in Miles City at the Bucking Horse Sale meet, then added Baker, Forsyth, and Glendive. Some years, Sidney's Old Fashioned Fourth, the Central Montana Fair in Lewistown, and the Phillips County Fair in Dodson also had parimutuel approval.

In the western half of the state, the Tri-County Fair in Deer Lodge raced horses in the 1960s, Hamilton ran annually until 1997, and Kalispell held races with few gaps from 1902 until 2011. In north-central Montana, Fort Benton had a historic tradition of horse racing at the Chouteau County Fair.

But first, back to Madison County.

Madison County: Beyond Spokane

We are getting far enough advanced now…so that all who wish…can have a heavy draft horse for farming and freighting, a good saddle animal for herding, and [a] goer to sit behind when out for pleasure.
—Rocky Mountain Husbandman, *December 11, 1879*

Twin Bridges was an early Montana racing hotbed. Noah Armstrong, who owned Spokane, was a prominent racehorse owner, but he was neither the first nor most longstanding horseman in the area. That honor probably goes to William Hillhouse Raymond. In 1868, he found ranchland on Sweetwater Creek, a never-freezing tributary of the Ruby River he called an "animal's paradise."[221]

To improve his stock, Raymond went to Kentucky in 1876, returning with twenty mares and a Standardbred stallion, Commodore Belmont. Raymond also brought the first Shetland ponies to Montana. In 1880, Commodore Belmont sired a colt that Raymond named Doncaster. This horse became a star on Montana's trotting tracks—and, as noted in chapter 5, has confused historians for decades about the origin of Noah Armstrong's ranch name. Marcus Daly later bought the colt and renamed him Dalgamo.[222]

By 1880, Raymond had built a large white horse barn, still standing today, and a one-mile training teack. Raymond dubbed his ranch Belmont Park for his favorite stallion, and in honor of the famous race then held at Jerome Park, New York.[223]

Raymond owned Belmont Park until his death in 1905 and became one of the largest breeders of trotting horses in the United States. In 1900, when the U.S. Senate refused to seat W.A. Clark, Raymond testified at a congressional hearing, noting under oath that he owned "six or seven hundred" "blooded" horses.[224]

Another local breeder was Samuel Larabie's brother Charles X. Larabie (also spelled Larrabee), co-founder of the Boston & Montana Consolidated Mining Company. He owned Brook Nook Ranch, 4,500 acres in the upper Ruby Valley. He spent $250,000 to set up the place and, by 1895, owned about two hundred well-bred trotting horses. He purchased Commodore Belmont from Raymond in 1891. The aged stallion was described as "full of spirit, courage and virility as when he was a colt."[225]

Madison County residents raced horses in addition to breeding them. In 1898, Twin Bridges' Southern Montana Fair Association advertised trotting, pacing, and running races. The 1899 premium book promised racegoers a restaurant serving "a meal that would tempt the Gods." A promotional brochure from about 1909 declared Madison County "has the largest number of thoroughbred horses of any county in the state," noting the fairgrounds contained "the finest mile track in the state of Montana" and "ample stables for horses."[226]

But by 1928, with hard times hitting agricultural counties, Madison County ran out of money to conduct a fair. The fairgrounds buildings, built in the 1800s, were in disrepair. Soon, the Great Depression left many residents out of work.

Enter the New Deal. Starting in 1936, the WPA rebuilt the Madison County Fairgrounds, including new barns and a grandstand. All the

"WPA Rustic," Madison County Fairgrounds, Twin Bridges. *Wahler.*

work was done by local craftspeople using local materials, most buildings resembling log cabins in a style later called "WPA Rustic."

Noah Armstrong's Doncaster Round Barn was purchased in 1932 by the Bayers family, who repaired it to shelter their Hereford cattle. Honoring the resurrected structure and A.C. Bayers's personal efforts as head of the fair board, the WPA built an octagonal exhibition pavilion. A half-mile racetrack and a baseball field completed the layout. By July 1938, the county fair returned. Horse races were seldom reported, though a 1964 article noted a feature race at the fair named in honor of Spokane.[227]

Madison County did not hold parimutuel races in the post-1965 period. Local lore mentions informal "lap and tap" races. ("Lap and tap" is one method of starting races without a starting gate or barrier.) Susan Nardinger, writing in the 1980s, noted the 6-1/2 furlong "Spokane Memorial."[228] Today, the grandstand remains in front of a rodeo arena. Parts of the half-mile oval are visible in aerial photos.

The Whole Town Turned Out

Small towns probably drew more visitors per capita than the larger communities. The 1915 gambling ban had little impact. In 1927, the Richland County Fair drew 4,000 spectators; the county seat, Sidney, had a population of 1,200.[229]

Forsyth's Rosebud County Fair offered horse races every September from 1906 until 1986. In those seventy years, they only canceled twice, in 1934 and 1945. Race conditions were tailored for local needs: the program for 1925 included a one-mile running race, a relay, a "girls" race, separate races for "cow ponies" and "saddle horses," and a "team novelty race" (apparently a relay) featuring husband-and-wife pairs. Local enthusiasm was such that in a town of roughly 1,500 people, 1,200 spectators braved "inclement weather"—icy rain that turned the track into a quagmire—to watch the races.[230]

The 1925 fair also featured an "Indian race." Forsyth is not far from the Crow and Northern Cheyenne Reservations. That year Frank Takes the Gun brought at least three horses to Forsyth. With his string, he won the 3/8-mile sprint and the "Indian race," and placed second in the open men's relay. Takes the Gun also took racehorses to Billings.*

---

* See chapter 11.

Rosebud County Fair, Forsyth, 1918. *Walter Dean, MHS Photo Archives PAc 76-26.312.*

Eastern Montana kept a racing circuit into the modern era, though Baker and Forsyth both ended parimutuel meets after 1986. Glasgow followed in 1987. Research to date has not determined why, but the most likely reason was the impact of legalized video gaming.[231]

RACING'S REBOUND AND THE RMAF

The 1926 *Toomey* decision kick-started a racing revival on Montana's tracks. In spite of drought and economic troubles, the Rocky Mountain Association of Fairs (RMAF) formed in 1928 and thirty counties hosted fairs that year. In 1929, when parimutuel wagering was legalized, thirty-seven counties held fairs.[232]

By 1932, at the height of the Great Depression, the RMAF circuit promised $60,000 in combined prize money. In 1935, the group announced $100 purses per race and a combined twenty-seven race days in Glasgow, Great Falls, Billings, Dodson, Havre, Sidney, Miles City, and Forsyth. Two years later, the RMAF announced twelve meets running forty-five total days. Missoula joined the RMAF, as did smaller venues in Lewistown, Chinook, and Baker.

Outside the RMAF circuit, Shelby began racing in 1929. Hamilton and Kalispell ran during the 1930s. Jefferson County split its fair off from

Twin Bridges and ran races in 1939. The Sanders County Fair at Plains held races in 1940. From Worden to Wisdom, even towns without county fairs, including Big Sandy, Helmville, Stockett, and Two Dot, advertised local races in conjunction with rodeos or other festivals. The Lincoln County Fair in Eureka hosted jackpot races. Young jockeys across Montana took inspiration from promises like "if you win at Denton, then you can ride at Lewistown."[233]

"Gopher Downs" on the Hi-Line

Billings had the biggest meet in the Big Sky Country, and Great Falls had more civic pride than the rest of Montana put together. But Montana racing's best party was at the Marias Fair. Nicknamed "Gopher Downs" by the horsemen—who spent much of their spare time filling holes made by enterprising rodents—Shelby hosted Montana's last surviving small-town county fair meet from 1929 until 2004.

Shelby is the transportation hub of Montana's Hi-Line. Today, Interstate 15 passes through on the way to the Canadian border, intersecting the BNSF "Empire Builder" line, originally part of the Great Northern Railroad. Shelby also sits halfway between the Blackfeet and Fort Belknap Reservations on U.S. Highway 2.

The sports-mad town hit the national press in 1923 when it organized the infamous Dempsey-Gibbons boxing match. The Tommy Gibbons Handicap was instituted in honor of the fight, and Gibbons himself returned to Shelby in 1951 to present a blanket to the winning Thoroughbred. The Gibbons Handicap ran every year thereafter.[234]

Toole County started a fair in 1929. Johnny Longden came down from Canada to ride, and he also pocketed $100 in a foot race. The Marias Fair started in 1939, combining Toole, Glacier, Liberty, and Pondera Counties. The fairgrounds on the eastern edge of Shelby drew horses from across the state. Horsemen from the nearby Blackfeet Nation sponsored races and helped keep the meet afloat in hard times. Canadians from southern Alberta, a horse-racing hotbed, came to Shelby to prep for their September races in Lethbridge.[235]

In the week prior to the annual meet, the backside filled with horses, trainers, jockeys, and their families. Rigs parked bumper to bumper. As fairgoers arrived, the motels and bars filled up. Organized chaos reigned, and a good time was had by all.

Boxer Tommy Gibbons (*left*) presents award blanket to Tommy Gibbons Handicap winner Miss Annie. Race sponsor Eddie Johnson holding blanket on right. Marias Fair, July 27, 1951. *Shelby Promoter.*

Because the track was used only once a year, horsemen wrestled with gopher holes and other prairie hazards: multiple interviewees for this book described rousting rattlesnakes out of the horse barns, saddling paddock—and jockeys' room. Trainer Sue Resch, bringing horses to Shelby in the 1980s and 1990s, recalls seeing galloping horses "slam on the brakes" during early-morning workouts when they saw rattlers sunning themselves on the freshly harrowed track. Resch mentioned another incident when a badger sauntered onto the oval as she ponied a racehorse.[236]

The Marias Fair decided to roll with its nickname and offered gopher races. A miniature starting box and 24-foot-long "track" with eight lanes was set up in front of the grandstands for the most chaotic event on the schedule. Children of the town and track captured the namesake rodents. They housed the gophers in cages and boxes until the "meet," feeding them the racehorses' alfalfa and grain until the little critters were so fat they could barely waddle. Gophers were given names, and management printed up a program. Adults sponsored top "competitors," entry fees went to charity, and small prizes were handed out to winning "owners." Rumor holds the event was eventually shut down by concerned citizens who argued it was cruel to the gophers.[237]

The valiant Shelby meet was the last to fall to the pressures that doomed other small-town tracks: low population and high expenses. Racing in Shelby survived the growth of video gaming machines in the local casinos, even though it cut racing handle in half. But other changes, such as the increased cost of accident insurance for jockeys, sent Marias

This page: Win photo, Shelby, circa 1950. *PCM.*

Fair into the red, and racing ended in 2004. Nonetheless, while the homestretch is fenced off by the rodeo arena today, the track and barns are mostly intact. Racing could return to the Marias Fair.

Tom Chapman: Painting the Ponies

The Hi-Line produced a jockey who made it to the big leagues: Tom Chapman of Cut Bank. He was a high school wrestler at 101 pounds and fond of animals. Inspired by the races at the Marias Fair, he began galloping racehorses. Seeking better career opportunities, he headed for Southern California. In 1973, he got a job as a hot walker at a ranch with a jockey apprentice program and worked his way up.

MARIAS FAIR
JULY 24, 2004
$2800.00..Purse

SPONSOR
BEN TAYLOR INC

CHANGING THYMES 109

Race# - 7 - 860 YARDS - 0:33.90
KEITH BIRD RATTLER MEMORIAL

TARASTRIP..........Place
SOUTHERN JONAH..........Show

TRIDENT

DON WEAVER...Owner
MEL BERKRAM...Trainer
CARL HEBERT...Up

Keith Bird Rattler Memorial, Marias Fair, 2004. Changing Thymes 109, Mel Berkram, trainer. *Courtesy Barrett.*

Marias Fairgrounds, 2018. *Wahler.*

He debuted at Santa Anita in 1977 and was the leading apprentice in Southern California in 1978. He rode Hoedown's Day in the 1981 Kentucky Derby, to date the only Montanan besides Smokey Saunders to gain a Derby mount. Montana governor Ted Schwinden declared Derby day, May 2, 1981, as "Tom Chapman Day."[238]

Chapman won the Grade I Hollywood Oaks on Moment to Buy in 1984 but spent most of his racing career in Northern California. He began painting in 1993, and when he won the Bay Meadows Handicap on Slew of Damascus, he celebrated by painting a portrait of the horse. The owners loved it, and the price they offered inspired a new career. Chapman retired as a jockey in 1996 with over 20,000 starts and 2,500 wins. Today, he creates fine art paintings with horse racing themes, one of which was used for the 2009 Woodford Reserve Bourbon Kentucky Derby bottle.[239]

FLATHEAD COUNTY: PAST AND FUTURE

Kalispell traces organized horse racing to at least 1902. The Northwest Montana Fair ran horses throughout the 1930s. Records are scarce for the 1940s and 1950s. In the regulatory era, Kalispell raced from 1966 through 2011.

A well-known owner-trainer in the Flathead, R.D. Mower, came to northwestern Montana from Idaho in 1948. He first ran horses in Kalispell in 1952 and was an annual participant in the races for almost sixty years. He started as a jockey at small meets in his native Idaho, and in Montana, he trained horses not only for the track but also for O-Mok-See speed events and barrel racing. One of his best horses, the powerful black gelding Sourdough Cake, won Great Falls' $30,000 Agribasics Derby in 1985.[240]

Like most Montana tracks, the Northwest Montana Fair meet did well in the 1970s and 1980s. Horses ran up to six days a year with handle over $400,000. Hamilton, Missoula, and Kalispell worked together to produce an attractive western Montana circuit, capped by the "Marcus Daly Triple Crown" series.

The modern track was the pride of the Quarter Horse racing community thanks to an extra-long homestretch chute that gave the half-mile oval a straightaway that could be set up for races at all of AQHA's recognized distances, including the eponymous quarter mile.

The Kalispell meet faced twenty-first-century financial difficulties, most stemming from issues that ended racing elsewhere. The county commissioners canceled the meet after 2005, having spent four years subsidizing losses. Racing fans worked to revive the meet. It took time, but five years later, with state support, sponsorships from Blackfeet tribal members, and the efforts of the All Breeds Turf Club, horses raced again in 2010 and 2011.

In October 2011, the county commissioners were presented a long-range plan for the Flathead County fairgrounds that, as with similar plans in Helena and Missoula, advised tearing out the track. Between the plan and the lack of state simulcast revenue, Kalispell ended racing in 2012.[241]

Since that time, racing equipment has been sold off piecemeal and the long homestretch chute has been torn out. But the rest of the track footprint remains and the facility has hosted Indian Relay competition. The fairgrounds expanded the rodeo arena in front of the grandstands and plans to add other horse facilities. Racing could theoretically return to the fairgrounds at Kalispell so long as the track remains, but other uses steadily eat away at the footprint.

Bird's-eye view of Kalispell, circa 1906. *J.R. White, LOC.*

Pascal wins at 400 yards, August 1981. Northwest Montana Fair, Kalispell. John Mello up, Barrett family, owners/trainers. *Courtesy Barrett.*

IN THE TWENTY-FIRST CENTURY, Flathead County exploded in population and wealth, becoming a destination for other equestrian sports. The Kalispell area hosts the Event at Rebecca Farm, an internationally ranked "CCI3"* eventing competition (a "triathlon for horses" that includes dressage, cross-country jumping and stadium jumping). Recognized by the Fédération Equestre Internationale (FEI), it draws horses from across the United States and Canada. Each July, hundreds of horses arrive, some by air.[242]

Many eventing horses are off-track Thoroughbreds, retrained for second careers. A 2014 survey found that, like Flying Catman, most retired racehorses go to private homes or rehab and rescue programs. Only 2.3 percent are sold via public auctions, the risky route that can lead to a foreign slaughterhouse.[243]

Thoroughbreds have another foothold in the Flathead. In 2018, Montana hit the national racing news because of Grade I winner and Kentucky Derby contender Bolt d'Oro. Bolt's sire, Medaglia d'Oro, though foaled in Kentucky, was bred by Great Falls residents Al and Joyce Bell.* Bolt himself came to Montana as a yearling and was started under saddle in the Big Sky before being shipped to major races.

Bolt's owner, Mick Ruis, is a throwback to the likes of Noah Armstrong and Marcus Daly, a self-made multimillionaire spending some of his large fortune on racehorses and a Montana ranch. He bought an 80-acre equestrian center near Bigfork, and his friend and trainer, Ike Green, runs the operation. Now known as Ruis Ranch, the facility starts young Thoroughbreds and conditions them for their race careers.

---

* See chapter 15.

Changing horses, Indian Relay, Great Falls, 1987. *GF 96.7.368.*

The future of small Montana tracks may include the Indian Relay circuit. The Fallon County track in Baker hosted relay competition in 2016. Dodson, in proximity to the Fort Belknap Reservation, hosted race meets dating back to at least 1927. It brought back horse racing with Indian Relay in 2018. Other Montana meets ran in Hardin and Busby along with historic locations at Browning and Crow Agency.[244] As discussed in chapter 16, Indian Relay's survival in the twenty-first century is promising for horses and horse racing.

MONTANA'S "LADY JOCKS"

There are some excellent horsewomen in Montana,
and the one who wins will have no walk-away.
—Butte Daily Post, *1903*[245]

NATIVE ROOTS

The first woman to gallop a horse across the Montana prairie in a match race was undoubtedly an American Indian. The earliest documented individual was Natawista Iksina, the Kainai woman who married Alexander Culbertson. In 1843, when Natawista was about eighteen, John James Audubon, the famed bird artist, visited Fort Union. Amazed by her beauty and boldness, he described her in a race:

> *The ladies had their hair loose and flying in the breeze, and then mounted on horses with Indian saddles and trappings. Mrs. Culbertson and her maid rode astride like men, and all rode a furious race, under whip the whole way, for more than one mile across the prairie; and how amazed would have been any European lady, or some of our modern belles who boast their equestrian skills, at seeing the magnificent riding of this Indian princess—for that is Mrs. Culbertson's rank.*[246]

The very first race at Montana's first Crow Fair, circa 1904, was a women's race. Photographer Fred Miller captured the start: eight Native women

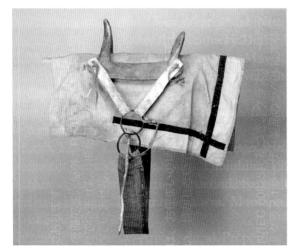

Left: "Blackfeet Saddle owned by Chief Three Plumes," circa 1850. Treed saddles derived from Spanish designs. "These are generally used by the elderly men and women." Meriwether Lewis, August 24, 1805. *X1959.06.02, MHS.*

Below: First race, first Crow Fair, women's race, circa 1904–5. *Fred E. Miller, MHS Photo Archives PAc 2016-38 OP-01-060.*

rode astride in an era when sidesaddles were so de rigueur they were mass-produced and sold in catalogues. Split riding skirts were deemed radical, yet these young women wore close-fitting—and safer—men's-style trousers. Most wore moccasins; some added leggings. Their horses, well-muscled and showing Thoroughbred influence, dance in anticipation. One half-rears, the rider sticking like glue.

LADIES' RELAY

Non-Native women also had a competitive spirit. When gold brought settlers to Montana in massive numbers, as noted in chapter 3, Virginia Slade rode in the Sunday races down the streets of Virginia City. Slade is famed for her desperate ride on Billy Bay, but she might also be the first documented white woman to ride horse races in Montana.

As the state settled, women bet on racehorses and rode them, though often in women-only competition. Women also drove sulkies. In 1903, Helena offered a ladies' trotting race with a $500 purse.

Ladies' relay debuted in 1903. Rules varied: generally, one woman rode several horses, switching at a designated area. Sometimes, elimination heats ran on consecutive days. The 1903 state fair in Helena offered a women's relay of twenty miles, divided into four-mile heats each day. Riders could choose whether to ride sidesaddle or astride. Butte recruited Bessie Kirkendall, Hugh Kirkendall's daughter, to "demonstrate she knows a thing or two about races of that sort." Another contestant was Fannie Sperry Steele, later the World Champion Lady Bucking Horse Rider and an inductee into the Cowgirl Hall of Fame.[17]

The 1903 *Great Falls Tribune* called the ladies' relay "the most popular and most exciting feature of the Cascade County Fair." The *Butte Daily Post* described a race in 1904: Mrs. Richardson was the favorite; her strongest competition was Miss Getts. Unfortunately, Miss Getts lost time at the first

Women's sidesaddle relay, Big Timber, circa 1900. *MHS Photo Archives 941-062.*

change of horses, "her attendant having pinned her divided skirt around the stirrup strap [in] some manner as to prevent her dismounting quickly." On the final lap, Miss Getts rode her fastest horse and briefly took the lead before fading in the stretch; Mrs. Richardson took the win.[248]

Given Montana's small population where most everyone knew everyone else, it is unlikely local women fooled race organizers by disguising themselves as men. Women determined to race in open competition probably just did so, while organizers either tsk-tsked or didn't care. Rural tracks in particular had few rules. Early twentieth-century newspapers reported races for "cowgirls" and "ladies," but race results show some women hit the board in competition against men.

"Mother" Berry

Worldwide, some women did conceal their sex to ride against men. Helena's own "Mother" Berry (1854–1969) was one. Berry had retired from race riding by the time she arrived in Montana but enjoyed telling colorful tales of her early years.

Berry was born Elizabeth Williams in Melbourne, Australia, on June 21, 1854. She said she began riding at age 6, won her first race at 10, and started racing professionally at 13. Her father, a bookie, "made a boy outa me 'cause he didn't 'ave one," she explained in an interview on her 113th birthday.

She rode under the name "Jack" Williams and disguised herself as a man, wearing bowler derbies and smoking cigars to maintain her façade. She also developed a sharp wit and a salty vocabulary. Later, she said she didn't like to be around the ladies of her time "because I'm afraid I might say something bad. I learned to curse from the jocks I ran around with. I don't do it often, but I can sure rip, tear, and bite if I want to."[249]

Berry said she won over 4,200 races in her Victorian-era career, a remarkable but not impossible accomplishment. She rode at tracks worldwide—from Australia to South Africa to France. She once claimed she rode in England against the Prince of Wales's jockey, telling him she would tie flowers to her horse's tail for him to smell, because "she would be right in front of him all the way."[250] She came to America about 1900 and rode races in Northern California.

Berry never said when she took off her bowler and retired "Jack Williams," but she married veterinarian James B. "Doc" Berry in 1903. The childless jockey got the nickname "Mother" from a Colorado judge

Mother Berry, undated. *PAc 82-60.1, MHS Photo Archives.*

who granted her custody of a runaway boy she had taken in. Berry stated that she "stopped riding horses" in 1911.[251]

Doc and Mother Berry took up residence in a house on the Helena fairgrounds in 1913. Until his 1927 death, Doc Berry vetted racehorses, the work horses at the Kessler Brewery, and the prize bull of Green Meadow Ranch, owned by Yellowstone Park entrepreneur Harry Child. Mother Berry, officially "Mrs. J.B. Berry," trained racehorses. Her favorite, the mare Rosa Lockwood, raced from the late 1920s into the early 1930s, last reported in training in 1932.

As noted in chapter 6, fire swept through the Helena fairgrounds in 1937, destroying many buildings, including the home of then-eighty-three-year-old Berry. Rosa Lockwood, fourteen and retired from racing, was saved from a burning barn. The mare, nicknamed "Babe," was nearly as famous as her owner, the pair being described as "best friends." Four years later, on the day Whirlaway won the Kentucky Derby on his way to a Triple Crown, the *Independent Record* reported that Rosa Lockwood had died that past week.[252]

As Berry entered her second century, her birthdays became annual news. At 111, she was declared Montana's oldest person. At 113, still living independently, she said, "I'm not fit fer the choppin' block yet, 'cause I'm too tough." She attributed her longevity in part to a love of horses—but noted that tea with breakfast and half a cup of beer with lunch and supper didn't hurt.[253]

On February 2, 1969, Kentucky's *Lexington Herald-Leader* described Berry as "probably the only lady jockey to compete successfully against men for any length of time." The story ran five days before Diane Crump accepted a mount in Florida at Hialeah, making history as the first woman to ride as a fully licensed jockey in a modern American parimutuel race.[254] Berry passed away at home on March 26, 1969, three months shy of her 115th birthday.[255]

In 1968, the Helena racing community honored her with the Mother Berry Handicap, later the Mother Berry Memorial. It ran annually through at least 1976, won that year, appropriately enough, by jockey Sue "Suzy" Wilson on Hy Grit.

WINNING WYOMINGITE

Horse-riding is more a game of technique and skill than strength—the same as playing chess with men.
—Kathy Kusner, 1967[256]

The late 1960s marked a sea change for women, finally allowed to ride races as licensed jockeys. In 1967, U.S. Olympic Equestrian team member Kathy Kusner sued when she was denied a jockey's license by the Maryland Racing Commission. The commission justified its denial by alleging Kusner lacked riding skill—even though she had jockeyed at unrecognized meets for years. A Maryland court overruled the commission on September 27, 1968, declaring that Kusner could be licensed. Ironically, an injury kept her off the track at the time.

States began licensing women, but male jockeys boycotted races where women appeared. On February 7, 1969, when Diane Crump had a race mount, racing officials ordered the male jockeys to ride—or else. The hostility was intense; Crump required a police escort to get to the paddock.

Montana began licensing jockeys in 1965 and never explicitly banned women from the track. But there is no record of applicants until February 6, 1969—the day prior to Crump's first race—when the *Billings Gazette* reported that two "jockettes," one from Montana and one from Wyoming, applied for licenses. Firmly refusing to sanction drama in the Treasure State, the executive secretary of Montana's Horse Racing Commission, Herb Schatz, stated that any male jockeys who refused to ride against women would fail to fulfill their contracts and "the racing commission has appropriate penalties." At least four women rode Montana races that year. The commission's 1969 report only stated that "persons" seeking licenses were "thoroughly screened."[257]

Women began riding Big Sky races that spring. The *Billings Gazette* reported Barbara Meyer (née Stein—the Wyoming applicant—was "Montana's first licensed woman jockey." On May 20, 1969, she rode at Miles City. Her win on the mare Two-Twelve set a track record of 0:16.19 for three hundred yards. Originally from Glasgow, Meyer and her husband, Jerry, lived near Acme, Wyoming, where the they trained and raced Quarter Horses. Meyer also rode in Fort Benton later that summer.[258]

Meyer had been licensed in Wyoming on August 22, 1968—a month before Kusner won her case. Thus, Meyer was probably the first woman with a jockey's license in America, though it is not known if Meyer rode any Wyoming parimutuel races that year.

Like Kusner in Maryland, Meyer was initially turned down by Wyoming's parimutuel board. In her case, Meyer took the issue to the state's attorney general, Jack Speight. "[W]e women jockeys should have the right to beat boys on horses if we're good enough," Meyer wrote, arguing that Wyoming was the first state to grant women the right to vote and should also lead the nation in licensing female jockeys. Speight agreed, stating, "Wyoming is indeed an equality state, and you do have the right…to compete with male jockeys." The Wyoming parimutuel board granted the license. The board's chair grumbled a bit, saying Wyoming had become the only state in the nation "which allowed women on the track."[259]

In 1970, Meyer's hometown *Glasgow Courier* put her story on page one. She explained that she had no trouble with male jockeys in Montana; they treated her fairly. But at a larger track in Denver, the jockeys were unwelcoming. The article stated the American Quarter Horse Association "wouldn't recognize me." This is a puzzling statement because jockey licensing is done by individual states, not private organizations. A news report in January 1969 stated that AQHA had "amended its racing regulations" to allow women to ride races. Yet staff at AQHA could not locate evidence the organization had ever formally banned women from racing.[260]

In May 1970, Meyer and another Wyomingite, Karen Greenough, rode at Miles City. Meyer also rode in Helena, where the press described the thirty-two-year-old as a "petite 115-pound housewife." No records of races ridden by Meyer after 1970 have been located, though longtime members of Montana's horse racing community recall meeting Barbara and Jerry Meyer at the track.[261]

The first "Montana applicant" in 1969 remains unidentified. License applications from that era have been lost. Four women raced in 1969. Patty Barton rode in Fort Benton, along with Meyer. A Canadian, Barbara Mooney, then age eighteen, rode at Kalispell, reported as the first female jockey to ride at the Northwest Montana Fair.[262] The fourth was a feisty sixteen-year-old teenager from eastern Montana…

FROM COLTS TO COBOL

Do no wrong, but take no shit.
—Suzy Wilson, 2018[263]

Suzy Wilson's career paralleled Montana racing's second golden age. She started riding racehorses for her uncle Vernon, who lived near Savage, Montana. Wilson ran her first match race at Sidney in 1965, when she was twelve. Before she was licensed, she rode in small towns like Wibaux and Ekalaka. These tracks seldom had starting gates, none had official recognition, and some had "auction pool" or "Calcutta"-style wagering—common but technically illegal.

Once licensed, Wilson won a Quarter Horse race at Glendive's Dawson County Fair in 1969. In 1971, Wilson was described as a high school senior and "three-year veteran" who won twenty races in 1970. Most of her wins were at small tracks with unreported results, like Baker, Forsyth, Glasgow, and Glendive, but the *American Racing Manual* verifies Wilson as a 1970 race winner.[264]

Wilson also was a National Merit semifinalist with a full-ride scholarship to Montana State University. She tried academia for about six months, choosing the racetrack over college by the spring term. Heading for the "cities"—Billings and Helena—she was a licensed apprentice jockey in 1972.[265]

Five-foot-two, spunky, good-looking, and articulate, Wilson was popular with the press. She stayed diplomatic while reporters described her as a "pretty 'bug boy'," "girl jockey," and the inevitable "jockette." She told reporters she had few problems with male jockeys, saying, "If you act like a lady, you'll be treated with respect."[266]

Reality was different. Tracks lacked separate showers or changing facilities for women. While most riders and trainers accepted her, some remained wary. Harassment could be blatant; Wilson told of being grabbed by a rodeo clown in makeup, who kissed her white jockey's breeches, leaving a large red lipstick stain in a suggestive location.[267]

The racing stewards were the bane of Wilson's existence. One in particular made it known that he did not think women belonged on the track. If Wilson did anything wrong, he viewed her error to be "twice as wrong." At one meet, her nemesis called her in for a steward's inquiry—until Wilson pointed out that he was criticizing a race she hadn't entered.[268]

She eventually tired of being a novelty. One year, Billings race organizers begged the reluctant jockeys' colony to "promote the meet" and attend a

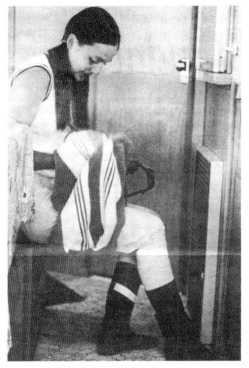

Left: Women often lacked separate jockey quarters. Suzy Wilson preparing to race, 1972. *Courtesy Wilson.*

Right: Suzy Wilson riding Circle Bypass to the winner's circle, Great Falls, circa 1976. *Courtesy Wilson.*

Lions' Club breakfast. During the meal, Wilson was asked—as always—if she had any trouble with male jockeys. Instead of her standard "act like a lady" reply, she deadpanned, "Once you sleep with a few of 'em, you don't have any problems." One of her colleagues, jockey Rob Price, had just taken a sip of coffee. In the stunned silence that followed, the only sound was Price, spewing the beverage out of his nose. She declared, "And that was the last time they asked me to speak anywhere."[269]

In spite of the challenges, Wilson enjoyed racing. She once won six races in a day. Her career peaked in 1976, when she rode 328 races from Arizona to Canada and earned over $41,000 in purses.[*] Her share was 10 percent. "Back in the day, that was big money," she said. But accidents were a way of life. In a 1973 fall, she broke vertebrae in her neck and back; in 1977, she

---

[*] At least $169,000 in 2017 dollars.

cracked her skull. Forty years later, she looked back and said, "I'm not quite sure how it is I'm still alive."[270]

Wilson began training in the 1980s. She worked in California at Hollywood Park, then returned to Montana. Then one day, a fractious horse dumped her onto a cold, muddy track. Picking herself up, old injuries aching, she decided racing was not as fun as it used to be and retired. She moved to the warmth of Texas, dusted off her academic skills, and earned a degree in computer programming. She began a second career operating a mainframe for Lockheed-Martin. Still fond of fast ponies, she drives a 1966 Mustang.

Several other talented young women also took to the track in the 1970s, among them Helena's Kim Bignell and Peggy "P.J." McGowan. In 1973, on Mother's Day at Helena's spring meet, Wilson, Bignell, and McGowan brought home four of nine winners.[271]

Twenty-First-Century Racing

Holly Gervais, raised in the Bitterroot, began racing professionally about the time Wilson retired. Gervais rode before she could walk, placed in the saddle in front of her mother, a trainer whose clients included Margit Sigray Bessenyey of the Bitter Root Stock Farm.

Gervais began competing in endurance riding at age six. In this sport, dominated by Arabian horses, horse and rider navigate trails over courses up to one hundred miles long. At ten, Gervais was the junior national champion endurance rider and ranked nationally five more times.

When she reached adulthood, Gervais began galloping horses at the track, riding her first races in 1989. In her career, Gervais rode not only the Montana-to-Canada circuit but also across the West, from Arizona to Washington State. She even tried California: "Wonderful horses, but lots of politics," she said.

Officially, Gervais's best year was 2000, riding for bigger purse money in Canada and at Playfair in Spokane. As she entered her forties, experience paid off. Riding better horses, she began pulling down awards, including a six-year streak as leading rider at the North American Indian Days meet in Browning.[272]

Recounting her racing injuries, as most jockeys do, Gervais described them as "nothing critically major."[273] Still, she has a plate and screws in

Right: L Bar D Countess in the winner's circle. Holly Gervais up. Owner-trainer Harlan Bird Rattler (*right*). North American Indian Days, 2018. *Wahler.*

Below: Great Falls homestretch, 2018. Nikeela Black (*left*) and Holly Gervais (*right*) challenge for the lead. *Wahler.*

her left ankle, and a broken arm in 2017 required another plate and more screws. Entering her fifties, Gervais still races, claiming it is "for fun." Loving the outdoors, she also has a landscaping and groundskeeping business.

While Mother Berry disguised herself with swearing and cigars, women today ride openly. But the jockeys' room is still a man's world. Gervais explained, "Some guys still don't really like girl riders, so we just have to be tough." Her career has spanned a period when "women on the track" are no longer a novelty, though they remain a distinct minority.

Riders like Kym Espy* and Holly Gervias thrived on small and mid-level tracks. Yet today, only 14 percent of North American jockeys are women, riding just 10 percent of all starts. NBC sportscaster Donna Brothers attributes some of the problems women face in twenty-first-century America to the decline of mid-level tracks. As Kusner noted in 1967, it is not a question of skill: the belief that men's upper body strength makes them better jockeys is debunked by research. A 2018 study by the University of Liverpool found that men and women perform at the same level on horses of similar quality. The same study found women only rode one race in one hundred at the highest levels.[274]

For Montana riders—both men and women—the nearby regional tracks where they can prove they are ready for bigger things are gone. Tracks such as Playfair in Spokane and Les Bois Park in Boise, Idaho, have been shuttered, making it a long jump from Montana to racing's upper rungs.

Gervais is undeterred. She said she will ride horses "until I can't—as long as I'm not scared, doing good, have a heart and a love for it…yup, I'll be doing it!"[275]

REACHING THE TOP

To date, one Montana woman has reached racing's top level: Jefferson County's Greta Kuntzweiler. At twelve, she learned to stay on her pony, Lady Luck, riding bareback at a racing gallop. She left Montana for Kentucky when she was twenty-one. Kuntzweiler found a mentor in Patty "P.J." Cooksey and debuted as a jockey at Churchill Downs on May 8, 1999. In 2000, Kuntzweiler was a finalist for the Eclipse Award as the top apprentice rider in America.[276]

---

* See chapter 11.

Kuntzweiler won over $2 million in 2001. She rode in the 2004 Breeders' Cup Classic and 2005 Kentucky Oaks. Following a period away from the track, Kuntzweiler came back in 2010 and won more graded stakes races, including the 2011 Gardenia Stakes on Groupie Doll—the 2012 and 2013 Eclipse Award–winning sprinter. Equibase shows Kuntzweiler retired in 2015 at age forty with over 6,600 starts and 555 wins, but other records indicate she has ridden races at small tracks since that time. As of 2018, she was still exercising and conditioning racehorses.

In 2005, Kuntzweiler described being a jockey to the *Helena Independent Record*: "To be on a thoroughbred in the morning as the sun rises and to feel their heartbeat through your legs…It's pretty spiritual."[277]

14

MILES CITY

Wild Horses Dragged Them In

Racing is a favorite pasttime with our people, all of whom own their own horses,
and every evening, quite a crowd congregates in front of Ringer and Johnson's
Livery Stable to witness trials of speed.
—Yellowstone Journal, *July 16, 1881*

Miles City uniquely combines horse racing with its annual "World Famous" Bucking Horse Sale. Rodeo and racing traditions each date back over a century, blending cowboys and soldiers, English noblemen and local entrepreneurs. Thriving horse country, the community has long been a center for Montana's livestock industry—its first radio station had the call sign "KATL."

FORT KEOGH

In 1876, following the Battle of the Little Bighorn, the U.S. Army built the Tongue River Cantonment near the confluence of the Yellowstone and Tongue Rivers. Commanded by Colonel Nelson A. Miles, by 1877 the outpost was called Fort Keogh, after Captain Myles Keogh, who died at the Little Bighorn with Custer's Seventh Cavalry detachment. Keogh was also the owner of the horse Comanche, the lone survivor recovered from the battlefield.[278]

Various entrepreneurs settled near the fort, but their primary business was selling alcohol, and Miles forced them to move. These enterprising souls set up Milestown a few miles away. Buffalo hunters, freighters, and sheepherders soon arrived, and the town grew into a trading hub named Miles City. The Northern Pacific Railroad reached town in 1881.

Meanwhile, at the fort, where there was a half-mile racetrack, organized horse races were first mentioned in 1880, with a $550 purse offered. The Custer County fairgrounds is on land once part of the military reservation, and the fort's track may have been where the fairgrounds track is today. On December 22, 1882, the *Miles City Daily Press* reported that officers brought out their trotters and sleighs to race over the snow, marking the earliest written record of cutter racing in Montana.

Fort Keogh transitioned to a remount station, and by 1916, just prior to America's entry into World War I, there were 1,773 horses at the facility. It was, at the time, the largest army remount station in the country. The military bred horses there, plus brought in more from "all over the west" to be trained in accordance with army-approved techniques—gentler than the "man-handling with quirt and spur" that characterized the local area. Later, the fort became an agricultural experiment station. Today, it is operated by the U.S. Department of Agriculture.[279]

Thoroughbreds Arrive

Horses did well in eastern Montana. As the Montana *Stock Growers' Journal* explained, "Of all the conditions that make climate, none conduce more to the development of the race horse than moderate altitude…the altitude makes lung power and capacity—that is, wind.…The Bunch Grass Region of Montana is superior to the blue Grass Districts of Kentucky."[280]

Cowboys arrived with fast horses. One of the first cattlemen in eastern Montana was Conrad Kohrs. Kohrs and Bielenberg brought cattle out from Deer Lodge in 1879 and kept herds year-round in the Tongue River Valley by 1882.[281] Their fast and nimble cow horses came along, and the fine chiseled heads shown by L.A. Huffman's photos of the K-B "cavvy" clearly show Thoroughbred influence.

In December 1885, the *Yellowstone Journal* mentioned that Sydney Paget, the "well known horseman on Otter Creek," hosted a social event with "several races…between the running horses of the neighborhood."[282]

"Saddle bunch listening at cocktail time." Kohrs ranch cavvy in a rope corral. *L.A. Huffman, courtesy Allen.*

Paget was an interesting character—a nobleman's son and amateur jockey in his native England. His Anglo-American Cattle Company brought two thousand head of cattle up from Texas to eastern Montana. When Paget arrived in 1881, he lived the life of a gentleman rancher. Photos of his ranch show horses with clear Thoroughbred influence. Paget sold out in 1897, returned east, and became the racing manager for William C. Whitney (Paget's uncle by marriage), who purchased Hamburg for $60,000 at Marcus Daly's 1901 dispersal sale.*

MILESTOWN RACES

Match races in Miles City occurred whenever a dispute arose in the saloons over who had the faster horse. Organizers on horseback cleared the streets, then stationed themselves at the intersections to warn people off the road until the question was settled. The year 1884 was a particularly busy one for impromptu racing. The *Yellowstone Journal* reported a June 14 event at "race track south, Bullard's Park." On August 23, there was a "lively little scrub race between three men on horseback" past the I.O. Hotel.[283]

---

* See chapter 8.

The town soon restricted street races, probably in the interest of public safety. Support arrived when the 1885 Montana legislature toughened laws, giving incorporated communities the power to ban "immoderate riding or driving" in the streets."[284]

That year, the *Yellowstone Journal* mentioned a half-mile race at the track "near stockyards" on June 27 and, in November, advertised two days of racing on the "Keogh reservation." News reports mentioned races in 1889 at "Fort Keogh." These locations may have been the same place; today the stockyards are across the road from the current track.[285]

The Custer County Fair and Racing Association organized an 1890 county fair, which, of course, included horse races. Miles City was part of a statewide racing circuit by 1892. The association went all-out for variety: various meets included harness races, a one-and-a-half-mile "steeplechase" over ten fences, and a polo match. A 1907 map clearly outlines the track in its present-day location, and that year the fair was promoted with humor: buttons for the event portrayed a racing sulky pulled by a large chicken, stating "just hatched."

The grounds were under a revocable lease from the federal government. When Montana banned gambling on horse races in 1915, some locals argued the anti-gambling law did not apply because the land was on a federal reserve.[286] That said, it is not known if legal wagering occurred at the Miles City track while the gambling ban was in effect.

Miles City, 1882. *L.A. Huffman, courtesy Allen.*

This page: "The Stretch, Custer County Fairgrounds, Miles City, Montana" (*top*) undated, circa 1900; (*bottom*) 2018. *L.A. Huffman. 981-969 MHS Photo Archives; Wahler.*

The federal government slowly turned the land over to the county. A patent deed issued in 1929 perfected a land transfer authorized by Congress in 1924. The patent required the property be used "as a fair ground for the benefit of the citizens of said county." Unique in Montana, Custer County's federal patent has a reversion clause that would return the land to the federal government "if it ceases to be used as such."[287]

The Custer County Fair became the Eastern Montana Fair in 1927. Horse racing at the fair continued though the 1930s, then declined. It revived in the 1960s as part of the Miles City Bucking Horse Sale, where horses still race today.

Wild Horses and the CBC

Slaughter all but eliminated American bison in the late 1800s, and the long winter of 1886–87 decimated Montana's cattle industry. Horses, able to paw through deep snow and travel miles to find food and water, multiplied to fill the empty cold, dry habitat, not unlike the ancient terrain that formed *Equus ferus*.

Before long, feral—"wild"—horses roamed the eastern Montana prairies by the thousands, raising dust that could be seen for miles. With few natural predators, horses became "as thick as the buffalo had been…all shapes, colors, breeds, and half-breeds."[288] Some were Mustangs; others were strayed remounts or "Indian horses."

Unbranded horses were free for the taking. In 1890, the Horse Sales and Fair Association formed and built a sales yard. At Fort Keogh, quartermaster sales of surplus horses were held until at least 1904. Remounts usually had significant Thoroughbred breeding, and these sales helped establish Miles City as a center for horse trading.

World War I brought a high demand for horses and mules, and the United States sent nearly one million horses to Europe. One broker was Ed Love, who formed the Miles City Horse Sales Company in 1910. He procured military contracts to ship horses to France. Thinking ahead, he put signs on the eastbound railroad cars stating, "These horses are from Miles City, Mont., the largest range horse market in the world."[289]

The war's end was a double whammy for horses: the surplus bred for shipment to Europe had no market, and mechanization reduced demand at home. The horse market collapsed. Prices fell from $187 a head during the war to $3–$4 a head after. Horses became so cheap that no one bothered to brand them.

The 1920s brought hard times. Drought and low prices bankrupted Montana homesteaders long before the Great Depression hit in 1929. People mortgaged their stock in a frantic attempt to hang on and, when they pulled out, abandoned the animals to fend for themselves. Local resident John Lockie described being hired by a bank to locate and round up mortgaged livestock left by departing farmers; he gathered around eighteen thousand horses over two years.[290]

With no local market, horses shipped east, but the only market there was the slaughterhouse. Americans generally viewed eating horsemeat with scorn and disgust but willingly shipped it abroad. There also was an American market: in 1922, Ken-L-Ration, the first canned dog food, was advertised as containing "government-inspected horsemeat."[291]

Thus began the era of the Chapple Brothers Cannery—the CBC. The Illinois-based company set up its western headquarters in Miles City. Starting in 1928, the CBC hired "runners" to round up horses. They offered unemployed cowboys $40 a month from April to November; a better wage than the dollar a day paid to ranch hands by the few places hiring. The CBC had a contract to supply horsemeat to Russia; a packing plant in Miles City converted to process it.

The CBC rounded up unbranded feral horses. Local historian John Moore said, "Any horse eating grass in the eastern half of Montana was fair game for the CBC."[292] They also brought in draft stallions to run loose with local mares to produce bigger, meatier animals. At the peak of CBC's empire, about sixty thousand horses ranged Eastern Montana, grazing for free, and harvested at will.

But not all horses were free for the taking. CBC runners sometimes scooped up other people's horses in their gathers. Local ranchers periodically joined roundups for a few extra dollars—and to rescue their own horses. Other times, locals retaliated by putting their own brands on any "slick" (unbranded) CBC stock they could catch.

The CBC dominated the prairie until the Taylor Grazing Act of 1934 ended the free use—and severe overgrazing—of the public domain. The act initiated rangeland leasing with a per-head fee for each animal—and horses cost twice as much to graze as cattle. As the government ended unchecked free grazing, the CBC packed up and left Miles City in 1937.

The Bucking Horse Sale

Rodeos were also part of Custer County history, starting with the 1913 Powder River Roundup, which included wild horse races. Later named Miles City Roundup, the nationally known rodeo featured the bronc Sky Rocket, who was as famous as any cowboy.

Sky Rocket's story illustrates the roots of many bucking horses. A lady in Sheridan, Wyoming, used him as a buggy horse. However, when she sold him, he refused to be ridden and bucked with such great agility that the Roundup Association bought him in 1914 and made him the star of its show. He only gave up a qualifying ride to a cowboy six times in his career, which lasted until he was twenty-two years old.

Fast-forward to 1940. As horse prices rebounded, ranchers rounded up the powerful, part-draft descendants of horses left by the CBC. Some made excellent rodeo horses. The ones trained to saddle had a combination of speed and weight to chase a full-grown steer and hold it at the end of a rope; the rank outlaws made powerful saddle broncs. Some ranchers and ex-CBC runners became rodeo stock contractors.

The first bucking horse sale in Miles City was an unofficial event in 1950 when some bucking stock was sold along with a consignment of roping steers. In 1951, the sale went public. Bucking horses were auctioned as cowboys, paid $5 to $10 a head, rode them out of the chute.[293]

Wild Horse Race, Miles City, circa 1914. *Doubleday-Foster Photo Company, RR.*

Bucking horses are auctioned between races. Miles City, 2017. *Peters.*

In 1952, 1,800 horses sold, and the "official" era of the "World Famous" Miles City Bucking Horse Sale began. Alice Greenough, later inducted into the Cowgirl Hall of Fame, helped organize the sale. A stock contractor herself, she also bought 66 head. The sale grew in fame, and in 1960, a young Ted Kennedy rode a horse out of the chutes as a campaign stunt on behalf of his brother, presidential candidate John F. Kennedy. The event settled on the third weekend of May, with Thoroughbred and Quarter Horse races added in 1963.

Modern Miles City

Today, the race meet during the Miles City Bucking Horse Sale remains popular. It allows "the small person, especially, to have a test spot to try their horses out and see what they have." The third weekend in May brings in 10,000 visitors from around the world. Gate admissions alone have topped $90,000, and lodging is often booked a year in advance.[294]

Trainer Leroy Coombs is a former jockey. He rode at Ruidoso Downs, where he got a small part in the film *Casey's Shadow*, released in 1978. He explained that he comes to Miles City to introduce young stock to race conditions: a starting gate, strange stables, crowds, and commotion.

A septuagenarian, Coombs still exercises his own horses. When interviewed by this author, he was limping at bit. The previous day, he had ridden a young racehorse. Excited by the rain and cold, the youngster spooked at the gate, dumping Coombs into the famous gumbo of the Miles City track. Telling the tale, he shook his head and commented—unconvincingly—"Maybe I'm getting a little old for this."[295] That July, he was in the saddle for hours every day as a track steward at Great Falls.

Miles City's racing is a Montana survivor. In 2012, when the Board of Horse Racing could not provide financial support to any Montana track, Miles City was the only venue to host a meet on its own. The only racing in the state that year, its parimutuel handle of over $117,000 was the highest the meet had seen in over twenty years.[296]

Bucking Horse Sale organizers knew the value of racing from hard experience. In the 1990s, they temporarily succumbed to the temptation to rid themselves of the time, hassle, personality dramas, and expense of running a race meet. In 1991, 1995, and 1996, the sale operated without racing. But revenues dropped. Crowds were smaller, visitors did not stay

Leroy Coombs with two-year-old filly, Miles City, 2018. *Wahler.*

Horse race, Miles City, 2017. *Peters.*

as long, and concession visits plummeted. Bringing the races back in 1997 improved finances.

This accidental economic study vividly demonstrated what racing supporters have long asserted: horse racing draws spectators and adds value to affiliated events. On paper, modern racing is lucky to break even. State simulcast revenue and local parimutuel takeout barely balance the books against purse money, staff salaries, and (at $11,000 a day in 2018) mandatory jockey accident insurance. But profits from increased gate admission, vendor sales, and concessions are seldom listed on racing's balance sheet.[297]

Today, the Miles City community enthusiastically supports the Bucking Horse Sale and the races. The two events have a symbiotic relationship where each improves the other. Civic pride in a tradition combining racing and rodeo preserved horse racing in Miles City.

GREAT FALLS

Racing in the Electric City

Horse racing is kind of a heritage in Great Falls.
—*Dale Mahlum,* Great Falls Tribune, *July 14, 2013*

In July 1805, the Lewis and Clark Expedition spent thirty-one difficult days portaging boats and supplies around the Great Falls of the Missouri River. In what was historically considered Blackfeet territory, fur trappers, explorers, miners, and missionaries came and went. Once settled, the area became notable for the vision and civic pride of its communities. From 1890 until 1910 and again from 1931 to the present, horses have raced in the Electric City. Great Falls proudly preserves Montana horse racing in the twenty-first century.

SUN RIVER

Mr. Vaughn has some of the best thoroughbred stock in the territory.
—Great Falls Tribune, *May 14, 1885*

In 1867, to protect travelers along the Mullan Road, Fort Shaw was built near the Sun River. Soon after, a new town, Sun River Crossing, offered hotels, a general store, and livery stables. By 1883, residents were thinking about hosting a race meet. Newspapers reported, "There is talk of starting a racing association, which will lay out a race course and build fair buildings."[298] It is not known if talk resulted in organized races.

In 1869, Robert Vaughn was the first homesteader in the area to file a claim. By 1873, the *Helena Weekly Herald* touted Vaughn as "a prominent rancher and stock-grower of Sun River."[299] He brought in blooded horses, and in 1879, the *Benton Weekly Herald* noted, "Vaughn has a fine band of race horses, mostly trotters."[300] He entered Chouteau Belle and Maid of Chicago in trotting races at the 1880 Helena Territorial Fair. They competed against Bielenberg's string and Harvey's Mambrino Diamond (a.k.a. "Black Diamond").

Vaughn owned one thousand horses by 1885. He made the news when he sold off his partbred horses and all his cattle to focus exclusively on "thoroughbreds"—purebred horses of several breeds. He stood "trotting" (Standardbred) and "running" (Thoroughbred) stallions at stud as well as a "Norman" (Percheron) draft horse. The press declared, "Mr. Vaughn is recognized as the foremost horseman of northern Montana."[301]

After the death of his young wife in 1889, Vaughn sold his ranch. The sale included over one hundred "high bred colts" and a racetrack. The buyer, Thomas Couch, manager of Butte's Boston & Montana Consolidated Mining Company, moved his family there and continued the horse operation. Vaughn and his baby daughter moved to Great Falls.[302]

"MINNEAPOLIS OF THE WEST"

Paris Gibson, founder of Great Falls, once ran woolen mills in Minneapolis. He came to Montana and started a sheep operation on Belt Creek. Inspiration struck when he visited Fort Shaw in 1879. There he read Lewis and Clark's account of their arduous portage and recognized the falls' potential water power. In May 1882, Gibson explored the area and dreamed of building a "Minneapolis of the west."[303]

Needing capital, Gibson met with railroad magnate James J. Hill. After surveying the land, they staked claims to 6,000 acres. As settlers arrived, Gibson filed his town plat for Great Falls, the "Electric City," on September 30, 1884. Hill laid track, and the St. Paul, Minneapolis & Manitoba Railroad arrived in 1887.

Watson Coulee

Thus at a bound, has Cascade County come to the front as a patron of horsemanship and sport in general.
—Great Falls Weekly Tribune, *May 1, 1889*

Great Falls was planned from the outset. While later accounts sanctimoniously claimed residents were "too busy building to go in for any organized sports,"[304] the opposite was true: the first mention of horse races was a Fourth of July match race in 1885.

Couch, Gibson, Vaughn, and others incorporated the North Montana Fair Association in 1889. They harrowed a one-mile oval on some of Gibson's land at Watson Coulee, off what is today Stuckey Road. A special train brought out spectators for a Fourth of July celebration, though no specific races were reported.

At the Fourth of July meet in 1890, the highlight was a hotly contested quarter-mile children's pony race where Texas Dixie, ridden sidesaddle by Miss Tillie Sheridan, lost by a mere head to Sleepy Dick, who woke up under the urging of Joseph Herring. In 1891, Couch footed the bill for the Boston & Montana Band from Butte to provide entertainment between races.

Organized meets ran at this "West Side Fair Grounds" through 1897. After that, the track was used for conditioning horses and occasional novelty events. The Great Falls Riding and Driving Club held a small meet there in 1908, and the Northern Montana Racing Association organized horse races in 1913. The track hosted motorcycle and stock car races in 1916, possibly the last events at the site. The area is now agricultural land, but a faint track footprint remains visible in aerial imagery.

Black Eagle Park

Who is there in all this broad land, be he cycle crank or Anabaptist deacon, who does not love a horse?
—Great Falls Tribune, *May 6, 1901*

In 1898, Black Eagle Park succeeded the "West Side" track at Watson Coulee and became the home of the Cascade County Fair. Horse races ran every year until 1910.

Montanus was the star of the 1901 meet. His owner, R.W. Fullerton, successfully raced harness horses across the state. Fullerton also owned Ostracism, a daughter of Marcus Daly's Prodigal.

In 1904, Fullerton led the Cascade County Fair Association when the location hosted its biggest event: Fort Assiniboine, located southwest of Havre, coordinated its annual practice march with the fair. Several troops of the Third Cavalry—plus the fort's band and artist Charlie Russell—joined four companies of infantry. They marched down to Great Falls. Arriving on September 24, they set up an encampment adjacent to Black Eagle Park, open to the public. Thousands visited, and the spectacle launched a tradition of military exhibitions coordinated with the fair.

For six days, the cavalry entertained the town. The troops held hurdle races (horse racing over jumps), Roman racing (standing with a foot on each of two horses at a racing gallop), Cossack hurdle racing (standing in crossed stirrups while jumping fences), and "rough riding"—a mass race of thirty-five riders at full gallop.

Most dramatic was the rescue race: a rider galloped into the arena, dismounted, and threw his horse to the ground. Using the prone live animal as a bulwark, the soldier fired at an imaginary enemy, then fell down, "wounded." A second rider galloped in, lifted the soldier onto his own horse, remounted behind the victim and returned to "safety."

Black Eagle Park, Great Falls, 1890s. *Courtesy Ken Robison.*

In 1910, the city of Great Falls bought Black Eagle Park, ending the fair and races. Today, Centene Stadium occupies the site. Between 1911 and 1927, newspapers reported a few races, most at the old Watson Coulee site. Once the 1915 statewide gambling ban went into effect, public enthusiasm faded.

Meanwhile, the private Montana Livestock Pavilion Company purchased undeveloped land in 1919 near the river on Great Falls' West Side. The company built a large "amphitheater" to host livestock shows and auctions, ultimately hosting the 1926 "North Central Exhibition." This facility was the seed for a new fairgrounds—and a new track.

RACING RETURNS

In planning a new fair grounds, they took a long look into the future.... They have planned one that will compare favorably with any other park of the city in verdant beauty, and will be as permanent as the city itself.
—Great Falls Tribune, *September 29, 1927*

In 1926, Cascade County bought the Livestock Pavilion and 102 acres. Planning carefully, the county envisioned stylish exhibition buildings, parkland, and a racetrack. The new fairgrounds grew on a "pay as you go" basis. Today, the facility is Montana ExpoPark.

By 1928, grandstands were up and a racetrack graded. The facility hosted a Fourth of July rodeo with a wild horse race, relays, and other "cowboy" races. Formal racing was on the horizon: with the *Toomey* decision allowing wagering in all but name, local politicians won election with promises to legalize parimutuels.[305]

Great Falls announced race days in 1929 but held no meet. It was a busy year. Two horse barns went up; bleachers for two thousand more people were added next to the grandstands. Prophetically, the biggest issue was convincing the city to run water mains to the barns for fire protection. The next year, another barn was finished, and the Fourth of July celebration offered horse races for children.

Finally, the new North Montana Fair—with parimutuel horse racing—was scheduled. A $250,000 investment in infrastructure carried no debt. Governor J.E. Erickson dedicated the facilities on opening day, August 24, 1931. Fair attendance that Monday was 29,168—with 15,000

This page: Stretch run, Great Falls, 1946, 2018. *PCM, Wahler.*

bettors. Even with Prohibition in effect, the *Great Falls Tribune* noted that "the concession stands were getting a big play…especially those handling food and soft drinks."[306]

A band concert opened the day's racing. Between harness race heats, spectators enjoyed performances such as the Novikoff Trapeze Act and Chicago's Jack Brancel and his Wonder Dogs. When the running races started, so did the rodeo, holding events in the infield arena between races.

Parimutuels headlined the sports section in the Tuesday newspaper: "Rank Outsider Wins Race to Pay $185 for $2 Ticket." The gelding Lieutenant Rust won the third race by a "scant few inches," resulting in the largest payout since the "parimutuel machines" arrived in Montana. Four people collected on their lucky bets.[307]

The North Montana Fair thrived during the Great Depression. The fairgrounds "added to the economic and 'spiritual' vitality of Great Falls."[308] Public Works Administration assistance helped build the grounds' distinctive art deco exhibition buildings. With Helena's fair out of the picture, supporters unofficially dubbed their event the North Montana *State* Fair in 1937. That year, 215,000 people visited—when Great Falls' population was only 46,000. The 400 horses entered in races overflowed the 304 stalls available.

The grounds were deemed finished in 1938, with the event officially declared the "state fair" in 1939. Available records indicate only five years without racing: 1943 and 1945, on account of World War II; then in 2002, 2011, and 2012.

Disaster

Forlorn and saddened jockeys in bedraggled silks, some in tears…sat atop the fence as they watched the firemen stream water on the charred animals.
—Great Falls Tribune, *August 10, 1946*

After World War II, people were ready to return to normal. In 1946, the state fair saw record attendance—as well as its greatest tragedy.

The Great Falls Army Air Base (now Malmstrom AFB) organized airshows for fair week. Brief flyovers Monday and Wednesday occurred without incident. On Friday, August 9, 1946, the military promised to "shoot the works"—described by some as a "damn fool thing to do." At 2:05 p.m., right after the first race, three A-26 Invader bombers roared in

1946 bomber crash, Great Falls. 15 on track is plane's tail section. *Courtesy Hinton.*

low over the fairgrounds. Airspeed was 390 miles per hour, altitude about 500 feet from the ground.

Horses spooked at the noise as the bombers closed into formation—too close. One plane's wing clipped off the tail section of the lead aircraft. That plane hit the ground at the track's final turn, then plowed through a horse barn. The gas tank exploded on impact and set the barn on fire. Both pilots perished. Debris rained everywhere; the severed tail of the plane landed on the track.

The plane that caused the collision, its left wing demolished, veered off. It crashed and burned in the empty hills five miles north of town, killing the two-man crew. The third plane, damaged but aloft, limped to the base airstrip where its pilots walked away from a crash landing.

The barn fire killed nineteen horses and three more people. Two victims were identified, Dorothy Szabo and Andy Seman. A third body, found a day later, was charred beyond recognition. Twenty-five people were injured, most from flying debris, including one man knocked off his horse. Amazingly, only three people were hospitalized. Injured horses were not tallied.

Heroes included the pilots of all three planes, who each aimed their aircraft away from spectators. The crowd was estimated at 20,000. (The day's total attendance was 34,367.) Some eyewitnesses claimed they saw the first pilot struggling to hold a straight course as the plane fell. The pilots of the second plane could have saved themselves by ejecting, but they avoided an uncontrolled crash by going down with their craft.

Another hero was rodeo announcer Cy Tallion, who averted a panic. Tallion grabbed the microphone from the stunned army PR officer announcing the airshow. With a resonant voice that "rang out sharp and clear," Tallion asked for calm and for "cool heads" to safely evacuate the stands. Visitors with medical skills volunteered at the Red Cross station; others guided victims to aid.[309]

The remaining Friday races were canceled. Debris was cleared from the track, and racing resumed on Saturday. While the courts wrestled with lawsuits, a new barn went up. Air shows continued in future years, with safety protocols.

Montana's Secretariat

One of the most celebrated race horses in the state.
—Great Falls Tribune, *May 23, 1982*

In the post-1965 regulatory era, organizers spotted a gap in the statewide schedule: county fairs, typically scheduled after harvest, made June a slow season for racehorses. To fill the gap, Big Sky Racing, led by Dick Forster, started a Great Falls spring meet in 1971. It peaked in 1982, hosting eighteen days and pulling in $1.6 million in handle. Due to assorted problems, the group folded after 1983, and the state fair took over the spring meet. At that

Bettors at the windows, Great Falls, 1987. *GF 96.7.338.*

time, a young man named Skip Sherman came on board to manage the track. Great Falls peaked at thirty-four racing days in 1989, pulling in $3.6 million in handle.[310]

A star of the track was Son of Harpo, foaled in 1969 on R.C. "Blackie" Bower's ranch near Cascade. Bower believed in "letting a horse be a horse." He turned out his stallion Harpo to pasture-breed Norkota Blue, and the ensuing chestnut foal, Son of Harpo, grew up on the open range. As trainer Frank Velock Jr. explained, "He'd never seen belly-deep straw."[311]

The two-year-old gelding arrived at the track in 1971 half-broke and gangly. His first two races were unimpressive. But Velock's father, Frank Velock Sr., saw potential. Bower agreed to let Velock senior train the young Thoroughbred. Under Velock's care, Son of Harpo's first win—by eight lengths—was on June 19, 1972, in Great Falls. Heading to Spokane, he won twice more in September.

In 1973, Secretariat made national headlines, the first Triple Crown winner since Citation in 1948. Secretariat's nickname was "Big Red," and Son of Harpo, 17 hands high, became Montana's own "Big Red" as he won seven of his fifteen recorded races that year. Son of Harpo raced at the Assiniboia track in Winnipeg, Manitoba, where he thrilled fans by winning four races. Then he beat a ten-horse field by three lengths in the Midwestern Melvin Stakes in Saskatoon. He returned to Canada in 1974. Bower said that at age four or five, "[Son of Harpo] could run with any allowance horse in America," adding, "We like to watch our horses run, and you can't do that at those big tracks."[312]

Son of Harpo's jockeys included Suzy Wilson* and Vic Sigouin. Sigouin came to racing from a unique background. Enlisted in the U.S. Air Force and stationed at Malmstrom, he fell in love with Montana—and horses. He became a jockey in 1973, with help from Frank Velock Sr. and morning gallops on Son of Harpo. Sigouin raced until he retired in 1990.[313]

Frank Velock Jr. said the range-bred horse "was smarter than a lot of people around him." Son of Harpo liked to stalk the pace and typically won by "hooking" the competition—he'd look his rivals in the eye, then take off. "If he wanted to," said Velock, "he'd win by open lengths." But in morning workouts, he was a loafer. He only got serious "in company"— workouts against another horse. Handicappers who didn't know his style put him at 20–1 on the morning line.[314]

In the afternoons, Son of Harpo was valiant in both defeat and victory. The 1-1/16th-mile King's Ransom Handicap in August 1975 was Billings's biggest race of the year. Son of Harpo faced his Montana rival, Lon Marsh's hard-running bay gelding, Mabel's Dancer (93:20-18-15). They had met twice before, and betting was heavy. Mabel's Dancer was fast out of the gate and in front until Son of Harpo hooked him at 6-1/2 furlongs and kicked off. Two lengths ahead in the stretch, jockey Suzy Wilson thought they were home free. Then suddenly, Last Wink, a 14–1 longshot, caught them at the wire.

In 1976, at Great Falls, with Wilson in the irons, Son of Harpo found his favorite race: the City Bar Inaugural, five furlongs sponsored by the track's favorite off-hours establishment. He won seven consecutive years. In 1977, the eight-year-old set a track record when most racehorses are retired: five furlongs in fifty-nine seconds. "Son of Harpo is the best horse I've ever ridden anywhere," Wilson said.[315]

Frank Velock Sr. passed away in 1978. His daughter Sharon and son-in-law, Ken Sevalstad, took over the racing stable, aided by Frank Velock Jr.[316] The winning streak continued. In 1981, with Vic Sigouin, Son of Harpo won his sixth consecutive City Bar Inaugural against another veteran of the Montana turf, the eight-year-old champion Charmhersweet (72:19:20:10).

---

* See also chapter 13.

"He was so proud." Son of Harpo, age twenty, on his special day, July 3, 1989. (*Left to right*) Laurel Velock, Sandy (Velock) Noble, Sharon (Velock) Svalstad, Frank Velock Jr. Vic Sigouin up. Trainer Ken Svalstad not shown. *Courtesy Frank Velock Jr.*

"Put him in the No. 1 hole for five furlongs and he's still the horse to beat," declared Bower.[317]

In May 1982, Sigouin piloted Son of Harpo to his seventh City Bar Inaugural win at age thirteen. The aged gelding reluctantly surrendered champion's status that June to the up-and-coming Oriental Showboy, owned by the Barrett family of Helena. Son of Harpo was the favorite to win the Northwestern Bank Feature for the second year in a row but finished third to the brilliant five-year-old in his prime.[318]

When Blackie Bower died in October 1982, his widow, Jean, retired Son of Harpo. His official record is 92:32-17-10, with earnings of $48,694. But not all his races were reported. By Velock's count, the old campaigner ran about 112 races and won 51. He probably earned almost $80,000—$1,000 at a time.[319]

Special Year, Special Days

The 1989 Great Falls meet, the biggest ever, sought "celebrities" to draw crowds. Organizers tracked down Sevalstad and Velock, hatching plans to make July 3 "Son of Harpo Day" and parade the horse at the track. They went out to a pasture near Cascade, where the twenty-year-old recognized the men and "trotted right up." His chestnut coat was glossy from a diet of prairie bunchgrass, and he was nicely muscled from once again roaming the open range. He jumped into a trailer, and everyone headed to town, where he got a bath and a hoof trim. Vic Sigouin was riding the meet and eagerly volunteered to saddle up the old fellow.

Son of Harpo walked onto the track under tack, to the cheers of the crowd. His head lifted. "Them old ears perked up," Velock said. Plans to simply parade him in front of the grandstand were abandoned. Sigouin eased him into a gallop. Taking a lap around the half-mile oval, he stretched out and savored every step. Crossing the finish line, he was brought back to the winners' circle and adorned with a garland. Velock smiled at the memory. "Proud as a peacock," he said. After posing for photos, head high and ears forward, the gallant campaigner returned to graze at the ranch. He lived to be twenty-seven years old, passing on in 1996.[320]

Another celebrity in 1989 was jockey Bill Shoemaker, visiting Montana on his farewell tour.* On August 2, Shoemaker started the day with a quick round of golf at the Meadow Lark Country Club. Then he headed for the track for two races. Shoemaker ran third on Crown a Matic, losing to Vic Sigouin. In the tenth race, with the seasoned gelding Gambeto, Shoemaker won.

As elsewhere in Montana, after 1989, Great Falls faced declining race days. In 1993, the June meet ended. Handle nosedived from $1.5 million in 1997 to $636,078 in 2000. But racing in the Electric City had three critical supporters: the county commissioners. They put aside their differences and declared that racing would continue, "period." The county ran the meet in 2001, though it went in the hole and they canceled 2002 to regroup. Races revived in 2003, running between five and ten days the rest of the decade.[321]

---

* See also chapter 11.

Medaglia D'Oro

Al and Joyce Bell came to Montana in 1967. Al started his career driving trucks, then became a successful businessman. The Bells had raced Thoroughbreds since the late 1960s, but as Montana's horse racing economy changed, they sent their mares to foal in other states, where large breeder incentives rewarded successful runners.

Their mare Cappucino Bay dropped her 1999 foal in Kentucky. The bay colt was by the Irish champion El Prado. Al initially named the little fellow "Bay Latte," because all of Cappucino Bay's foals got "coffee names." His daughter insisted he class it up. She suggested a famous brand of coffee, and the colt became Medaglia d'Oro.

The foal came to Montana when he was three months old. He grew up under the Big Sky on the Bells' land. Shipped east, he won on his second trip out the gate, and a determined agent made two attempts to buy him. The Bells took the second offer, $500,000. Medaglia d'Oro landed connections who took him to the top: the agent scouted for hall of fame trainer Bobby Frankel. The buyer, Edmund Gann, was an owner of Chicken of the Sea.

Medaglia d'Oro (17:8-7-0) is the only Montana-raised horse to contest all three races of the Triple Crown.* He earned a paycheck in the Kentucky Derby, finishing fourth after being bumped at the start and hung out eight wide on the final turn. He finished poorly in the Preakness but was second in the 2002 Belmont, losing by a heartbreaking half-length to Sareva. Like Marcus Daly's Senator Grady, the colt ran second in his very biggest races—including the 2002 and 2003 Breeders' Cup Classic and 2004 Dubai World Cup. Still, Medaglia d'Oro won respect—and seven other graded stakes, including the Travers and the Donn Handicap.

Possibly the greatest racehorse to grow up on Montana bunchgrass, Medaglia d'Oro's biggest success was in the breeding shed: he sired multiple graded stakes winners, the most famous being Rachel Alexandra, the 2009 Kentucky Oaks and Preakness winner. By 2017, his stud fee was $250,000. As noted in chapter 12, Medaglia d'Oro's son Bolt d'Oro (8:4-1-1), who grew up in Bigfork, made national news as a 2018 Kentucky Derby contender.

Cappucino Bay lived happily at the Bell's place in Great Falls until the valiant mare passed away in early 2019, a few days short of her thirtieth birthday.[322]

---

* Montana-owned Alysheba won the Derby and Preakness and finished fourth in the Belmont. But, as noted in chapter 10, he never lived in Montana.

THE LONG LOOK

Everywhere we go, people are asking what they can do to help us.
—Kelly Manzer, 2013

ExpoPark had rough years in 2011 and 2012. Infrastructure was aging. The private company that ran the race meet pulled out, and no one took over. For the first time since 1931, Great Falls went two consecutive years without racing. Some people wondered out loud if it was time to end horse racing altogether.[323]

Race supporters, led by Great Falls veterinarian Kelly Manzer, swung into action. They incorporated the nonprofit Great Falls Turf Club (GFTC) in November 2011. The next year, they pitched an offer to organize the meet. The county commissioners tentatively agreed. The community was already there: Commissioner Jane Weber, running for election in 2012, won on a platform that supported horse racing; her opponent was publicly dubious.[324]

In 2013, the state fair advisory board and county commissioners formally voted to support GFTC—they had two years' data from the fair without racing. Commissioner Joe Briggs worried about the budget but commented, "If we view horse racing as an attraction to get people to come to the fair, then it doesn't necessarily have to break even to be successful." The Board of Horse Racing granted race dates and some startup funds, the county kicked in $50,000, and the meet was on.[325]

The deferred maintenance challenges were daunting: GTFC fixed the rail and hauled in four thousand tons of sand. Manzer sought assistance from Skip Sherman, who managed Sunland Park after he worked in Great Falls. Supporters—including John Hayes, Sparky Kottke, racing secretary Lonnie Dalke, and dozens of other volunteers—found sponsors, recruited horsemen, and promoted the meet.

Hard work paid off: 225 horses filled the stables. On July 20, when the track ponies brought their charges out for the first race, the crowd of two thousand—far larger than anticipated—cheered wildly and gave the horses a standing ovation. Thirteen thousand spectators attended over four days, and handle of $374,457 was the most since a ten-day meet in 2005.[326]

At the end of the year, the county commission voted unanimously to renew the meet. Concession profits went to the county coffers. The Turf Club maintained the track, ran the races, and handled the backside.

Starting gate crew, Great Falls, 2018. *Wahler.*

Ginwillmakeusin, Western Montana Turf Club feature, Great Falls 2018. Owner/trainer Jackie Smith, jockey Nikeela Black. Toni Hinton and Jim Johnson, WMTC *(third and fourth from left)*. *Wahler.*

But by 2018, the aging grandstands had reached the end of the road. Chunks of concrete were falling from the underside, rendering the concession and betting areas unsafe. Temporary solutions allowed the six-day meet to run, and the commissioners unanimously agreed to replace the structure.[327]

Days after the 2018 meet wrapped, the grandstands were demolished and new construction began. As of 2019, the Great Falls Turf Club continues to take point to secure the future of racing in the Electric City. Great Falls is a twenty-first-century success story and a model for Montana's tracks. Community support, long range planning, and a deep love of the turf saved the day.

16

NATIVE FUTURE

Indian camps are not Indian without horses.
—Chris Roberts, Pow Wow Country[328]

Today, the "horse nation" thrives with Montana's First People. As discussed in chapter 1, traditional match races and relays long predate white settlement in Montana. Once non-Indian people arrived, horse racing became not only intertribal but also interracial; tribes put up their best horses against those of soldiers, cowboys, and other settlers.

Several extended families from Montana's Indian Country have run horses at organized meets for generations. Among these are the Bird Rattlers of Browning and the Real Birds from Crow Agency. Both families still race horses today.

Additionally, the Blackfeet and Crow Indian Reservations now host two of the four remaining horse race meets in Montana. Because of issues surrounding tribal sovereignty, reservation meets run independent from the Montana Board of Horse Racing. Races are not simulcast, and results are not officially reported. Most rules are local, enforced by tradition. Crow Fair offers parimutuel betting some years, but most wagering is conducted in traditional forms less obvious to the casual visitor.

Off the reservations, an expanding circuit for modern Indian Relay competition, also outside the purview of MBOHR, helps preserve half-mile tracks across the Intermountain West.

Holly Gervais and L Bar D Countess leading down the backstretch. North American Indian Days, 2018. *Wahler.*

APISTIKINII

The beautiful black horse was the pride of the Crow Nation. In the late 1800s, when tribes ran match races on straight tracks, he was a champion.

Bird Rattle of the Blackfeet loved fast horses. Those of the Apsáalooke, many of remount breeding, were noted for speed. A young man already renowned for his leadership of war parties, Bird Rattle decided the horse had to be his. Trade was out of the question. The closely guarded horse stood out, having flashy white hind leg markings running over his hocks and up his hind legs.

Bird Rattle entered the Apsáalooke camp and boldly captured the horse. But it was not enough to elude the party of furious men who chased him. He came back, to the very center of the camp, and also took "a fine medicine shield" displayed high on a pole in a place of honor. Bird Rattle named the magnificent horse Apistikinii, and he became the pride of the Blackfeet Nation, never beaten in a race.[329]

Another time, Bird Rattle owned a pair of buckskins identical in every way—except speed. In match races on straight tracks, he devised a ruse. At multiday gatherings, he'd bring his slower horse the first day, bet heavily,

204

and lose much of his money. The next day, as Bird Rattle's grandson Joe Bird Rattler explained, "He'd bring the fast one and fool everybody and win all his money back." Reviewing my notes, I asked, "Which horse did Bird Rattle steal from the Crow?" He smiled. "All three of them," he said.[330]

Later in life, Bird Rattle became Chief Bird Rattler—no one knows how the extra *R* was added. A greatly honored leader by his people, he also protected their rights. He traveled to Washington, D.C., seeking fair payment for land claims. At home, he led the tribal police before becoming the tribal judge, a job from which he retired in 1935. His 1937 obituary declared him "a good hunter, a good warrior, a good policeman, a good judge and an exceptionally good man."[331]

Reservation Era

Montana's reservation era began as American Indian Nations were forced onto ever-shrinking parcels of land. After the Dawes Act of 1887, the process accelerated. The Office of Indian Affairs (now Bureau of Indian Affairs) began enforcing a policy of assimilation. Any large gathering was suspect, and by the 1890s, holding traditional Native dances and ceremonies was forbidden. In one example, on the Flathead Indian Reservation, the Salish and Pend d'Oreille attempted to hold a traditional celebration, an *esyapqeyni*, in 1891. The reservation agent, Peter Ronan, threatened to use military force to break it up.[332]

As a result, ceremonies were held secretly. Resistance sometimes took the form of misdirection: if a tribe asked permission to gather for a "Fourth of July celebration," given the holiday, the government could hardly say no. People gathered for officially sanctioned activities, then quietly held their traditional ceremonies away from the watchful eye of the agent.

Tribal oral history places the first "Arlee powwow" about 1898. But in 1897, five hundred people gathered at Arlee for horse racing on the Fourth of July. The newspapers reported a number of races held along a straightway with the items staked for each race stacked at the finish line. The most popular event was the five-mile race.[333] An *esyapqeyni* has not been directly correlated with this race meet, but it seems likely.

It didn't take long before Indian agents and local communities realized that dances performed in traditional regalia could draw tourists. At the dawn of the twentieth century, Fourth of July advertisements for "Indian

"Indian Pony Race," Fort Belknap Reservation, Montana, 1906. *Detroit Publishing Company, LOC.*

celebrations" with horse races began appearing in Montana newspapers. Well into the 1930s, horse races headlined traditional celebrations from Arlee in the west to Poplar, on the Fort Peck Reservation in eastern Montana.[334]

Another common "legal" gathering was when trading or commodity distribution was held at the agency headquarters, which allowed opportunities for match races.

As county fairs grew, scattered news reports listed American Indian jockeys, including Frank Takes the Gun, winning both "Indian" races and open events against all comers at tracks large and small, from Butte to Forsyth.* Purses in "Indian races" were often much lower than in events open to whites. Results seldom made headlines save in exceptional cases, such as in 1899, when a horse owned by Plenty Coups won over four furlongs in :54 at Billings.

---

* See chapters 11 and 12.

CROW FAIR

At Crow Agency, reservation agent S.G. Reynolds and tribal leaders, including Plenty Coups, agreed to host a celebration using a "county fair" format. Records disagree if the first Crow Fair occurred in 1904 or 1905, but in either case, the agent hoped to promote assimilation by exhibiting crops and livestock, while tribal elders wanted to preserve traditional Apsáalooke culture.[335]

Apsáalooke leaders planned both individual and relay races. Though traditional races ran on a straightaway, the committee agreed to install an oval track for the same reason circular tracks developed elsewhere—to make the whole race visible to spectators. The Apsáalooke name for Crow Fair, Chichia'xxaawasuua, translates as "running in a circle." The first race at the first Crow Fair was a women's race.* In 1909, the agency set aside 40 acres as a permanent facility that hosted a half-mile oval and grandstands seating 800 people. By 1920, twice-daily trains brought visitors to and from the venue.[336]

The original event continued until 1923. There are no news reports of Crow Fair between 1924 and 1932. In that period, the government declared war on the Crows' horse population. Until the end of World War I, the Apsáalooke had high-quality horses and easily sold their surplus. But after World War I, the horse market crashed. Reservation herds grew large, and non-Indian ranchers complained that "wild" horses competed with their cattle.

In 1919, the secretary of the interior demanded the Crow Tribe get rid of their horses. Such an order was "like ordering a man to kill his best friend or brother" to the Apsáalooke. They refused.[337]

Therefore, in 1923, the government authorized a bounty on "wild" horses. "Runners" were paid four dollars for every dead horse, collected by bringing an ear. Slaughtering horses disgusted local cowboys, and many refused to cooperate. At least one cattle outfit brought in Texas gunmen. The government estimated forty thousand horses were destroyed over three years. The Apsáalooke said the toll was higher—and included tame animals. By 1930, both the Crow and Northern Cheyenne tribes lost most of their horses. The cultural trauma was deemed greater than any military defeat.[338]

In spite of the challenges, somehow, the Northern Cheyenne hosted a rodeo with horse races in 1929—on the Fourth of July.

---

* See chapter 13.

Above: "Indian Race." Deer Lodge, circa 1947. *Hartly Photo. PCM.*

Opposite, top: Spectators at Crow Agency, 1941. *Marion Post Wolcott, LOC.*

Opposite, bottom: Horse race. 2017 Crow Fair. *Chris Jorgensen.*

With the New Deal, matters improved. The Indian Reorganization Act of 1934 granted tribes some freedom to manage their own affairs. The Crow Fair revived in 1932, and by 1934, the Crow Nation had complete control of the event. It became a true cultural celebration. Using the 1934 Act, tribal superintendent Robert Yellowtail started a horse-breeding program to restore the Apsáalooke herds. He took advantage of army remount programs, leasing and buying stallions to improve local stock. With a stated goal to raise "cow horses," he named one fine Morgan stallion "Roosevelt" in honor of the president.

The herds of the Apsáalooke revived, but the war on "wild" horses continued. Following World War II, 100 horses in the Rotten Grass Breaks were shot from planes and helicopters. The only surviving population was "a little band of 70 horses...in almost inaccessible box canyons used only by themselves and some deer." Later confirmed by modern genetic testing to be of nearly pure Spanish horse ancestry, they

are now federally protected on the Pryor Mountain Wild Horse Range of Montana and Wyoming.[339]

Today's mid-August Crow Fair hosts the largest encampment in North America, dubbed "the tepee capital of the world." The Edison Real Bird Memorial Complex, with a rodeo arena and half-mile oval, hosts both Indian Relay and modern-style races with a starting gate and jockeys in track silks. Eight horse barns, complete with hot walkers, stable racehorses, while the nearby encampment hosts countless more, from children's ponies to parade horses. Many impromptu races run on the edge of the camp.

CROW SOVEREIGN

Robert Yellowtail declared a practical goal of breeding "cow horses" to manage cattle herds in the 1930s. Before long, Apsáalooke rodeo cowboys were well known for their skill in roping events—where a sprinting horse "fast out of the box" was prized. They knew "cow horse" breeding could also succeed on the racing straightaway.[340]

The modern American Quarter Horse developed from Thoroughbred stock crossed on agile local horses used in cattle country. AQHA was founded in 1940. Noted for quickness and "cow sense," the Quarter Horse is also a racehorse, known today as the "World's Fastest Athlete." But early AQHA breed registry policies excluded horses with "excess" white. Thus, the American Paint Horse Association (APHA) formed in the early 1960s, registering—and racing—pinto-spotted horses of Quarter Horse and Thoroughbred lines.

Flashy "painted horses" also were a part of Native culture, and the APHA was made to order for the Real Bird family of Crow Agency. Lawrence "Chuck" Real Bird had the horse culture of his people bred in the bone. His father, Mark Real Bird, was given the traditional name IisaashkeXaxxe, "Owns Painted Horses." As an adult, Chuck Real Bird started breeding—and racing—registered Paints.[341]

In 2002, Real Bird's mare Hurrah for Spots gave birth to a little tobiano colt that carried lines to the Thoroughbred Alydar and Quarter Horse Hall of Fame champions Easy Jet and Dash for Cash. Real Bird named him Crow Sovereign, and he ran across the west: Colorado, Oklahoma, Wyoming—and Montana.

As a three-year-old, the powerfully built young horse found his distance at 300–350 yards. He won the 2005 Western Montana Fair Derby in Missoula and then won again three weeks later in Billings at Yellowstone Downs. That November, he won an allowance race at Los Alamitos in California. He was named the American Paint Horse Association's three-year-old champion gelding.[342]

Crow Sovereign was the first horse from any Indian nation to win a national APHA racing title. In 2006, Crow Sovereign and Chuck Real Bird were jointly honored with the APHA Legendary Achievement Award. APHA president Carl Parker presented the plaque at Crow Fair, honoring Real Bird for his lifelong support of the American Paint Horse, then tribal members sang ceremonial praise songs. Chuck's son, Shawn Real Bird, explained the significance of the award:

> *On an Indian reservation it is harder to achieve goals and dreams. This one great success will inspire the young Crow racehorse men to dream the dream, live the dream, and to accomplish the dream.*[343]

North American Indian Days

Browning, Montana, hosts North American Indian Days the second week of July. For four days, the campground fills as the Blackfeet Nation hosts the largest Powwow in Montana next to Crow Fair. Charging Home Stampede Park runs the rodeo and horse races. Some races use a starting gate, measured distances, and modern equipment. Others, including Indian Relay, take a more traditional form with bareback riders taking off from a standing start.

Reservation-era racing was influenced by the cross-border reach of the Blackfoot Confederacy. As noted in chapter 2, trade routes from Fort Benton to Canada went through tribal territory. In 1869, Fort Hamilton, also known as Fort Whoop-Up, was built near present-day Lethbridge, Alberta. Unstructured match races quickly became a part of trading post culture, and after the North-West Mounted Police (now the RCMP) settled things down, horse racing in Canada was formalized.

People from the Babb and Browning areas, including Joe Kipp, Charlie Powell, and Bill Johnson, brought horses to race in southern Alberta in 1898. Southern Alberta also produced a number of excellent jockeys, notably

Start of "Chief's Race." North American Indian Days, 2018. *Wahler.*

George "Iceman" Woolf, who lived in Babb as a child and probably honed his chops against boys of the Blackfeet Nation.

As occurred elsewhere in Montana, the Blackfeet Reservation held agent-sanctioned gatherings on the Fourth of July. In 1905, an encampment of several hundred tepees set up in Browning with dancing and horse racing. Exhibiting "an excess of patriotic fervor" may well have been another example of misdirection, as agent J.Z. Dare had banned the Sun Dance.[344]

Horse racing was reported again at the "first annual Blackfeet fair" in 1915. Like the early Crow Fair, the event supposedly highlighted agricultural products. In 1919, the tribe again hosted horse racing as part of their Fourth of July celebration. The Browning Rodeo offered horse racing in 1933. Consolidating all celebrations, North American Indian Days officially started in 1951 and has run annually since.

The Blackfeet Nation has produced a number of jockeys. One was Shannon Wippert, who started racing as a child, running Indian Relay, then went on to make his name in Canada and Montana. From 1994 until 2007, Equibase recorded Wippert in over 2000 races from Alberta to Arizona with wins on Thoroughbreds, Quarter Horses, Paints, and Arabians.[345]

The Bird Rattlers

All the horses that I had, they listen to me.
—Joe Bird Rattler, 2018

Joe Bird Rattler was an infant when his grandfather, Chief Bird Rattler, died. But the love of racehorses was in his blood. He won his first race as a twelve-year-old jockey, then turned to training in adulthood. At one point, he had a racing stable of twenty-five horses, running both Thoroughbreds and Quarter Horses in Montana and Canada.[346] Today, he is a respected member of Montana's horse-racing community. The family tradition carries forward: at North American Indian Days in 2018, his fourteen-year-old grandson, also named Joe, won his first race.

The Bird Rattlers are a force to be reckoned with. At least thirteen members of the extended family appear as trainers in racing's Equibase; six ran horses in 2018. Because small race meets are seldom reported and reservation meets not at all, the family's breadth of experience cannot be described by simple online statistics. Joe Bird Rattler's siblings, in-laws,

Lifetime chief of the Blackfeet Nation, Earl Old Person (*right*) honors Joe Bird Rattler (*center*), Great Falls 2018. *Wahler.*

children, nephews, nieces, and grandchildren are owners, trainers, jockeys, and race sponsors—stalwarts of the Montana racing circuit.

At Great Falls, Joe's son Ed, once a jockey and now a trainer, was the official starter. Joe's nephew Merlin Bird Rattler Jr. ran the gate truck. In 2018, the family sponsored the 660-yard Joe Bird Rattler Feature: Eighteen-year-old Shance Bird Rattler, another grandson and the youngest jockey at the meet, rode L Bar D Countess for his uncle, Joe's son Harlan. Shawn Bird Rattler, Joe's nephew, put Holly Gervias* on his horse Wait; they ran second. The winning horse, Bv Imgunabesomebody, had Native connections: owner-trainer Duane Lafferty and jockey Brian Beetem, from Oglala, South Dakota. Beetem described himself as Shance's "Native brother in the jocks room."[347]

INDIAN RELAY

Professional jockeys wouldn't touch Indian relay with a 10-foot stick. The degree and skill it takes to be an Indian relay rider is night and day from any other sport.
—Kendall Old Horn, 2013[348]

Relay riding dates to antiquity. In the fifth century BCE, Persia's Royal Road stocked over one hundred stations with fresh horses to speed messengers across the empire. The American Pony Express used a similar model in 1860–61 to convey mail from St. Joseph, Missouri, to San Francisco, California.

The Shoshone claim credit for developing Indian Relay.[349] In Montana, photographs show a 1906 Indian Relay, probably at Crow Fair. For decades, newspapers promoted "Indian Races"—tribal members in Native regalia were often a tourist draw. In 1922, with the state's gambling ban in full force, the state fair in Helena offered a five-day "Intertribal" meet that drew competitors from the six reservations in existence at the time.

Modern Indian Relay is popular with both Native and white spectators. The modern form dates to the mid-1970s. The sport's governing bodies ebb and flow, but rules are becoming standardized. Most events have teams of four people and three horses, each horse running one lap of a half-mile oval track. The race begins with a standing start: no starting gate.

---

* See chapter 13.

"Indian relay race," probably Crow Fair, circa 1906. *T.A. Morris, MHS Photo Archives. Lot 035 B5F6.03.*

Team members are:

- the rider, who must move from horse to horse, riding bareback;
- the "mugger," who must catch the incoming horse as the rider dismounts;
- the "set up guy" or "exchange" holder, who has the fresh horse that is next to run, and
- the backup holder, who handles the other animal.

The exchange holder is particularly critical: if a horse gets loose, the team is disqualified. But if the holder lets go too late, the rider loses time.

A team might maintain a string of twelve horses to maintain the health and soundness of individual animals. Some horses are racing Quarter Horses and Paints, but an increasing number are seasoned off-track Thoroughbreds, retrained for a second career.[350]

Teams usually wear matching shirts, and horses are often painted with traditional designs. Riders do not necessarily wear regalia—athletic performance is key. They mostly eschew helmets, but goggles are useful, and proper running shoes are critical.

The exchange, Indian Relay, 2015 Crow Fair. *Chris Jorgensen.*

Top of the stretch, Indian Relay, North American Indian Days, 2018. *Wahler.*

Indian Relay runs from Emerald Downs, nestled between Seattle and Tacoma, to the Pine Ridge Indian Reservation in South Dakota and as far east as Canterbury Downs in Minnesota. Purses are growing; the 2015 championship in Billings awarded $10,000. Indian Relay itself is enlivening tracks across the Intermountain West, drawing large crowds and providing a link between horse racing past and present.

Afterword

THE HORSE AND ITS FUTURE

R acing is about the horse, and the horse is born to run. Crowds still gather for live racing. Parents anxiously pull children back from the paddock fence as they press forward with bright eyes. Thoroughbreds and Quarter Horses still dance to the Call to the Post as they are handed off to track ponies. The two-dollar bettor keeps live meets going. Young and old, spectators cheer as the winning horse thunders down the homestretch.

In the twenty-first century, horse racing is under fire but doggedly survives. But as far back as 1998, a gambling report prepared for the Montana legislature expressed concern about an aging base for parimutuel gambling and the draw of "more exciting" screen-based forms of wagering.[351]

The world of horse racing must adapt to survive, but live racing was never about gambling alone. As meets at Crow Fair and North American Indian Days prove, horse racing is also a place for people to gather, to spend hours instead of seconds interacting with one another and the world around them. Humans and horses have been a team for millennia. The bond forged by a Neolithic struggle for survival is stronger than the lure of screens.

Perhaps Dale Mahlum said it best: "Go watch the horses, because it's a beautiful thing."[352]

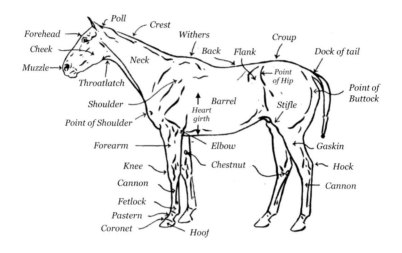

Common Horse Markings

Face Markings

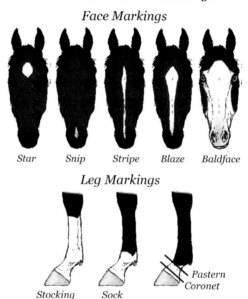

Star   Snip   Stripe   Blaze   Baldface

Leg Markings

Stocking   Sock

Top: Points of the horse. *From* Riding Simplified, *Margaret Cabell Self, 1948; labels updated by author.*

Bottom: Horse markings. *Wikimedia Commons; labels by author.*

GLOSSARY

See endnotes for sources consulted.[353]

advance-deposit wagering (ADW). Gambling where bettors pre-fund an account. Used for internet wagering.

allowance. 1) Race where weights carried by the horses are based on conditions—such as the horse's age, sex, or past performance. 2) Adjustment in weight a horse carries, examples include when an apprentice is riding, for three-year-olds running against older horses, or for female horses running against males.

American Quarter Horse. Horse breed that excels at sprinting short distances and handling cattle. Breed registry founded in 1940. Name derives from the ability to outdistance other breeds in races of a quarter mile or less. *See also* Quarter-miler.

Andalusian. *Pura Raza Española* or "Pure Spanish Horse." Powerfully built, agile, valued by the Spanish as a war horse. Pedigrees date to the 1300s. *See also* Spanish horse.

Appaloosa. Horse breed developed by the Nez Perce. Recognized by a pattern of small spots distributed over the hindquarters or entire body. Appaloosas are raced in the western United States. *Compare* Pinto, Paint.

AQHA. American Quarter Horse Association.

Arabian. "Oriental" breed that provided foundation bloodstock for the Thoroughbred and many other light horse breeds, including some Spanish horses. Recognized by refined appearance and high-carried tail. Dominant today in endurance racing. Arabians do some flat-track racing.

auction pool, "Calcutta." Wagering where bettors bid on a contestant. Collected wagers are pooled and paid out to the winners.

backside. Location of the horse stables, usually on the side of the track opposite the grandstands.

backstretch. 1) Track straightaway farthest from the grandstands. 2) The backside.

bay. Reddish-brown body with a black mane and tail. Lower legs are black unless white markings are present. The Jockey Club records darker variants as "dark bay or brown."

book. 1) Bookmaker's records. 2) Jockey's riding commitments. 3) List of mares scheduled to be bred to a stallion.

bookmaking. Accepting bets from multiple people, recording bets in a ledger or "book." Bookmakers ("bookies") offer fixed odds to a client at the time of the bet, hold money, pay out winnings, and keep a set fee for themselves. Historically, bookmaking was considered disreputable and corruption was common. *Compare* Parimutuel.

bowed tendon. Torn tendon, a common racehorse injury. Requires months of healing and can be career-ending. Most occur on a front leg.

buckskin. A yellow-gold body color and a black mane, tail, and lower legs. Often confused with dun.

bug. An apprentice jockey, allowed a lower weight. Term comes from the "bug" or asterisk in the racing program designating such riders.

Bute. Slang for phenylbutazone, trade name Butazolidin. Used on horses to treat fever, pain, and inflammation.

chestnut. 1) Reddish-brown coat color; mane and tail the same shade or lighter. Varies from a bright reddish-brown (sometimes called "red" or "sorrel") to a dark chocolate brown ("liver chestnut"). 2) Callus-like growths on the inside of all four legs.

chute. Track extensions at the backstretch or homestretch. Used as the starting point for certain distances so horses do not have to start on a turn.

claiming race. Lower-level race. Horses entered can be purchased by other licensed owners at a set price. Horses in such races may be called "claimers."

closer. Horse that runs best late in the race, a "come from behind" horse.

clubhouse turn. First turn on the track. Named for the racetrack clubhouse, often nearby.

colors, racing colors (silks). 1) Colored jacket and cap worn by a jockey. 2) Recorded designs to uniquely identify the owner of the horse. 3) At smaller tracks, "track silks" designate post positions. (For example, red for post position one, white for two, etc.).

colt. In racing, a male horse four years old and younger. In other contexts, age three and under. Baby horses of either sex are "foals."

conditions. 1) Requirements to enter a race, such as horse's age, sex, money, or races won, etc. 2) Other race details, such as weight carried by the horse and distance. The "conditions book" outlines the races offered.

conformation. Horse's build and general physical structure.

connections. A horse's owner, trainer, jockey, etc.

cutter. Lightweight sleigh. In modern racing, a stripped-down chariot-style vehicle pulled over snow.

dash. Race decided in a single run, not by multiple heats. Most common type of race today, though the term has faded from use.

derby. Special stakes races for three-year-olds, such as Kentucky Derby, Montana Derby, and so forth. Similar races for fillies only are titled "Oaks."

dun. Light tan or gold coat, with dark mane, tail, legs, and "primitive markings," including a dark dorsal stripe down the spine. Often confused with buckskin.

exacta. Wager where the bettor chooses the first two horses to finish, in order.

exotic bet. Any wager other than to win, place, or show. Examples include exacta, trifecta, pick three, and so on.

fast track. Track condition where the footing is dry and even.

filly. In racing, a female horse four years old and younger. In other contexts, one three and under.

flat race. Running race that is not over fences.

foal. Baby horse of either sex, under a year old.

furlong. One-eighth of a mile. Used to measure the distances on a track.

futurity. Special stakes races for two-year-olds.

gallop. Fastest gait of the horse, averaging 25–30 miles per hour. Quarter Horses have been clocked for short distances at 55 miles per hour; Thoroughbred record is just under 44 miles per hour.

gelding. Castrated male horse, any age.

graded stakes. Highest-quality Thoroughbred races in North America, ranked Grade I, II, or III. *See* stakes.

grade horse. Horse of mixed or unknown breeding.

gray. Horses born with a dark coat color that slowly lightens with age until mostly white. Skin remains dark (except under markings). Intermediate stages sometimes confused with roan. Mature grays are still called gray, not "white."

Hambletonian. 1) Rysdyk's Hambletonian, foaled 1849, foundation sire of the Standardbred. 2) Hambletonian Stakes, a major trotting race.

hand. Four inches. Measures horse height at the highest point of the withers. 15 hands equals 60 inches, 15.3=63 inches, 16.0=64 inches, and so on.

handicap. 1) Race where the track handicapper assigns the weights carried by each horse, based on past performances. 2) Selecting horses in a race on the basis of past performances.

handle. Total amount of money wagered for a day, a meet, or a year. *Compare* takeout.

heat. 1) A preliminary trial. Used in harness racing, Indian Relay and Quarter Horse racing, no longer common in Thoroughbred racing. *Contrast* dash. 2) Informal term for estrus in a filly or mare.

hit the board. To finish a race in the top four, and thus to win some purse money. Literally, to appear on the tote board.

homestretch, stretch. Final racetrack straightway leading to the finish line.

in the money. 1) Finishing in the top three, where bettors win money. 2) Finishing in the top four, where horses win prize money.

Lasix, Salix. Trade names for furosemide, a medication common on modern racetracks. Prevents and treats exercise-induced pulmonary hemorrhage (EIPH), which produces blood in the lungs, or "bleeding."

length. Eight feet, a horse's average length from nose to tail. Denotes distance between racehorses. Increments under a half-length are designated by the body part ahead of the trailing horse, i.e. neck, head, nose.

maiden. 1) Horse that has never won a race. 2) Race for maiden horses.

mare. In racing, a female horse age five and older. In other contexts, one four and older.

markings. White patterns on a horse, unique and often used to assist identification. *See* Horse Markings diagram on page 220.

match race. Head to head race between two competitors (occasionally more).

Morgan. American horse breed founded circa 1790 by the stallion Figure, aka Justin Morgan.

morning line. Odds calculated by the track handicapper, an estimate of probable final odds.

Mustang. Feral horses of the American west. From Spanish, *mesteño*, "wild, untamed." Originally Spanish Colonial stock, most modern Mustangs have mixed ancestry from horses brought by successive waves of settlers.

off-track betting (**OTB**). Race betting outside of a racetrack. *See also* simulcasting.

O-Mok-See. Timed pattern racing and games on horseback. Called "Gymkhana" outside the American West.

Oriental horse. Ancient horses of the Middle East, specifically the Arabian, Barb, and Turkoman. Foundation stock for the Thoroughbred and other light horse breeds.

pace. 1) The speed of any race. 2) Specific two-beat gait used in harness racing where the horse's legs move in lateral pairs, clocked up to 34 miles per hour when racing, slightly faster than the trot.

pacer. Harness horse that races at the pace. *Compare* trotter.

Paint. 1) American Paint Horse, pinto-spotted breed developed from Quarter Horses and Thoroughbreds, raced in the United States. 2) Historically, one of many words describing pinto horses. *See* Pinto.

palomino. A golden body color and a white or cream-colored mane and tail.

parimutuel. Primary method of horse race betting in the United States. From the French *parier mutuel*: "mutual stake," "betting among ourselves." Totals wagered determine the odds on each horse, which fluctuate until betting closes at post time. All money bet—minus the takeout—is divided up among winning tickets. Calculations of wagering pools and odds are continually updated prior to post time via a Totalizator and displayed on a tote board.

pinto. Pattern of large patches of body white over a darker base color. Many different words describe various pinto patterns. *Compare* Appaloosa, Paint.

place (bet). Wager for a horse to finish first or second. *See also* win, show.

pole. Markers placed along a racecourse showing the distance to the finish. One-sixteenth mile poles are black and white striped; eighth poles, green and white; quarter poles, red and white.

pony. 1) Small horses maturing under 14.2 hands. 2) Colloquial diminutive for horses regardless of height, e.g. "track pony," "playing the ponies."

post. 1) Starting point for a race. 2) Post position.

post parade. When the horses in a race are brought onto the track and led past the grandstands.

post position. Numbered stall in the starting gate, corresponds to the number on the horse.

post time. When horses are ready to load into the gate and betting closes for the race.

Quarter horse. *See* American Quarter Horse.

quarter-miler. Sprinters with powerful hindquarters. Ancestors of the American Quarter Horse.

quinella. Wager for two horses to finish first and second, in either order.

rabbit. Horse entered to set a sacrificial fast pace early, encouraging other horses to use up their speed too soon.

ringer. Horse entered in place of another, usually to fool bettors and opponents.

roan. Coat color of intermixed white and dark body hairs. Sometimes confused with gray. The Jockey Club records some horses as "gray or roan."

running race. Race at a gallop. Contrasted with harness races at a trot or pace.

show (bet). Wager for a horse to finish first, second, or third. *See also* win, place.

silks. See colors.

simulcast. Live broadcast of a horse race to multiple locations for the purpose of wagering.

sorrel. Western term for a chestnut horse, especially Quarter Horses.

Spanish horse/Colonial Spanish horse. Horses brought to the Americas by the Spanish. Stocky and agile ancestors of many American horse breeds.

sprint. Race of less than a mile.

stakes. 1) Prizes offered to winners. 2) Higher-level races entered by invitation or by paid fees to nominate, enter, and start.

stalker. Horse that runs just behind the front-running horses, within striking distance of the lead.

stallion. In racing, an uncastrated male horse five years old and older. In other contexts, one four and older.

Standardbred. Breed developed for harness racing by crossing Thoroughbreds on trotting and pacing horses. Registry founded 1879.

steeplechase, hurdle race. Race over jumps.

straight bet. Wager to win, place or show. All others are exotic bets.

sulky. Light two-wheeled cart used for harness racing.

superfecta. Wager where the bettor chooses the first four horses to finish, in order.

tack. 1) Horse equipment. 2) Putting tack on a horse ("tacking up"). 3) Jockey's weight with equipment ("He tacked at 126").

takeout, "take." Percentage of money deducted from parimutuel pools prior to payouts. Some is used by the track for certain expenses, some goes to taxes. *Compare* handle.

Thoroughbred. 1) Racing breed with ancestry tracing to any of three foundation sires circa 1680–1724: the Darley Arabian, Byerley Turk, and Godolphin Arabian. Must also meet the current rules and requirements of The Jockey Club. "Any other horse, no matter what its parentage, is not considered a Thoroughbred for racing and/or breeding purposes."[354] 2) (*archaic*) Any purebred animal.

Tobiano. A pinto coat pattern characterized by rounded and distinct markings.

Totalizator, "tote." Automated parimutuel calculation equipment. Records bets, dispenses tickets, calculates odds and payoffs, pays winning tickets.

tote board, odds board. Public totalizator display. Shows official time, minutes to post, odds, results, and payouts.

track pony. Horse (any size) used to lead a racehorse on the track.

trifecta. Wager where the bettor chooses the first three horses to finish, in order.

trot. Two-beat gait where the horse's legs move in diagonal pairs. Ordinary horses average 8 miles per hour, racing trotters clocked up to 33 miles per hour. *See* pace.

trotter. 1) Harness horse that races at the trot. 2) Generically, all harness racing horses.

turf. 1) Horse racing or racetracks generally ("the turf"). 2) A grass-covered track ("turf course").

walkover. Race with only one horse, who still must travel from start to finish to be awarded the win.

white. Horse born with a white coat and pinkish skin. Distinguished from mature grays by skin color. Inaccurately, "albino"—albinism does not occur in horses.

wild horse race. Competition where teams attempt to saddle and ride unbroken horses around the track.

win (bet). Wager for a horse to finish first. *See also* place, show.

yearling. Horse of either sex between one and two years old.

NOTES

Abbreviations

The following abbreviations appear in the endnotes:

DRF: *Daily Racing Form*
MBOHR: Montana Horse Racing Commission (1966–1972)/Montana
    Board of Horse Racing (1973–present)
MHS: Montana Historical Society, Helena
MNAI: Montana Newspaper Association Inserts
NRHP: National Register of Historic Places

Introduction

1. "Montana and Its Racing," Keeneland Racing Association Library
   and the University of Kentucky, Daily Racing Form Historical Online
   Archive, https://drf.uky.edu. Source of all *DRF* entries prior to 1940.
   September 12, 1896.
2. *Montana Constitution*, Article III, section 9.

Chapter 1

3. Sweeney, "When Old and New Worlds Met."

4. Bennett, *Conquerors*, 193–97, 329–31; Sweeney, "When Old and New Worlds Met"; Kirkpatrick and Fazio, "Surprising History"; Gokey, "Feral vs. Wild Horses."

5. Powell, "Story of the Horse"; Haines, *Horses in America*, 51–53; Cowdrey et al., *Horses & Bridles*, 9–12, 41; Forbes, "Appearance of the Mounted Indian," 189–212.

6. Smithsonian, *Song for the Horse Nation*, "Horses Spread Across the Land"; Kelekna, *Horse in Human History*, 371–72.

7. Viola, "Horse Culture," 90–91; Haines, "Northward Spread of Horses," 434; Haines, *Horses in America*, 51; Ambrose, *Undaunted Courage*, 273; Cowdrey et al., *Horses & Bridles*, 8–9.

8. Smithsonian, *Song for the Horse Nation*, "Horse Trading Among Nations"; Cowdrey et al., *Horses & Bridles*, 2, 8–10.

9. "Flathead Indian Book Coming Soon," MNAI, July 27, 1936; Turney-High, *Flathead Indians*, 106–8; Cowdrey et al., *Horses & Bridles*, 8–10.

10. Cowdrey et al., *Horses & Bridles*, 8–9; Medicine Crow, *Crow Country*, 13, 100–101; "Apsáalooke Historical Timeline," Little Big Horn College, 2018, http://lib.lbhc.edu/index.php?q=node/129.

11. Smithsonian, *Song for the Horse Nation*, "Naming a New Ally"; Frantz and Russell, *Blackfoot Dictionary*, 192.

12. Cowdrey et al., *Horses & Bridles*, 8–9; Wissler, "Influence of the Horse," 5; Haines, "Northward Spread of Horses," 434; Wischmann, *Frontier Diplomats*, 18, 73.

13. Ambrose, *Undaunted Courage*, 276–77, 283, 285; Moulton, *Lewis and Clark Journals*, Meriwether Lewis journal, August 14, 1805; William Clark journal, September 5, 1805.

14. Moulton, *Lewis and Clark Journals*, Meriwether Lewis journal, February 15, 1806, and July 2, 1806.

15. Hamilton, *My Sixty Years*, 121–22, 184–85, 236.

16. Ibid., 189–92.

17. Medicine Crow, *Crow Country*, 101–4.

Chapter 2

18. Overholser, *Fort Benton*, 133.
19. Barbour, *Fort Union*, 29–30, 130; Plain, *This Strange Wilderness*, 81; Agonito, *Brave Hearts*, 53.
20. Dempsey, "Natawista"; Wischmann, *Frontier Diplomats*, 20–21, 91; National Park Service, "Powerful Woman Then and Now."
21. From oral history, circa 1855, told to Bob Doerk by Rufus Good Striker, November 20, 2000, relayed by Doerk circa 2005 to Ken Robison, historian, Overholser Historical Research Center, Fort Benton, Montana; Dempsey, *Amazing Death of Calf Shirt*, 62–63, 234.
22. Harden, "Across the New Northwest," 289, 292; Overholser, *Fort Benton*, 165; Robison, *Montana Territory*, 23; Grant, *Very Close to Trouble*, 88.
23. "Caused by His Son's Violent Death," *Butte Miner*, October 10, 1888; "Last Day at the Races," *Butte Weekly Miner*, August 28, 1889.
24. "Race Meet Shatters Handle Record," *Big Sandy Mountaineer*, May 30, 1974.
25. Bev Tomaskie and John Tomaskie, author interview, July 22, 2018; Tom Tucker, author interview and email correspondence, June–October 2018.

Chapter 3

26. Dimsdale, *Vigilantes*, 181.
27. *Montana Post*, November 19, 1864; Baumler, "Montana's Horse Racing History Runs Deep"; Towle, *Vigilante Woman*, 125, 144.
28. Sanders, *History*, 229.
29. Dimsdale, *Vigilantes*, 176–77.
30. Baumler, NRHP, 2; Ronan and Ronan, *Girl from the Gulches*, 39–41; Sanders, *History*, 229; Towle, *Vigilante Woman*, 123–51.
31. Ronan and Ronan, *Girl from the Gulches*, 40–41.
32. *New North-West*, November 4, 1870, November 18, 1870; Writers' Program of the Work Projects Administration [hereafter WPA], *Montanans' Golden Anniversary*, 112.
33. Untitled, November 6, 1890, vertical file, "Slade, Virginia," MHS.
34. Baumler, *Spirit Tailings*, 8–14; Towle, *Vigilante Woman*, 150–51.
35. *Montana Post*, September 2, 1865; "Forty-Eight Years Since Famous Race," *Anaconda Standard*, July 4, 1913; WPA, *Montanans' Golden Anniversary*, 112–13.

Chapter 4

36. Stuart, *Forty Years*, 183.
37. Grant, *Very Close to Trouble*, 16, 40, 86–87.
38. Ibid., 45–46, 50, 62, 76, 88, 91.
39. Kohrs, *Conrad Kohrs*, 50–51, 72
40. "Grant-Kohrs Ranch National Historic Site (proposed)," EIS, National Park Service, 1973.
41. "A Stallion for the $1500 Purse," *Independent Record*, August 19, 1876; John Milner Associates Inc., "Grant-Kohrs Ranch Cultural Landscape Report, part 1," National Park Service, July 2004; obituary, "Death of John Bielenberg," *Breeder's Gazette*, July 13, 1922, 47; Kohrs, *Conrad Kohrs*, 72; Melin-Moser, "In the Winner's Circle," 23.
42. Grant-Kohrs Ranch Foundation, Facebook post, May 15, 2015.
43. Kohrs, *Conrad Kohrs*, 96–97.
44. *New North-West*, October 18, 1878, October 17, 1879.
45. "Noteworthy Turf Events," *The Sun*, February 6, 1887; "John D. Morrissey," *Nebraska State Journal*, April 13, 1887; "Sporting Notes," *St. Louis Post-Dispatch*, November 19, 1888; Klotz, "Deer Lodge Firm," January 1, 1922.
46. *New North-West*, July 30, 1869.
47. *New North-West*, July 9, 1869, August 6, 1869; Meikle, KQRV interview.
48. *Anaconda Standard*, August 31, 1926, September 5, 1938; MBOHR reports.

Chapter 5

49. Alexie, "Horses."
50. Lowney, "Noah Armstrong"; Nardinger, *Spirit Horse*, 13–20; Sowers, *Kentucky Derby*, 370; Mooney, "Spokane."
51. Axline, NRHP.
52. Nardinger, *Spirit Horse*, 34.
53. Keyes, *Fifty Years' Observations*, 272–73.
54. Treaty with the Yakima, June 9, 1855, 12 Stat., 951, Ratified Mar. 8, 1859, Proclaimed Apr. 18, 1859; Meyers, "It Happened"; "Yakama Nation History," http://www.yakamanation-nsn.gov/history3.php; McFarland, *Edward J. Steptoe*, 176; Keyes, *Fifty Years' Observations*, 272–73; Lutey, "Marker Recalls 1858 Slaughter"; Nardinger, *Spirit Horse*, 5–14; Petit, "Slaughter of Horses"; Ruby and Brown, "Fire on the Prairie," in *Spokane Indians*, 114–40.

55. Alexie, "Horses."

56. Nardinger, *Spirit Horse*, 3.

57. *The Madisonian*, June 1, 1889.

58. "Snoqualmie Tribe Remembers Esteemed Member Harriet Estelle Turner," *Native News Online*, June 26, 2015; Nardinger, *Spirit Horse*, 34; Susan R. Nardinger, author interview, August 20, 2018; Ruby and Brown, *Spokane Indians*, 8.

59. Emery, "1889 Derby Winner." The article names the filly "Madelin," but other records show Interpose's 1885 filly was named Helena.

60. Mooney, "Spokane."

61. Nardinger, *Spirit Horse*, 49–60; Mooney, "Spokane."

62. Sowers, *Kentucky Derby*, 39.

63. Briggeman, "1889 Derby Winner."

64. *Bourbon News*, December 2, 1898; *Courier-Journal*, December 1, 1898; Rees, "1889 Spokane."

65. *Anaconda Standard*, April 22, 1898; *Courier-Journal*, May 10, 1898; Nardinger, *Spirit Horse*, 140, 143–44; Nardinger, interview.

66. Spokane Chamber of Commerce newsletter, in "Spokane," vertical file, History Museum, Great Falls, Montana.

Chapter 6

67. Ashley, "Off the Record."

68. *Montana Post*, August 31, 1867.

69. *Montana Post*, August 28, 1868; Baumler NRHP, 5; Baird, "Fairgrounds."

70. Putz, *Lewis and Clark County Fairgrounds*, 4, fn 3; Baird, "Fairgrounds."

71. Baumler, NRHP, 5; Wahler, "Race Day in Great Falls," 38; WPA, *Montanans' Golden Anniversary*, 82.

72. Baumler, NRHP, 5–6; Putz, *Lewis and Clark County Fairgrounds*, 4–5, fn 3.

73. "The Turf," *New York Times*, August 2, 1876; *Helena Weekly Herald*, October 5, 1876.

74. "Among the Horses," *Missoulian*, January 27, 1895; "Hugh Kirkendall Dead," *Dupuyer Acantha*, April 22, 1897; "Butte Horses Will Enter the Events," *Butte Daily Post*, July 27, 1903; Baumler, NRHP, 6–7.

75. Baumler, NRHP, 6–7.

76. Ibid.

77. *Codes and Statutes of Montana*, §530, §§1,195–196 (1895); Jockey Club, "History of the Jockey Club."

78. Putz, *Lewis and Clark County Fairgrounds*, 6.

79. "Betting Revival on Races," *Great Falls Tribune*, February 1, 1921; Baumler, NRHP, 7–8; Putz, *Lewis and Clark County Fairgrounds*, 6.
80. *Butte Miner*, May 17, 1910, August 7, 1912; "Fourteen States Have Ponies Here," *Anaconda Standard*, June 27, 1913; obituary, "George Cooney, 76, Helena Pioneer and Racehorse Breeder, Dies," *Great Falls Tribune*, April 9, 1942.
81. Baird, "Fairgrounds"; Baumler, NRHP, 8; Putz, *Lewis and Clark County Fairgrounds*, 9; Tomaskie, interview.
82. "Racing Official, Cash Missing," *Billings Gazette*, December 11, 1977; Hutchinson, "Helena Horse Racing"; Pace, "Board Won't Relieve Threat."
83. Tomaskie, interview.
84. Ibid.
85. Ibid.
86. David Neu, "Montana's Fast Horses," undated article in Tomaskie clipping file; Abraham, "Granny's Not Exactly"; Equibase, "Montskaia"; Tomaskie, interview.
87. Equibase, "Super Ciel"; Tomaskie, interview.
88. "Results," *Racing Journal*, December 1995; Mendyke, "Dance De Kas."
89. Equibase, "Super Ciel."
90. *Montana Constitution*, Article III, section 9; Geise, "Many Questions"; Tucker, "Live Racing Breakdown"; Tomaskie, interview.
91. Testimony on SB 446, Senate Committee on Taxation, March 14, 1991; *History and Final Status*, Montana 52nd Legislature Regular Session, 1991.
92. Mohr, "Yeas and Neighs"; Kline, "Whoa There!"; *Save the Track Found., Inc. v. Tinsley*, First Judicial District Court, Lewis and Clark County, Cause no. CDV 2005-497; Kline, "Pricey!"
93. Anderson, "Railbird Predicts Good Year."

Chapter 7

94. Powell, *Copper, Green and Silver*, 95.
95. "Butte Track Twenty Years Old," *DRF*, July 3, 1907; *Butte Weekly Miner*, August 20, 1878; *New North-West*, October 18, 1878; *Butte Weekly Miner*, July 13, 1880.
96. *Butte Weekly Miner*, June 30, 1886; "Paris Mutuals," *River Press*, August 18, 1886; untitled clipping, vertical file "Horse Racing," MHS.
97. Shoebotham, *Anaconda*, 147.

235

98. *Butte Miner*, April 28, 1886; *Butte Daily Post*, June 29, 1887; *New North-West*, July 8, 1887; Kohrs, *Conrad Kohrs*, 96–97.

99. Shoebotham, *Anaconda*, 150; "A New Turfman," *DRF*, October 7, 1902.

100. *Butte Daily Post*, March 31, 1890; *Independent Record*, May 23, 1890; Shoebotham, *Anaconda*, 150; Van Duyne, "Old Race Track"; Young, "Bob Wade."

101. *Goodwin's*, 1899, vol. 1, cxxii; Chamberlain, "Bob Wade"; Denhardt, *Foundation Sires*, 64–65.

102. Markham, "Montana Sports Tales."

103. *Anaconda Standard*, August 15–August 30, 1890; Young, "Bob Wade."

104. *American Racing Manual* 1959, 800–801; *American Racing Manual* 1958, 811; AQHA, World Records, aqha.com.

105. Glasscock, *War of the Copper Kings*, loc 1906.

106. Racetrack Park memorial marker; untitled clipping, vertical file "Horse Racing," Butte-Silver Bow Public Archives.

107. Kohrs, *Conrad Kohrs*, 96.

108. "Butte Has the Racing Fever in Its Most Virulent Form," *Anaconda Standard*, April 29, 1901.

109. "Broken Second Time on Butte Track," *Anaconda Standard*, August 24, 1906.

110. "Record Broken Again," *Anaconda Standard*, August 8, 1906; Markham, "Montana Sports Tales"; "World Turf Record Falls at Anita," *Montana Standard*, February 2, 1946; "Horse Breaks World Record Set in Butte," *Montana Standard*, December 2, 1967.

111. Laidlaw, "Not Hostile."

112. Chapter 92, *Laws of Montana*, 1909.

113. *State v. Rose*, 40 Mont. 66 (1909); *State v. Sylvester*, 40 Mont. 79 (1909); "Ed Sylvester Convicted," *Butte Miner*, June 22, 1909. For a different telegraph betting scam, see *State v. Postal Tel. Cable Co.*, 53 Mont. 104 (1916).

114. "The Racing Situation," *Butte Miner*, August 5, 2011; "Test Case Before District Court," *Butte Daily Post*, April 17, 1912; "Jockey Club Wins Race Track Case," *Anaconda Standard*, April 18, 1912; *State v. Gemmell*, 45 Mont. 210 (1912).

115. "The Racing Situation," *Butte Miner*, August 5, 2011; "Test Case Before District Court," *Butte Daily Post*, April 17, 1912; "Jockey Club Wins Race Track Case," *Anaconda Standard*, April 18, 1912; *State v. Gemmell*, 45 Mont. 210 (1912).

116. Chapter 55, *Laws of Montana*, 1915.

117. "Horse Racing in State of Montana," *DRF*, April 12, 1919.

118. "House Fights; Pari-Mutuel Bill Survives," *Great Falls Tribune*, February 9, 1921.

119. "State Fair Racing Held Legal," *Independent Record*, April 17, 1926; "Butte's Five Big Days," *Anaconda Standard*, June 27, 1926; "Montana Court to Decide Legality," *Anaconda Standard*, November 13, 1925; *Toomey v. Penwell*, 76 Mont. 166 (1926); Early, "Gambling Is Evil."

120. "Woolf of Montana Outstanding Jockey," *Montana Standard*, February 28, 1943; "Sports Jabs," *Missoulian*, January 10, 1946; Lewyn, "Fiery Iceman"; "Red Pollard," "George Woolf," *American Experience*, pbs.org; Allison, *Southern Hoofprints*, 269–79; Hillenbrand, *Seabiscuit*, 52–54, 94; Laura Hillenbrand, personal correspondence, February 8, 2018. One Woolf biography says he rode in "Chinook." The February 25, 1935 *Missoulian* identified Woolf as "of Glacier Park, Mont." The March 10, 1938 *Montana Standard* stated Woolf was "of Browning, Mont."

121. Chapter 103, *Laws of Montana*, 1929.

122. *DRF*, May 26, 1930; "One Record Falls," *Great Falls Tribune*, July 5, 1930; "Flames Destroy Butte Race Plant," MNAI, September 21, 1936.

123. "Montana Horses in Plenty," *DRF*, June 12, 1897.

124. "Copper and Green Win," *Anaconda Standard*, July 3, 1892.

125. Bryson, "Creating," 157; Shoebotham, *Anaconda*, 162; Mike Menahan, author interview, 2018.

126. Morrison, Anaconda Saddle Club NRHP.

Chapter 8

127. Shoebotham, *Anaconda*, 153.

128. Owen, *Journals and Letters*, vol. 1, 125–26.

129. Salish language information from http://www.salishaudio.org/documents.

130. "Mr. Daly's Stable," *Butte Daily Post*, August 20, 1888.

131. "The Passing of Rancho Del Paso," *New York Times*, October 8, 1905; *Norris v. Haggin*, 136 U.S. 386 (1890); Robertson, *History*, 143.

132. "Cholly Francisco Observes," *San Francisco Examiner*, March 19, 1946.

133. Shoebotham, *Anaconda*, 177–78; Powell, *Dalys*, 4–5.

134. Powell, *Copper, Green and Silver*, 46–48; annotations to image DA-03.025, RCM.

135. Powell, *First 100 Years*, unpaginated; *Stallions at the Marcus Daly Bitterroot Farm*, 1892, oil on canvas, Henry H. Cross, Daly Mansion Collection, Mansfield Library, University of Montana.

136. Powell, *Copper, Green and Silver*, 31; Robertson, *History*, 147; Shoebotham, *Anaconda*, 168, 179. Today, the Hagyard clinic is the Hagyard Equine Medical Institute, https://www.hagyard.com/about.

137. "Horses for the Japanese," *Ravalli Republic*, August 11, 1905; *Montana Standard*, March 29, 1929.

138. Daly annotation, 1896; "Montana's Greatest Turfman," *DRF*, December 22, 1912; Shoebotham, *Anaconda*, 162; Robertson, *History*, 146; Powell, *Copper, Green and Silver*, 49.

139. Daly annotation, 1896; Powell, *Copper, Green and Silver*, 10–22; Shoebotham, *Anaconda*, 157.

140. *Butte Daily Post*, October 10, 1893, October 30, 1893; Powell, *Copper, Green and Silver*, 21.

141. Powell, *Copper, Green and Silver*, 38; Shoebotham, *Anaconda*, 157–58.

142. Daly annotation, 1896.

143. Ibid.; "The Chieftain," *Western News*, June 2, 1897.

144. Powell, *Copper, Green and Silver*, 24–33; "Hamburg," National Museum of Racing and Hall of Fame.

145. Powell, *Copper, Green and Silver*, 24–33; "Hamburg," National Museum of Racing and Hall of Fame.

146. "Hamburg," National Museum of Racing and Hall of Fame.

147. Cathro, "Commentary."

148. Gocher, *Fasig's Tales*, 162–65.

149. "Daly Estate Horse Sale," *New York Times*, December 25, 1900.

150. "Whitney Buys Hamburg," *New York Times*, January 31, 1901.

151. Ibid.

152. "Madden Buys Ogden," *Courier-Journal*, December 17, 1901; "Notes of the Turf," *DRF*, December 25, 1901; "Ogden a Successful Sire," *DRF*, February 2, 1923; Palmer, "Ogden," 312–13.

153. Gocher, *Fasig's Tales*, 162–65; progeny research by Victoria Short.

154. Powell, *Copper, Green and Silver*, 39; Robertson, *History*, 186–88; "Mounted skeleton and model of racehorse Sysonby, at moment of suspension in fast run, left side view," K13812, American Museum of Natural History.

155. *Western News*, July 7, 1909; *Ravalli Republic*, July 23, 1909; Powell, *Copper, Green and Silver*, 40; Robertson, *History*, 147.

156. Owen, *Journals and Letters*, vol. 2, 28, 143.

157. Fairgrounds deed, June 6, 1913, courtesy Daly Mansion; Delaney, "Hamilton Fair Grounds."

158. Land records, Ravalli County Clerk and Recorder.

Chapter 9

159. "What It Takes: The Campaign for Montana State University," *Confluence 2016–2017*, College of Letters and Science, Montana State University, December 22, 2016, 36.

160. *Bozeman Avant-Courier*, October 18, 1871; "Gallatin City Items," *Bozeman Avant-Courier*, January 25, 1872; Meikle, KQRV interview.

161. *Goodwin's* 1905, vol. 2 (no page given); "Premium Lists and Rules," 1926, 1927 MHS Archives 394.6 P91g.

162. Merritt, "Index to the MNAI Inserts"; MNAI, October 3, 1935.

163. "Jockey Had Early Interest in Races," *Billings Gazette*, May 6, 1935; "William (Smokey) Saunders, Hall of Fame Inductee, 1976," *Canadian Horse Racing Hall of Fame*; Saunders obituary, *Evening Independent*, August 1, 1986; "Derby Wins of the Triple Crown Victors: Omaha," *Blood-Horse*, April 25, 2017; Allison, *Southern Hoofprints*, 279–80.

164. Obituary, "Lloyd Shelhamer, Jr.," *Helena Independent Record*, October 23, 2010; Thomas, "High-Tech Firm."

165. "Ranch Girl to Circus Boss," *Cincinnati Enquirer*, April 22, 1943; Shelhamer obituary.

166. Helton, "Beaumont Club"; Malby, "Faded Glory"; Thomas, "High-Tech Firm"; Holly Burrows, author interview, July 27–28, 2018.

167. Helton, "Beaumont Club"; Malby, "Faded Glory"; Thomas, "High-Tech Firm"; Holly Burrows, author interview, July 27–28, 2018.

168. "Thrills, Spills, Excitement Assured for First Cutter Races at the Beaumont," *Gallatin County Tribune and Belgrade Journal*, February 3, 1955.

169. Smith, "Faded Glory"; Thomas, "High-Tech Firm."

170. Jessica Hanke, AQHA manager of racing, email correspondence May–September 2018; Smith, "Faded Glory"; Tucker, interview.

171. MBOHR 1966 report; Smith, "Faded Glory"; Thomas, "High-Tech Firm"; "United Tote Company," Bloomberg.com; Tucker, interview.

172. Research by Victoria Short.

173. Tucker, interview.

174. Smith, "Faded Glory"; Malby, "Faded Glory"; Tucker, interview.

Chapter 10

175. Phyllis Tryon, "The Last Goodbye," copyright 1995, Phyllis Tryon, used with permission.
176. Moulton, *Lewis and Clark Journals*, William Clark journal, July 2, 1806.
177. Gordon, "Progress at a Price," 133–34; Mathews, *Guide*, 7–17.
178. *Anaconda Standard*, July 20, 1895; Koelbel, *Missoula*, 82.
179. *Helena Weekly Herald*, September 5, 1889; *New North-West*, February 22, 1889; Cave, "Real Fair Record"; Kim Briggeman, email correspondence, March–December 2018.
180. Koelbel, *Missoula*, 82.
181. Cohen and Jordonnais, *Western Montana Fair*, 21; Cohen, *Missoula County Images*, 173; Caywood, Missoula NRHP, 20; Briggeman, correspondence.
182. Cohen and Jordonnais, *Western Montana Fair*, 40, 42, 49–52.
183. *Missoulian*, September 17, 1954; Rocene, "Sports Jabs"; Caywood, Missoula NRHP, 23.
184. Ruth Rodenberger obituary, *Missoulian*, May 1, 2010.
185. Beecham, "Fair Fire."
186. "Horse Barn Fire Toll Tabulated," *Missoulian*, August 27, 1967; *Haynes v. County of Missoula*, 163 Mont. 270 (1973).
187. Lori Freeman, author interview, September 15, 2018, and email correspondence; Martin Elison, author interview, September 30, 2018.
188. Sec. 11, Ch. 196, L. 1965, first codified at sec. 62-511 Revised Codes of Montana
189. "Work Is Started on Track," *Great Falls Tribune*, November 24, 1966; "Torts, Tomes, 'n Racing Silks," *Billings Gazette*, February 26, 1967.
190. Elison, interview.
191. "Schubert Guides Le Cherro to Marcus Daly Triple Crown," *Missoulian*, September 4, 1978; Equibase, "Le Cherro."
192. Freeman, interview; Elison, interview.
193. Tucker, "Live Racing Breakdown."
194. Madden, "Racing Commission"; Hutchinson, "Board Seeks Ouster"; Early, "Parimutuel Fray."
195. Early, "Parimutuel Fray."
196. MBOHR, Fifth Annual Report.
197. Equibase, "Flying Catman"; Toni Hinton, author interview and email correspondence March–November, 2018.

198. Paulick, "Death"; "Agricultural Processing Industry Directory," Alberta Ministry of Agriculture and Forestry, http://www.agric.gov.ab.ca/a68/foodindustry.
199. Tucker, "Live Racing Breakdown."
200. Cohen, "Turf Club"; "Western Montana Turf Club Promotes Horse Racing," *Racing Journal*, August 2002; Briggeman, correspondence; Hinton, interview; Tucker, "Live Racing Breakdown."
201. Andrews, "They're Off."
202. Christian, "Missoula County Commissioners"; Kidston, "Turf Club."

Chapter 11

203. Van West, *Images of Billings*, 14; Wright, *Billings*, 35.
204. Reich, *Billings*, 75; Van West, *Images of Billings*, 37.
205. "Retrospective: A Century on the Midway," *Billings Gazette*, August 6, 2015; Stevens and Redman, *Billings*, 42, 75; Van West, *Images of Billings*, 37.
206. Wischmann, *Frontier Diplomats*, 67–75; Diamond, *Guns, Germs and Steel*, 78, 212.
207. Clawson and Shandera, *Billings*, 17, 20; obituary, "Roger Wayne Clawson," *Billings Gazette*, October 10, 2015. On smallpox generally, see Diamond, *Guns, Germs and Steel*, chapter 11.
208. Clawson and Shandera, *Billings*, 20.
209. "Close Finishes Furnish Thrills for Grandstand," *Billings Gazette*, September 7, 1928; "4-H Club Exhibits," *Great Falls Tribune*, September 8, 1928; "Printer Takes Feature Event," *Billings Gazette*, September 12, 1931.
210. Goodman, "Supaman."
211. Bighaus, "Amundson Coming Back"; Bighaus, "Amundson to Retrace."
212. Emmers, "…But No Petticoats."
213. Equibase, "William Shoemaker"; Tucker, correspondence.
214. Equibase, "Kym Powell/Kym Espy."
215. Tucker, "Live Racing Breakdown."
216. "New World Record Posted at Yellowstone Downs," *Racing Journal*, October 19, 2005.
217. Bighaus, "Despite Turmoil"; Bighaus, "Billings' Horse Racing"; "No Horse Racing in Billings in 2014," *Billings Gazette*, November 20, 2013.
218. Kordenbrock, "Riders."

Chapter 12

219. Krings, "Jockey Says."

220. *Montana Post*, April 25, 1868.

221. Leeson, *History*, 1277–78.

222. *Anaconda Standard*, April 26, 1895.

223. *Helena Weekly Herald*, August 23, 1883; Smith, *Montana's Madison County*, 110; Brown, Juisto and Ferris, *Hand Raised*, 100–101.

224. *Report of the Committee on Privileges and Elections of the United States Senate Relative to the Right and Title of William A. Clark to a Seat as Senator from the State of Montana United States*, 56th Cong., 1st sess., vol. 1052 (Washington, D.C.: Government Printing Office, 1900), 244; Brown, Juisto and Ferris, *Hand Raised*, 100–101; Leeson, *History*, 1277–78.

225. "Madison Equine Talk," *Anaconda Standard*, April 26, 1895; Gibson, "Mining City History."

226. "All Roads Lead to Twin Bridges Montana," brochure, circa 1909, Archives and Special Collections, Mansfield Library, University of Montana.

227. "Rapid Progress Made at Twin Bridges Fairgrounds," *Montana Standard*, April 12, 1936; McVey, "Great Horse"; "Derby Winner Once Trained in Bayers Barn," *Dillon Tribune*, November 7, 1981; Mikel N. Kallestad, delineator, MT-52 National Historic Buildings Survey, National Park Service, Library of Congress, 1984.

228. Sue Resch, author interview, February 12, 2018; Nardinger, *Spirit Horse*, xvi.

229. "Sidney Progressive Town, Says Cohen," *Anaconda Standard*, July 8, 1927.

230. Linebarger, "Larger and Better"; "Rosebud Fair Horse Racing Draws Crowds," *Great Falls Tribune*, September 11, 1925.

231. "A Brief History," rosebudcountyfair.com, November 2018; Tucker, "Live Racing Breakdown."

232. Sievert, NRHP.

233. Marylynn Donnelly, author interview, 2018; R.D. Mower, author interview, July 17, 2018.

234. "Birdrattler Memorial Highlights Shelby Races," *Great Falls Tribune*, July 24, 2004; Kavanaugh, *Shelby*, 1, 111.

235. Allison, *Southern Hoofprints*, 260, 269, 278–79; Joe Bird Rattler, author interview, July 14 and 27, 2018; Kavanaugh, *Shelby*, 142.

236. Resch, interview.

237. "Gopher Racing Returns to Marias Fair," *Missoulian*, June 12, 1986; Resch, interview.

238. Montana Legislature, Legislative History, Ch. 557, L. 1989, 16–17.

239. Baird, "Art of Tom Chapman"; Ehrman, "Equine Artist"; "Woodford Reserve Bourbon Releases 2009 Kentucky Derby® Bottle," Brown-Forman.com, March 30, 2009; August, "Tom Chapman's Second"; Burke, "Tom Chapman"; Equibase, "Thomas Chapman"; Tom Chapman, email correspondence, February–November 2018.

240. Reece, "Training Racers"; Mower, interview.

241. Priddy, "Mapping the Future"; "No Horse Racing at 2012 Northwest Montana Fair," *Flathead Beacon*, February 6, 2012.

242. Mintz, "Fast Facts."

243. Priddy, "Life."

244. Vogel, "Fallon County Fair"; Sutton, "Indian Relay Races"; Horse Nations Indian Relay Council, 2018 schedule.

Chapter 13

245. *Butte Daily Post*, July 27, 1903.

246. Agonito, *Brave Hearts*, 53.

247. *Butte Daily Post*, July 27, 1903; Baumler, NRHP, 7–8.

248. *Great Falls Tribune*, October 1, 1903; *Butte Daily Post*, July 5, 1904.

249. Hansen, "Happy Birthday."

250. Annotations, photo PAc 82-60.1m, MHS.

251. "Mother Berry, Queen of the Turf Makes First Plane Trip at 92," *Montana Standard*, June 25, 1946; Montana Newspaper Association, "Mother Berry's Home Destroyed"; "'Mother Berry' Will Mark 110th Birthday Today," *Independent Record*, June 21, 1964.

252. *Independent Record*, May 3, 1941.

253. "Woman Jockey Celebrates 104th Birthday," *Independent Record*, June 22, 1958; "Hardin Woman Notes 107th Birthday Today," *Missoulian*, April 30, 1966; Hansen, "Happy Birthday."

254. Wall, "Women Raced."

255. "Services Set Friday for Mother Berry," *Independent Record*, March 27, 1969.

256. Lipsyte, "Gal Jockey."

257. Chapter 196, Laws of Montana, 1965; Francis, "There's Penny"; MBOHR, Fifth Annual Report.

258. "Record Price for Bucker," *Billings Gazette*, May 20, 1969; "It Will Be Goodbye to Jockettes," *Great Falls Tribune*, July 4, 1969.

259. "Wyoming Oks Female Jockey," *Billings Gazette*, August 22, 1968.

260. "Acme Woman Off in Races," *Billings Gazette*, January 25, 1969; *Glasgow Courier*, "Montana's First Lady Jockey Is Native of County," August 6, 1970; Hanke, correspondence.

261. "Racing Season Opens at Miles," *Billings Gazette*, May 6, 1970; *Glasgow Courier*, "Montana's First Lady"; Lee, "Petite Lady Jockey."

262. "Girl Jockey Rides in Fair Opener," *Daily Inter-Lake*, August 14, 1969.

263. Suzy Wilson, author interview, February 9, 2018, August 30, 2018, and email correspondence.

264. Moore, "Girl Jockey"; *American Racing Manual*, 1971, A-327.

265. Wilson, interview.

266. Clawson, "Pretty 'Bug Boy'"; Robertson, "Favorites"; Krings, "Jockey Says."

267. Wilson, interview.

268. "Wilson Only Female Jockey at Marias Fair Races," *Shelby Promoter*, undated clipping, circa 1975; Robertson, "Favorites"; Wilson, interview.

269. Wilson, interview.

270. Equibase, "Sue Wilson," "S. Wilson"; *American Racing Manual*, 1977, A-499; Wilson, interview.

271. Robertson, "Women Have Big Day."

272. Equibase, "Holly Gervais"; Holly Gervais, author interview, June 28, July 14, July 27, 2018, and email correspondence.

273. Mansch, "Gervais Still Riding"; Gervais, interview.

274. Wood, "Female Jockeys"; Rainone, "Tough Game."

275. Von Hippel, Rutherford and Keyes, "Gender and Weight," 3; Gervais, interview.

276. McGee, "Greta Kuntzweiler's Second."

277. Lincoln, "Need.

Chapter 14

278. Contrary to popular legend, Comanche was not the only cavalry horse to survive, but suffering from seven bullet wounds, he was left on the battlefield and thus was the only living creature recovered.

279. Montana collection, Miles City Public Library; county maps, Custer County Clerk and Recorder; Hoopes, "Races"; Anglum, "Horseflesh," 69–72; Warhank, "Fort Keogh," 116, 119, 124.

280. Anglum, "Horseflesh," 69–72.

281. Rosenberg, "Hard Winter Endurance," 27.

282. *Yellowstone Journal*, December 20, 1885.

283. Gordon, *Recollections*; Hoopes, "Races."

284. *Sullivan v. Helena*, 10 Mont. 134 (1890).

285. Hoopes, "Races"; Warhank, "Fort Keogh," 118.

286. "Custer County Track Exempt," *Billings Gazette*, March 27, 1915.

287. 1929 Patent, courtesy Custer County Commissioners.

288. Moore, "Lockie Recalls 'Horses on Every Hill'," in *World Famous Miles City Jaycee Bucking Horse Sale*.

289. Freese, "From Idaho"; Warhank, "Fort Keogh," 66.

290. Anglum, "Horseflesh," 69–72; Moore, "Lockie Recalls 'Horses on Every Hill'."

291. "Half a Million Cayuses on Range," *Billings Gazette*, May 20, 1924; Moore, "Sale Evolved from a Need," in *World Famous*; Forrest, "Troubled History."

292. Moore, "The 30s—Era of the CBC," in *World Famous*.

293. Woerner, *Belly Full*, 107–8.

294. Ray Norgaard, interview in Collard, *World Famous*; "Annual Bucking Horse Sale Sets Records," *Billings Gazette*, May 22, 2005.

295. Leroy Coombs, author interview, May 12, 2018.

296. Tucker, "Live Racing Breakdown."

297. Gary Koepplin, author interviews, March 13, May 12, July 27–28, 2018; Don Richard, author interview, May 12, 2018, and email correspondence; Tucker, interview.

Chapter 15

298. *Rocky Mountain Husbandman*, January 11, 1883.

299. *Helena Weekly Herald*, January 23, 1873; *Sun River History II*, 63–64.

300. *Benton Weekly Record*, August 29, 1879.

301. *Great Falls Tribune*, July 16, August 8 and August 22, 1885.

302. *Sun River Valley History II*, 29–32, 64.

303. Robison, *Cascade County and Great Falls*, 8.

304. *Portraits of Progress*, 17.

305. "Broncos Holding Own at Great Falls Rodeo," *Great Falls Tribune*, June 2, 1928, November 9, 1928; Sievert, NRHP, 3, 17–19, 23.

306. "North Montana Fair Plant Ready," *Great Falls Tribune*, August 2, 1931; "29,000 Attend Fair on Opening Day," *Great Falls Tribune*, August 25, 1931; Sievert, NRHP, 14, 23.

307. "North Montana Fair Plant Ready," *Great Falls Tribune*, August 2, 1931; "29,000 Attend Fair on Opening Day," *Great Falls Tribune*, August 25, 1931; Sievert, NRHP, 14, 23.

308. Sievert, NRHP, 24.

309. "Army to 'Shoot the Works' at Fair Air Show Today," *Great Falls Tribune*, August 9, 1946; "6 Die in Double Air Crash at Fair," *Great Falls Tribune*, August 10, 1946; "201,177 Persons, All-Time Record," *Great Falls Tribune*, August 11, 1946; Blair Goyins, "The Great Falls Air Crash," in Moore, *World Famous*; Patrick Dawson, "Disaster that Took the Lives of 19 Race Horses," vertical file "Horse Racing," MHS.

310. "Billings Native's Hands-On Approach Works at Sunland," *Billings Gazette*, March 4, 1990; Tucker, "Live Racing Breakdown."

311. Frank Velock Jr., author interview, August 31, 2018.

312. Guttormson, "Son-of-Harpo"; Cherneski, "Midwestern"; *Calgary Herald*, October 14, 1975; Geise, "Son of Harpo Not Ready"; Geise, "Son of Harpo Honored."

313. "Vic Sigouin," *Independent Record*, May 12, 1984; Equibase, "V. Sigouin"; Velock, interview.

314. Velock, interview.

315. Krings, "Jockey Says"; *Great Falls Tribune*, June 13, 1977; Wilson, interview.

316. "Vic Sigouin," *Independent Record*, May 12, 1984; Equibase, "V. Sigouin"; Velock, interview.

317. Geise, "Son of Harpo Not Ready."

318. "Son of Harpo Does It Again," *Great Falls Tribune*, May 23, 1982, June 7, 1982; Equibase, "Oriental Showboy"; Bob and Lisa Barrett, author interview, July 10, 2018.

319. Equibase, "Son-of-Harpo"; Velock, interview; Wilson, interview.

320. Geise, "Son of Harpo Honored"; Velock, interview.

321. "Horse Racing Gets Boost from Unexpected Source," *Great Falls Tribune*, January 26, 2001.

322. Backa, "Kentucky Dreamin'"; Haskin, "Medaglia Magic"; Mansch, "Montana's First Family"; Mitchell, "Cappucino Bay."

323. Briggeman, "Horse Racing Company"; Puckett, "Research Highlights."

324. "Party Control at Stake in Race," *Great Falls Tribune*, October 5, 2012.

325. Beall, "To Race"; Beall, "County Joins"; Puckett, "Horse Racing Returning."

326. Mansch, "State's Top Horse"; Mansch, "Longshot"; "Horse Racing Kicks Up Fine Results," *Great Falls Tribune*, July 31, 2013; MBOHR reports; Tucker, interview.

327. Rosenbaum, "Cascade County General Fund"; Rosenbaum, "Cascade County to Rebuild"; Warren "Sparky" Kottke, author interview, June 14, July 27–28, October 3, 2018.

Chapter 16

328. Roberts, *Pow Wow*, 100.
329. Obituary, "Bird Rattler, One of the Most Famous Indians, Is Called," *Independent Record*, November 3, 1937; Joe Bird Rattler, author interview, July 14 and 27, 2018; Brittany Bird Rattler, correspondence, 2018.
330. Mansch, "Bird Rattlers"; Bird Rattler, interview.
331. Bird Rattler obituary.
332. "History," Arlee Celebration, http://www.arleepowwow.com/history.
333. "Indians Have a Good Time," *Ravalli Republic*, July 7, 1897.
334. "Indian Celebration Planned at Poplar," *Great Falls Tribune*, July 5, 1935.
335. "Chief Plenty Coups Dies," *Billings Gazette*, March 5, 1932; Heidenreich and Wishart, "Crow Fair."
336. Graetz, *Crow Country*; Hardin High School, *History*, 2, 6.
337. *Billings Gazette*, September 14, 1923; Medicine Crow, *Crow Country*, 106; Bird Rattler interview.
338. Medicine Crow, *Crow Country*, 105–8.
339. Ibid., 106; Fazio, "Fight to Save a Memory," 28–47.
340. *Billings Gazette*, October 23, 1932, September 4, 1934; Hardin High School, *History*, 3, 12; Medicine Crow, *Crow Country*, 108; Heidenreich and Wishart, "Crow Fair."
341. Gould, "APHA Honors Crow Nation"; Pius Real Bird obituary, *Billings Gazette*, March 2, 2014.
342. "Crow Sovereign," APHA Online–Performance Records, research by Victoria Short.
343. Gould, "APHA Honors Crow Nation."
344. *Great Falls Tribune*, July 8, 1905.
345. Equibase, "Shannon Wippert."
346. Mansch, "Bird Rattlers."
347. Equibase, "Brian Beetem"; Brian Beetem, author interview, July 27, 2018.
348. Lincoln, "Daring Indian Relay."
349. "The Oldest Extreme Sport in America," Shoshone-Bannock Tribes, http://www2.sbtribes.com/relay-racing.

350. Dye, *Indian Relay*; Lincoln, "Daring Indian Relay"; Niedermeier, "Exhilirating Indian Relay"; Craig Phillips, "How Indian Relay Works," *Independent Television Service*, pbs.org, 2013; "About Us," Horse Nations Indian Relay Council, http://www.horsenationsrelay.com/about-us.

Afterword

351. Montana Legislative Services Division, *The 1998 Montana Gambling Study* (Helena: Montana Legislative Services Division, 1998), a report to the governor and the 56th Legislature,
352. Mansch, "State's Top Horse Racing Official."

Glossary

353. Belknap, *Horsewords*; Equibase, "Industry Glossary"; "Glossary of Horse Racing Terms," *DRF*; "Horse Racing Glossary of Terms," CalRacing.com; "Glossary," Standardbred Canada; "Horse Racing Betting Terms & Glossary," Twinspires.com; "Quarter Horse Markings and Color Genetics Ebook," AQHA; Jockey Club, "American Stud Book"; USTA, United States Trotting Association Rulebook.
354. Jockey Club, "American Stud Book."

SELECTED BIBLIOGRAPHY

Abraham, Doug. "Granny's Not Exactly a One-Horse Wonder." *Calgary Herald*, September 23, 1995.

Agonito, Joseph. *Brave Hearts: Indian Women of the Plains*. Lanham, MD: Rowman & Littlefield, 2016.

Alexie, Sherman. "Horses." In *Old Shirts & New Skins*, 28–30. Los Angeles, CA: American Indian Studies Center, 1993.

Allen, Frederick. *A Decent, Orderly Lynching: The Montana Vigilantes*. Norman: University of Oklahoma Press, 2004.

Allison, Gary. *Southern Hoofprints: A History of Horse Racing in Southern Alberta*. Victoria, BC: Friesen Press, 2015. eBook.

Ambrose, Stephen E. *Undaunted Courage: Meriwether Lewis, Thomas Jefferson, and the Opening of the American West*. New York: Simon & Schuster, 1996.

American Racing Manual. Chicago: Daily Racing Form Publishing. (Issued annually 1906–present.)

Anderson, Ray. "The Railbird Predicts Good Year at Fairgrounds." *Independent Record*, January 3, 1992.

Andrews, Mea. "And They're Off." *Missoulian*, March 29, 2006.

Anglum, Gerald. "Horseflesh for the World." In *Centennial Roundup*, 69–72. Miles City, MT: Miles City Star Publishing, 1989.

Anthony, David W. *The Horse, the Wheel, and Language: How Bronze Age Riders from the Eurasian Steppes Shaped the Modern World*. Princeton, NJ: Princeton University Press, 2007.

Ashley, Mayo. "Off the Record." *Independent Record*, August 11, 1964.

August, Don. "Tom Chapman's Second Successful Career in Racing." *Horse Racing Nation*, March 29, 2011.

Axline, Jon. "Doncaster Round Barn." National Register of Historic Places Registration Form, Montana State Historic Preservation Office, 2015.

Azzaroli, A. "Ascent and Decline of Monodactyl Equids: A Case for Prehistoric Overkill." *Annales Zoologici Fennici* 28, no. 3/4 (1992): 151–63.

Backa, Curt. "Kentucky Dreamin'." *Great Falls Tribune*, May 2, 2002.

Baird, Kennon. "The Fairgrounds." Helena As She Was. http://www.helenahistory.org.

Baird, Steven. "The Art of Tom Chapman." *Thoroughbred Owners of California Online* (Summer 2008). toconline.com

Barbour, Barton. *Fort Union and the Upper Missouri Fur Trade.* Norman: University of Oklahoma Press, 2001.

Baumler, Ellen. "Montana's Horse Racing History Runs Deep." *Independent Record*, April 16, 2006.

———. "Montana State Fairgrounds Racetrack." National Register of Historic Places Registration Form, Montana State Historic Preservation Office, March 2006.

———. *Spirit Tailings: Ghost Tales of Virginia City, Butte, and Helena.* Helena: Montana Historical Society Press, 2002.

Beall, Michael. "County Joins in Mane Event." *Great Falls Tribune*, February 28, 2013.

———. "To Race or Not to Race?" *Great Falls Tribune*, February 27, 2013.

Beecham, Bill. "Fair Fire Loss Set at $66,000." *Missoulian*, August 25, 1967.

Belknap, Maria. *Horsewords: The Equine Dictionary.* 2nd ed. North Pomfret, VT: Trafalgar Square Publishing, 2004.

Bennett, Deb. *Conquerors: The Roots of New World Horsemanship.* 1st ed. Solvang, CA: Amigo Publications, 1998.

Bighaus, Bill. "Amundson Coming Back as Horse-Racing Secretary." *Billings Gazette*, July 4, 1999.

———. "Amundson to Retrace Racing Roots." *Billings Gazette*, July 11, 2009.

———. "Billings' Horse Racing Meet in Jeopardy." *Billings Gazette*, April 5, 2012.

———. "Despite Turmoil, Y-Downs Plans for Horse Racing." *Billings Gazette*, January 12, 2012.

Bitter Root Stock Farm. *Catalogue 1892.* Hamilton, MT: Bitter Root Stock Farm, 1892.

Briggeman, Kim. "1889 Derby Winner Directed National Attention to Iconic Round Barn in Twin Bridges." *Missoulian*, May 2, 2015.

————. "Horse Racing Company Leaves," *Missoulian*, December 7, 2010.

Brown, Christine, Chere Jiusto and Tom Ferris. *Hand Raised: The Barns of Montana*. Helena: Montana Historical Society, 2011.

Brown, Mark H., and W.R. Felton. *Before Barbed Wire: L.A. Huffman, Photographer on Horseback*. New York: Henry Holt and Company, 1956.

Bryson, Jeremy Glen. "Creating the Old and New Wests: Landscape and Identity in Anaconda and Hamilton, Montana." Master's thesis, Montana State University, 2006.

Budiansky, Stephen. *The Nature of Horses*. New York: Simon and Schuster, 1997.

Burke, Matt. "Tom Chapman: Painting a Brighter Future." danonymousracing.com, April 21, 2013.

Callaway, Llewellyn L. *Montana's Righteous Hangmen: The Vigilantes in Action*. Norman: University of Oklahoma Press, 1982.

Carl, Matthew R. "The Columbia Gardens Amusement Park: Company Sponsored Community in Butte, Montana." *Graduate Student Theses, Dissertations, & Professional Papers*, 971. Missoula: University of Montana, 2011.

Cathro, Morton. "Commentary: Legend of the Bitterroots." *Blood-Horse*, July 17, 2007.

Cave, Will. "The Real Fair Record." *Missoulian*, December 13, 1931.

Caywood, Janene, Suzanne Julin and Dan Hall, Preserve Historic Missoula. "Missoula County Fairgrounds Historic District." National Register of Historic Places Registration Form. Montana State Historic Preservation Office, May 2010.

Chamberlain, Richard. "Bob Wade." *American Quarter Horse Racing Journal* (June 2005): 10.

Cherneski, John. "Midwestern Melvyn to Son-of-Harpo." *Star-Phoenix*, August 20, 1973.

Christian, Peter. "Missoula County Commissioners Vote for an End to Horse Racing at Fairgrounds." *KGVO*, May 22, 2013. https://newstalkkgvo.com/missoula-county-commissioners-hear-protests-support-for-removing-fairgrounds-racetrack-audio.

Clawson, Roger. "Pretty 'Bug Boy', 20-Year Old Push Veterans." *Billings Gazette*, August 16, 1972.

Clawson, Roger, and Katherine A. Shandera. *Billings: The City and People*. Helena, MT: American & World Geographic Publishing, 1993.

Cohen, Betsy. "Turf Club Grounded in Fair Horseracing." *Missoulian*, August 10, 1999.

Cohen, Stan. *Missoula County Images*. Vol. 2. Missoula, MT: Pictorial Histories Publishing Company, 1993.

Cohen, Stan, with Katy and Les Jordonnais. *The Western Montana Fair: A Pictorial Heritage*. Missoula, MT: Pictorial Histories Publishing Company, 1995.

Collard, Sneed B. *The World Famous Miles City Bucking Horse Sale*. Missoula, MT: Mountain Press Publishing, 2010.

Courchene, Dorene, ed. *Powell County: Where It All Began*. Deer Lodge, MT: Powell County Museum and Arts Foundation, 1989.

Cowdrey, Mike, Ned Martin and Jody Martin; contributions by Nakia Williamson-Cloud and Paul Raczka. *Horses & Bridles of the American Indians*. Nicasio, CA: Hawk Hill Press, 2012.

Daly, Marcus. Handwritten annotations. *Catalogue of Thoroughbred Stock*. Hamilton, MT: Bitter Root Stock Farm, 1896.

Delaney, Connie. "Hamilton Fair Grounds." Accessed at https://web.archive.org/web/20120214010634/http://hamiltonmontana.com/montana/hamilton_1890.html.

Dempsey, Hugh A. *The Amazing Death of Calf Shirt and Other Blackfoot Stories*. Norman: University of Oklahoma Press, 1996.

———. "Natawista." *Dictionary of Canadian Biography*. Vol. 12. Toronto, ON: University of Toronto, 2003. http://www.biographi.ca/en/bio/natawista_12E.html.

Denhardt, Robert M. *Foundation Sires of the American Quarter Horse*. Norman: University of Oklahoma Press, 1989.

Diamond, Jared M. *Guns, Germs and Steel: The Fate of Human Societies*. New York: W.W. Norton and Company, 1999.

Dillon, Mark C. *The Montana Vigilantes 1863–1870: Gold, Guns and Gallows*. Logan: Utah State University Press, 2013.

Dimsdale, Thomas. *Vigilantes of Montana*. 2nd ed. Virginia City, MT: D.W. Tilton, 1882.

Dye, Charles, director; M.L. Smoker, writer; Aaron Pruitt, executive producer. *Indian Relay* (video), Independent Lens/Montana PBS, 2013.

Early, Dave. "Gambling Is Evil—Betting on Horses Is Honorable." *Independent Record*, July 10, 1970.

———. "Parimutuel Fray Accomplished Little." *Independent Record*, January 25, 1970.

Ehrman, Kit. "Equine Artist Tom Chapman." *Equestrian Ink*, July 28, 2009.

Emery, Tom. "1889 Derby Winner Was Illinois Bred." *Jacksonville Journal-Courier*, May 8, 2016.

Emmers, Robert H. "…But No Petticoats for This Cowgirl." *Billings Gazette*, August 21, 1977.

Equibase. Equibase Company, LLC. Thoroughbred Racing Association. https://www.equibase.com.

Equineline. Jockey Club Information Systems, Inc. http://www.equineline.com.

Erigero, Patricia, Elizabeth Martiniak, Ann Peters, et al. *Thoroughbred Heritage*. http://www.tbheritage.com.

Ewers, John C. *The Blackfeet: Raiders on the Northwestern Plains*. Norman: University of Oklahoma Press, 1958.

———. *The Horse in Blackfoot Indian Culture*. Bulletin 159. Washington, D.C.: Smithsonian Institution, Bureau of American Ethnology, 1955.

Fazio, Patricia M. "The Fight to Save a Memory: Creation of the Pryor Wild Horse Range." *Annals of Wyoming* 69, no. 2 (Spring 1997): 28–47.

Forbes, Jack D. "The Appearance of the Mounted Indian in Northern Mexico and the Southwest, to 1680." *Southwestern Journal of Anthropology* 15 (1959): 189–212.

Forrest, Susanna. "The Troubled History of Horse Meat in America." *The Atlantic*, June 8, 2017.

Francis, Ken. "There's Penny on Beatlebaum." *Billings Gazette*, February 6, 1969.

Frantz, Donald G., and Norma Jean Russell. *Blackfoot Dictionary of Stems, Roots and Affixes*. 2nd ed. Toronto: University of Toronto Press, 1995.

Freese, Jean. "From Idaho to New York, All Horse Buyers Knew Ed Love." *Miles City Star*, December 6, 1970.

Furdell, William J., and Elizabeth L. Furdell. *Great Falls: A Pictorial History*. Norfolk, VA: Donning Company, 1987.

Geise, George. "Horses and Jockeys Change but Racing Thrill Is the Same." *Great Falls Tribune*, February 24, 1985.

———. "Many Questions, Few Answers." *Great Falls Tribune*, May 23, 1992.

———. "Son of Harpo Honored." *Great Falls Tribune*, July 1, 1989.

———. "Son of Harpo Not Ready to Be Put Out to Pasture." *Great Falls Tribune*, May 29, 1981.

Gibson, Richard. "Horse, Greyhound Racing Have Rich History in Butte." *Montana Standard*, July 4, 2016.

———. "Mining City History: Two Less Well-Known Butte Bankers Who Made Their Mark." *Montana Standard*, January 16, 2017.

Glasscock, C.B. *The War of the Copper Kings*. Riverbend Publishing, 2002. Kindle edition.

Gocher, W.H. *Fasig's Tales of the Turf with Memoir*, 1903, 162–65.

Gokey, Monica. "Feral vs. Wild Horses." *High Country News*, April 11, 2013.

Goodman, Leslee. "My Responsibilities as a Native Artist | An Interview with Supaman." *Moon Magazine*, March 31, 2018.

Goodwin's Official Annual Turf Guide. New York: Goodwin Brothers. (Issued annually 1882–1908.)

Gordon, Greg. "Progress at a Price." *Big Sky Journal* (Summer 2012): 133–34.

Gordon, S. *Recollections of Old Milestown*. Miles City, MT, 1918.

Gould, Bob. "APHA Honors Crow Nation Racehorse Owner with Legendary Achievement Award." https://www.ebarrelracing.com/articles/?p=571, August 31, 2006.

Graetz, Rick, and Susie Graetz. "The Blackfeet Nation Has Long, Epic History." *This Is Montana*. http://www.umt.edu/this-is-montana/columns/stories/blackfeet.php.

———. *Crow Country: Montana's Crow Tribe of Indians*. Billings, MT: Northern Rockies Publishing Company, 2000. http://lib.lbhc.edu/index.php?q=node/73.

Grant, Johnny. Edited with historical annotations by Lyndel Meikle. *Very Close to Trouble: The Johnny Grant Memoir*. Pullman: Washington State University Press, 1996.

Guttormson, Elmar. "Son-of-Harpo Proves Looks Are Deceiving." *Winnipeg Free Press*, July 5, 1973.

Haines, Francis. *Horses in America*. New York: Crowell, 1971.

———. "The Northward Spread of Horses Among the Plains Indians." *American Anthropologist* 40, no. 3 (July 1938): 429–37.

Hamilton, W.T. *My Sixty Years on the Plains, Trapping, Trading, and Indian Fighting*. Edited by E.T. Sieber. New York: Forest and Stream Publishing, 1905.

Hansen, Ben. "Happy Birthday." *Helena Independent Record*, June 21, 1967.

Harden, M.D. "Across the New Northwest in 1860." *The United Service*. Vol. 2, 279–305. New York: L.R. Hamersly, 1903.

Hardin High School History Club. *History of Crow Fair: A Family Tradition*. 2010. https://arc.lib.montana.edu/ivan-doig/objects/2602-B039-F11.pdf.

Harvie, Robert A. *Keeping the Peace: Police Reform in Montana, 1889–1918*. Helena: Montana Historical Society Press, 1994.

Haskin, Steve. "Medaglia Magic." *Blood-Horse*, August 9, 2012.

Heidenreich, C. Adrian, and David J. Wishart, eds. "Crow Fair." *Encyclopedia of the Great Plains*. Lincoln: University of Nebraska–Lincoln, 2010.

Helton, Dorothy. "Beaumont Club at Belgrade New Year-Round Attraction." *Helena Independent Record*, July 18, 1954.

Hillenbrand, Laura. *Seabiscuit: An American Legend*. New York: Random House Publishing Group, 2003.

Hoopes, Lorman L. *This Last West: Miles City, Montana Territory, and Environs, 1876–1886*. Miles City, MT: Skyhouse Publishers/Falcon Press, 1990.

Howland, Joan S., and Michael J. Hannon. *A Legal Research Guide to American Thoroughbred Racing Law for Scholars, Practitioners, and Participants*. Buffalo, NY: William S. Hein & Company, 1998.

Hutchinson, Arthur. "Boards Seek Ouster of State Racing Officials." *Missoulian*, January 25, 1970.

———. "Helena Horse Racing Hit on 2 Sides." *Independent Record*, December 13, 1977.

Jiusto, Chere. *Montana Mainstreets*. Vol. 4, *A Guide to Historic Hamilton*. Helena: Montana Historical Society Press, 2000.

Jockey Club. http://www.jockeyclub.com.

Kavanaugh, John F. *Shelby: The First 100 Years*. Shelby, MT: Shelby Promoter, 2010.

Kearney, Pat. "Racetrack." In *Butte Voices: Mining, Neighborhoods, People*, 225–27. Butte, MT: Skyhigh Communications, 1998.

Kelekna, Pita. *The Horse in Human History*. New York: Cambridge University Press, 2009.

Kelly, Matt J. *Anaconda: Montana's Copper City*. Anaconda, MT: Soroptimist Club of Anaconda, 1983.

Kenworthy, J.P., et al. "Paleontological Resource Inventory and Monitoring, Upper Columbia Basin Network." *National Park Service* TIC# D-259, 2005, 17–25. http://www.npshistory.com/publications/nepe/paleontological-res-im-2005.pdf.

Keyes, Erasmus Darwin. *Fifty Years' Observations of Men and Events, Civil and Military*. New York: C. Scribner's Sons, 1884.

Kidston, Martin. "Turf Club Ramps Up Horse-Racing Pitch to Missoula County." *Missoulian*, November 14, 2015.

Kirkpatrick, Jay F., and Patricia M. Fazio. "The Surprising History of America's Wild Horses." *Live Science*, July 24, 2008. https://www.livescience.com/9589-surprising-history-america-wild-horses.html.

Kline, Larry. "Pricey! Grandstand Project Bids Nearly Double in Cost." *Independent Record*, April 6, 2007.

———. "Whoa There!" *Independent Record*, August 31, 2006.

Klotz, George. "Deer Lodge Firm Maintained One of the Most Successful Stables of Thoroughbred Racers in History of the Turf." *Anaconda Standard*, January 1, 1922.

Koelbel, Lenora. *Missoula the Way It Was.* Missoula, MT: Gateway Publishing, 1972.

Kohrs, Conrad. *Conrad Kohrs: An Autobiography.* Edited by Conrad Kohrs Warren. Deer Lodge, MT: Platen Press, 1977.

Kordenbrock, Mike. "Riders Try to Tame Muddy Track." *Billings Gazette*, September 22, 2017.

Krings, Marcia. "Jockey Says If You Act Like Lady, You'll Get Treated with Respect." *Great Falls Tribune*, August 1, 1976.

Laidlaw, Walter. "Not Hostile to Racing." *New York Times*, June 24, 1911.

Lay, Mark. "James W. Gidley: Expert in Cenozoic Mammals." Smithsonian National Museum of Natural History. Accessed 2018. https://web.archive.org/web/20181127185653/https://paleobiology.si.edu/history/gidley.html.

Lee, Marcia. "Petite Lady Jockey to Ride in Race Meet." *Independent Record*, July 2, 1970.

Leeson, M.A. *History of Montana, 1739–1885.* Chicago: Warner, Beers & Company, 1885.

Lewyn, Myra. "The Fiery Iceman." *Thoroughbred of California*, April 17, 1985.

Lincoln, Marga. "Daring Indian Relay Racing Featured in Film." *Independent Record*, October 20, 2013.

———. "Need for Speed." *Independent Record*, January 6, 2005.

Linebarger, R.G. "Larger and Better Exhibits than Ever." *Billings Gazette*, September 16, 1915.

Lipsyte, Robert. "Gal Jockey Takes Case to Court." *Billings Gazette*, November 30, 1967.

Lowney, Jacob. "Noah Armstrong." https://www.glendalemontana.com.

Lutey, Tom. "Marker Recalls 1858 Slaughter of Horses." *Spokesman-Review*, February 26, 2007.

MacFadden, B.J. "Cladistic Analysis of Primitive Equids with Notes on Other Perissodactyls." *Systematic Zoology* 25, no. 1 (1976): 1–14.

Madden, Jerry. "Racing Commission Has Fiery Session." *Great Falls Tribune*, January 25, 1970.

Malby, Andy. "Faded Glory: Beaumont Owner's Death Brings Racing Legend to an End." *Belgrade News*, October 29, 2010.

Malone, Michael P., Richard B. Roder, and William L. Lang. *Montana: A History of Two Centuries.* Seattle: University of Washington Press, 1991.

Mansch, Scott. "Bird Rattlers Love State Fair Race Meet, and Vice Versa." *Great Falls Tribune*, July 23, 2017.

———. "Gervais Still Riding Winners at State Fair." *Great Falls Tribune*, July 28, 2017.

———. "Longshot Comes In." *Great Falls Tribune*, July 21, 2013.

———. "Montana's First Family of Horse Racing Has Another Connection to the Kentucky Derby." *Great Falls Tribune*, May 3, 2018.

———. "State's Top Horse Racing Official Very Optimistic." *Great Falls Tribune*, July 14, 2013.

Markham, Joe L. "Montana Sports Tales of Other Days." *Montana Newspaper Association Inserts*, July 27, 1936.

Mathews, Allen James. *A Guide to Historic Missoula*. Helena: Montana Historical Society Press, 2002.

McDonald, G. "Hagerman 'Horse'—Equus simplicidens." *Fossil Record* (March 1993).

McFarland, Ron. *Edward J. Steptoe and the Indian Wars: Life on the Frontier, 1815–1865*. Jefferson, NC: McFarland and Company, 2016.

McGee, Marty. "Greta Kuntzweiler's Second Chance." *DRF*, June 25, 2010.

McGrath, Christopher. *Mr. Darley's Arabian*. New York: Pegasus Books, 2017.

McHorse, Brianna K., et al. "Mechanics of Evolutionary Digit Reduction in Fossil Horses (Equidae)." *Proceedings of the Royal Society B: Biological Sciences* 284, no. 1861 (2017).

McVey, George. "Great Horse Spokane." *Spokesman-Review*, July 5, 1964.

Medicine Crow, Joseph. *From the Heart of the Crow Country: The Crow Indians' Own Stories*. Lincoln: University of Nebraska Press, 1992.

Meikle, Lyndel. KQRV interview notes, July 25, 2016.

———. "Risky Business." *Distinctly Montana* (Summer 2009): 42–47.

Melin-Moser, Catharine. "In the Winner's Circle." *Montana: The Magazine of Western History* (Winter 2014): 22–41.

Mendyke, Thomas. "Dance De Kas to QH Futurity Qualifier." *Independent Record*, May 27, 1996.

Merritt, Richard. "Index to the MNAI Inserts." 1981–1983. Digitized 2013–2015, Montana Historical Society. https://mhs.mt.gov/Portals/11/research/docs/IndexToTheMNAInserts.pdf.

Meyers, Donald W. "It Happened Here." *Yakima Herald*, June 4, 2017.

Mintz, Leslie. "Fast Facts: The Event at Rebecca Farm and NAYC." *United States Eventing Association*, July 17, 2018.

Mitchell, Eric. "Cappucino Bay, Dam of Medaglia d'Oro, Dies at 30." *Blood-Horse*, January 25, 2019.

Mohr, Jason. "Yeas and Neighs." *Independent Record*, June 8, 2005.

Montana Board of Horse Racing (MBOHR Reports). Montana Horse Racing Commission/Montana Board of Horse Racing. Annual Reports, 1966–1973. Helena, MT: Montana Historical Society Archives.

Montgomery, E.S. *The Thoroughbred*. 4th ed. New York: Arco, 1971.

Mooney, Bill. "Spokane, the Kentucky Derby Winner of 1889, a Part of Montana Folklore." *Daily Racing Form*, May 30, 2014.

Moore, John. "Girl Jockey Says There's Not Much to Do in Summer." *Miles City Star*, May 12, 1971.

————. *The World Famous Miles City Jaycee Bucking Horse Sale*. Miles City, MT: Jordan Stage, 1982. (unpaginated)

Morris, Patrick F. *Anaconda, Montana: Copper Smelting Boom Town on the Western Frontier*. Bethesda, MD: Swann Publishing, 1997.

Morrison, Kimberly Currie. "Anaconda Saddle Club." National Register of Historic Places Registration Form. Montana State Historic Preservation Office, July 1996.

————. "Historic & Architectural Properties of Anaconda Deer Lodge County, Montana." National Register of Historic Places Registration Form. Montana State Historic Preservation Office, December 1995.

Moulton, Gary E., ed. *The Lewis and Clark Journals*. Lincoln: University of Nebraska Press, 2003. https://lewisandclarkjournals.unl.edu/journals.

Nardinger, Susan R. *Spirit Horse of the Rockies*. Great Falls, MT: Falcon Press Publishing, 1988.

National Park Service. "Earl Douglass." Dinosaur National Monument, February 24, 2015. https://www.nps.gov/dino/learn/historyculture/douglass.htm.

————. "A Powerful Woman, Then and Now: Natawista Iksana (Medicine Snake Woman)." Fort Union National Historic Site, January 5, 2018. https://www.nps.gov/fous/learn/historyculture/natawista-iksina-medicine-snake-woman.htm.

Niedermeier, Jordon. "The Exhilarating Indian Relay." *Cowboys and Indians*, July 20, 2016.

Overholser, Joel. *Fort Benton: World's Innermost Port*. Great Falls, MT: Falcon Press Publishing, 1987.

Owen, John. *The Journals and Letters of Major John Owen, Pioneer of the Northwest, 1850–1871*. New York: E. Eberstadt, 1927.

Pace, Roy. "Board Won't Relieve Threat to Local Racing." *Independent Record*, June 23, 1978.

Palmer, Joe H. "Ogden." In *Names in Pedigrees*, 306–13. Lexington, KY: Thoroughbred Owners and Breeders' Association, 1974.

Paulick, Ray. "Death of a Derby Winner: Slaughterhouse Likely Fate for Ferdinand." *Blood-Horse*, July 25, 2003.

Peterson, Don, and the History Museum. Images of America: *Great Falls*. Charleston, SC: Arcadia Publishing, 2010.

Petit, Stefanie. "Slaughter of Horses Leaves Lasting Mark." *Spokesman-Review*, October 1, 2009.

Plain, Nancy. *This Strange Wilderness: The Life and Art of John James Audubon*. Lincoln: University of Nebraska Press, 2015.

Portraits of Progress: Great Falls, Montana. Great Falls, MT: Diamond Jubilee, 1959.

Powell, Ada. *Copper, Green and Silver*. Hamilton, MT: A. Powell, 1993.

————. *Dalys of the Bitter Root*. Hamilton, MT: A. Powell, 1989.

————. *The First 100 Years: Hamilton 1890–1990*. Hamilton, MT: A. Powell, 1990.

Powell, Eric A. "The Story of the Horse: Return to the New World." *Archaeology Magazine*, June 4, 2015.

Priddy, Molly. "Life After Racing." *Flathead Beacon*, June 14, 2017.

————. "Mapping the Future of the Fairgrounds." *Flathead Beacon*, October 8, 2011.

Puckett, Karl. "Horse Racing Returning to Great Falls." *Great Falls Tribune*, May 17, 2013.

————. "Research Highlights Untapped Potential." *Great Falls Tribune*, February 3, 2011.

Putz, Paul. *Lewis and Clark County Fairgrounds Historic Sites Review*. Helena/Lewis and Clark County Historic Preservation Commission, December 2003.

Rainone, Cathy. "Tough Game for Women." *NBC Sports*, June 7, 2018.

Real Bird, Shawn. Author interviews July 28 and November 7, 2018.

Reece, Myers. "Training Racers for Six Decades." *Flathead Beacon*, August 10, 2011.

Rees, Jennie. "1889 Spokane." *Courier-Journal*, April 17, 2015.

Reich, James M. *Billings*. Charleston, SC: Arcadia Publishing, 2009.

Riess, Stephen A. *The Sport of Kings and the Kings of Crime: Horse Racing, Politics, and Organized Crime in New York, 1865–1913*. Syracuse, NY: Syracuse University Press, 2011.

Roberts, Chris. *Pow Wow Country*. Helena, MT: American and World Geographic Publishing, 1992.

Robertson, Gene. "Favorites Have Bad Day at the Track." *Independent-Record*, July 5, 1973.

Robertson, Ken. "Women Have Big Day at Track." *Independent Record*, May 14, 1973.

Robertson, William. *The History of Thoroughbred Racing in America*. Englewood Cliffs, NJ: Prentice-Hall, 1964.

Robison, Ken. *Cascade County and Great Falls.* Charleston, SC: Arcadia Publishing, 2011.

———. *Montana Territory and the Civil War: A Frontier Forged on the Battlefield.* Charleston, SC: Arcadia Publishing, 2013.

Rocene, Ray T. "Sports Jabs." *Missoulian*, June 12, 1955.

Ronan, Mary, and Margaret Ronan. *Girl from the Gulches: The Story of Mary Ronan.* Edited by Ellen Baumler. Helena: Montana Historical Society Press, 2003.

Rosenbaum, Traci. "Cascade County General Fund to Pay for Fix for Crumbling Grandstands." *Great Falls Tribune*, March 22, 2018.

———. "Cascade County to Rebuild Montana ExpoPark Grandstands for $2.8 Million." *Great Falls Tribune*, May 10, 2018.

Rosenberg, Anna Fay. "Hard Winter Endurance: Conrad Kohrs' Cattle Raising Operation, 1887–1900." *Graduate Student Theses, Dissertations, & Professional Papers.* 2509. Missoula: University of Montana, 1996.

Ruby, Robert H., and John Arthur Brown. *The Spokane Indians: Children of the Sun.* Norman: University of Oklahoma Press, 2006.

Sanders, Helen Fitzgerald. *A History of Montana.* Vol. 1. Chicago: Lewis Publishing, 1913

Sherrets, Harold. *The Taylor Grazing Act, 1934–1984, 50 Years of Progress, Impacts of Wild Horses on Rangeland Management.* Boise: U.S. Dept. of Interior, Bureau of Land Management Idaho State Office, 1984.

Shoebotham, H. Minar. *Anaconda: Life of Marcus Daly the Copper King.* Harrisburg, PA: Telegraph Press, 1956.

Sievert, Ellen. Cascade County Historical Society, "Northern Montana State Fairground Historic District," National Register of Historic Places Registration Form, Montana State Historic Preservation Office, December 1988.

Simon, Mary. *Racing Through the Century: The Story of Thoroughbred Racing in America.* Irvine, CA: BowTie Press, 2002.

Smith, Barb. "Faded Glory: Belgrade's Beaumont Track Once Buzzed with Horses, Parties, Parades." *Bozeman Daily Chronicle*, November 17, 1985.

Smith, Phyllis. *Montana's Madison County: A History.* Bozeman, MT: Gooch Hill Publishing, 2006.

Smithsonian Institution. *A Song for the Horse Nation: Horses in Native Cultures.* National Museum of the American Indian, October 2011–January 2013. https://americanindian.si.edu/exhibitions/horsenation/index.html.

Sowers, Richard. *The Kentucky Derby, Preakness and Belmont Stakes: A Comprehensive History.* Jefferson, NC: McFarland, 2014.

Stevens, Karen D., and Dee Ann Redman. *Billings A to Z.* Billings, MT: Friends of the Library, 2000.

Stuart, Granville. *Forty Years on the Frontier as Seen in the Journals and Reminiscences of Granville Stuart, Gold-Miner, Trader, Merchant, Rancher and Politician.* Edited by Paul C. Phillips. Cleveland, OH: Arthur H. Clark, 1925.

Sun River Historical Society. *A Pictorial History of the Sun River Valley.* Sun River, MT: Sun River Historical Society, 1989.

———. *Sun River History II.* Helena, MT: Sweetgrass Books, 2014.

Sutton, Hailey. "Indian Relay Races Bring a Small Community Together." KULR8.com, August 7, 2018.

Sweeney, Louise. "When Old and New Worlds Met." *Christian Science Monitor,* November 12, 1991.

Thomas, Steve. "A High-Tech Firm, A Down-Home Image." *The Blood-Horse,* January 24, 1987, 640–42.

Thoroughbred Times Racing Almanac 2007. Lexington, KY: Thoroughbred Times, 2006.

Toole, K. Ross. *Montana: An Uncommon Land.* 5th ed. Norman: University of Oklahoma Press, 1977.

Towle, Virginia Rowe. *Vigilante Woman.* New York: A.S. Barnes and Company, 1966.

Tucker, Tom. "Live Racing Breakdown." Spreadsheet, IMS Consulting Group, Inc., 2012–18.

Turney-High, H. Holbert. *The Flathead Indians of Montana.* Menasha, WI.: American Anthropological Association, 1937. https://catalog.hathitrust.org/Record/000288076.

Van Duyne, Frank. "The Old Race Track." Unpublished manuscript, vertical file. Butte-Silver Bow Public Archives.

Van West, Carroll. *Images of Billings: A Photographic History.* Billings, MT: Western Heritage Press, 1990.

Viola, Herman J. "The Horse Culture." In *Seeds of Change: Readings on Cultural Exchange after 1492,* 88–91. Smithsonian Institution. Palo Alto, CA: Addison-Wesley Publishing, 1993.

Vogel, Sherry. "Fallon County Fair Offers New Attraction." *Fallon County Times,* July 29, 2016.

Von Hippel, Paul T., Caroline G. Rutherford and Katherine M. Keyes. "Gender and Weight among Thoroughbred Jockeys: Underrepresented Women and Underweight Men." *Socius* (January 2017).

Wahler, Brenda. "A Race Day in Great Falls." *Best of Great Falls* (Summer 2015): 38–40.

Wall, Maryjean. "Women Raced in England as Long Ago as 1804." *Lexington Herald-Leader*, February 2, 1969.

Warhank, Joseph James. "Fort Keogh: Cutting Edge of a Culture." Master's thesis, Department of History, California State University, Long Beach, 1983.

Waters, Michael R., et al. "Ice Age Horse and Camel Hunting in North America" *Proceedings of the National Academy of Sciences* 112, no. 14 (April 2015): 4263–67.

Weinstock, J., et al. "Evolution, Systematics, and Phylogeography of Pleistocene Horses in the New World: A Molecular Perspective." *PLoS Biology* 3, no. 8 (2005).

Wischmann, Lesley. *Frontier Diplomats: Alexander Culbertson and Natoyist-Siksina' among the Blackfeet.* Norman: University of Oklahoma Press, 2004.

Wishart, David J., ed. "Crow Fair." *Encyclopedia of the Great Plains.* Lincoln: University of Nebraska–Lincoln, 2010.

Wissler, Clark. "The Influence of the Horse in the Development of Plains Culture." *American Anthropologist* 16, no. 1, (1914): 1–25.

Woerner, Gail Hughbanks. *A Belly Full of Bedsprings: A History of Bronc Riding.* Austin, TX: Eakin Press, 1998.

Wood, Greg. "Female Jockeys as Good as Men but Get Fewer Top Rides, Says Report." *The Guardian,* January 30, 2018.

Wright, Kathryn. *Billings: The Magic City and How It Grew.* Billings, MT: Reporter Printing Supply Company, 1953.

Writers' Program of the Work Projects Administration in the State of Montana. *Montanans' Golden Anniversary: Humorous History, Handbook and 1940 Almanac.* Helena, MT: State Publishing Company, 1939.

Young, Burrus. "Bob Wade." *Western Horseman.* Undated clipping, vertical file "Horse Racing," Montana Historical Society.

INDEX

ABOUT THE AUTHOR

Brenda Wahler is a fourth-generation Montanan with a lifelong interest in horses and history. She showed horses in the 1970s and 1980s, when the racing community was a major presence at fairgrounds across the country. Through college and beyond, she taught riding and judged horse shows. Today, she is an attorney and operates an equine education and consulting business. She and her husband live near Helena, Montana, with assorted horses and house pets. Visit her blog at https://wahlerequine.wordpress.com.

Billings, 1975, *Potter photo*; inset, 2016. *Roth photo*.

Visit us at
www.historypress.com
··